Culture
Clash

A Guide for Filipino Immigrants
Raising
American Children

Culture Clash: A Guide for Filipino Immigrants Raising American Children
Copyright © 2021 Lutie Orteza Lee
ISBN: 9781949109702
Library of Congress Control Number: 2021938361
Anchor Book Press, Ltd
440 W. Colfax Street, Unit 1132 Palatine, IL 60078
Printed in the United States

Cover Design by Kathryn Dunn

Culture Clash

A Guide for Filipino Immigrants Raising American Children

Lutie Orteza Lee

To Aida & John,
May there be "AHA" moments as you read along ... the journey continues ... now with our Apos! Happy Thanksgiving to you both! Love, Lutie

Anchor Book Press · Palatine

DEDICATION

For **Hiro** and **Kenzo**, your lives are just beginning to unfold, may you find your Lola's groundbreaking work on "culture clash" an inspiration to uphold your own mark in the world you live in.

For **Kristi** (1949-2013), in memoriam:
> ...into the darkness and warmth of the earth,
> ...into the sadness and smiling of our memories,
> ...into the cycle of living, of dying, of rising again,
> > ...rest in peace, in the loving embrace of our
> > > Creator. Amen.

Foreword

Parenting is tough enough under "normal" circumstances, ie having adequate financial resources and psychosocial support, including both parents sharing in the responsibilities.

It helps, as well, to be raising children in a familiar environment, one's hometown or at least home country with both parents sharing a common culture.

But these ideal circumstances might actually be more of the exception than the rule, especially in our age of mobility. People are on the move all the time. On a daily basis, one or both parents may be working outside the home. Add the Filipino diaspora, with one or even both parents having to be separated from their children for extended periods. Note that this migration is both domestic (as in household helpers who leave their children in impoverished rural areas to work in cities) as well as international.

Mobility and migration pose great challenges to individuals, mainly in terms of adjusting to a new environment and culture. These challenges are amplified when the migrants begin a new family in these unfamiliar environments, with partners or spouses coming from cultures different from their own.

Parenting guides rarely address these challenges that come about from mobility and migration. Lutie Orteza Lee's book is timely, compiling her own parenting experiences as a Filipina who migrated to the United States and had a Chinese husband. Also significant are her experiences as a teacher, and a lay minister, aptly described, together with parenting, as a journey and a search for personal truths.

An earlier book by Lutie Orteza Lee was based on her own experiences, which remain important in this second book. Her child now grown, she has the luxury of time to reflect on her experiences, as well as those of other parents, and to discover the scholarship around Sikolohiyang Pilipino (Filipino psychology) that goes back to the 1970s. The pioneer here was the late Virgilio Enriquez, who had studied in the States and returned to the University of the Philippines with many questions about the relevance of western psychology to the Philippine situation.

Enriquez and his students, some of whom later became his professional colleagues, conducted rigorous research to revisit the western-oriented work that had been done on the Filipino personality. He was particularly critical of "Filipino values" research which tended to "naturalize" these values as innate, and to blame the country's woes on such values. For example, "hiya" was simplistically defined as "shame" and was identified as the cause for Filipinos' lack of initiative, a kind of national inferiority complex.

Enriquez and his colleagues urged a more contextualized study of Filipino personality and values, context here referring to the historical, social, and cultural circumstances that shape the Filipino psyche. This attention to context is particularly relevant when we look at how Sikolohiyang Pilipino might apply to child-rearing and parenting.

Sikolohiyang Pilipino interacted heavily with anthropology, recognizing individuals as culture-bearers, carrying cultural baggage (some might argue excess baggage) to shape the way we perceive and interpret the world, and society. Rather than blaming culture as the root of our problems, Enriquez urged a deeper understanding of how that culture shapes us, and how we shape that culture.

For want of a better term, I will use the term "cross-cultural parenting" to describe part of what Lutie Orteza Lee tackles in this book. Lee's book focuses on Filipino families in the United States and her own circumstances having a Chinese husband.

Many more configurations are possible if we recognize that "Filipino" and "Chinese" and "American" are always tentative labels, as ethnicity, and even as place. I think of the Filipino writer Carlos Bulosan's novel, America (or the Philippines or China) is in the heart, just as the Philippines, or China, remains in the heart of a new migrant in the United States.

Bulosan's novel, and other works, speak of an America that is loved, that is aspirational, and that sometimes disappoints, more often from what seems to be paradoxes. Lutie uses the term "cultural clashes" and indeed they can be frightening.

The migrant experience reminds us of how culture inscribes itself on our bodies, in the way we move, the way we speak, the way we laugh or even cry. Even emotions are culturally shaped, some cultures more permissive than others when it comes to expression of those emotions. And there lies the potentials for clashes. Filipinos, already quite ebullient and expressive with emotions, are still shocked with Americans being even more spontaneous, even excessive in demonstrating one's emotions. The new migrant parent is in a dilemma, at once fascinated by the new cultural norms and cognizant of how those norms are important for survival and success, and yet worried that their children might go too far in being assertive and demonstrative.

Lutie describes one of the most important clashes that impinge on parenting, and this is the authoritarian parenting style in the Philippines, clashing with a more, and I'm using my term, liberal Dr. Spock method favored by many Americans. Lutie proposes an authoritative model, at once firm, but with more room for the child to participate in the decision-making. The most important case study she uses is that of her own daughter, who she practically had to rescue from a difficult situation. Lutie includes a letter from that daughter, years after the rescue, expressing gratitude for what happened. The case study is likely to be debated, and will reflect the dilemmas we face around parenting, in an age of increasing concerns over balancing rights and responsibilities.

I do not want to preempt Lutie Orteza Lee's book and instead want to urge reflexivity on the part of the reader, to better benefit from the book. It is a reflexivity that should lead readers to think of their own "self", as "culture-bearer," in relation to their being parents. There will be tough questions to answer, maybe starting with questions like, Am I Filipino American or American Filipino, and what do I want my children to be? (And then maybe suddenly realizing, but who am I to want my children to be what I want them to be?)

The reflexivity builds on the concept of the culture-bearer, and it will be helpful to be aware that we are often culture-bearers. I think of the many Tsinoy (Chinese Filipinos) who migrated to the States, a migrant twice over, now seeking identity in a gloriously multicultural American society. I have yet to meet someone self-identifying as Tsinoy-American; yet I see the elements of this intriguing blend in the Tsinoy in North America.

I also urge readers to strongly reflect on marginality. The problems faced by migrant families is not just cultural but political. Driven to the margins by discrimination and exclusion, migrant families might find themselves trying to reassert their home culture, as a reaction against, maybe even a shield, to the daily affronts. We see this in the Tiger Mom paradigm: my parents did not spare the rod with me and look at me now, I'm successful. Ergo, being a Tiger Mom will help my children to be successful as well, especially in this permissive American society.

The other tendency is to erase one's own home identity, in an attempt to be American (some will say more American than Americans), hoping for assimilation. Think too of the identity crises that children face today, migrants or non-migrants, around gender and sexual orientation. Lutie talks, too, of class and I wanted to add to her observations.

Class differences do exist – it has always been easier for upper class Filipinos to become American; the process having started even at home. I see it, for example, in private school students having to be tutored in Filipino because, with the recent Mother Language policy of the Philippines' Department of Education, a mother language must be used in schools up to 3rd grade. The problem is that the mother language for many upper-class Filipino children is not Filipino, but English. Class marks, or mars, our discussions. It is always easy for the upper classes to hector the middle classes and the poor about value change, forgetting that so many of the structural impediments were in fact created by the elite, disempowering the tiny and fragile middle class, and the teeming lower classes. As an educator, I see this all the time among our students at the University of the Philippines, the best and the brightest we are told, yet handicapped by the low priorities given to basic education, and by extension, to parenting.

Lutie invokes the saying "it takes a village to raise a child." Our migrant families will do well to recognize that even in the mega-cities of America, there are villages, there are kind and caring souls, from different cultures, who are ready to help raise a child. All said, the multicultural experience, while daunting, is a blessing for parents, and their children.

Michael Tan, Ph.D.
Office of the Chancellor
University of the Philippines Diliman
Quezon Hall, UP Campus
Diliman, Quezon City, Philippines

CONTENTS

INTRODUCTION

I wrote *Culture Clash: A Guide for Filipino Immigrants Raising American Children* as a direct result of the life-changing experience I encountered with the rebellion of my teenage daughter 32 years ago. She has been my motivation to write this book, and the event gave birth to my passion for bridging the generational gap between Americanized children and their immigrant parents. In my teen years, I had no experience in sneaking out at night with friends to the wee hours of the morning. It became my nightmare as a mother when I discovered my daughter's dummy pretending to be asleep! Where had I gone wrong in my childrearing practices? It was not my lack of being a good mother, but the result of culture clash. I have provided answers to my questions that I hope will help the millions of immigrant parents living in the United States, and in the Philippines as well.

This book begins where my previous work, *Culture Clash: The Americanized Teenagers Implications for Parenting, Teaching, and Mentoring* (2006) ends. This resource adds much to the original narrative. The original book was based on my master's thesis project in 2005 as a part of my Religious Education degree from Claremont School of Theology in Claremont, California. Because of ever-changing cultural dynamics, new research, and my own self-awareness, I was compelled to provide a fresh look at the subject. *Culture Clash: A Guide for Filipino Immigrants Raising American Children* also contains the influence of another book I wrote in 2001, *Teaching Cultural Diversity Through Children's Literature: Applying the Kluckhohn Model,* which is my master's thesis project for my degree in Human Development with a specialization in Bicultural Development from Pacific Oaks College in Pasadena, California.

Thirty-two years ago, as I walked back and forth through the aisles of Borders, Barnes and Noble, and B. Dalton bookstores frantically looking for culture clash related books, I found nothing that would address what I was facing with my rebellious teenager. Standing alone in the Borders aisle, I vowed that one day I would write a book that would provide answers to my questions. I really did not know what shape the book would take, but here it is, 32 years later. I want to believe that there are desperate Filipino parents living in the USA needing answers and this book could provide answers for them. Someone queried why my title is not inclusive of other cultures? As a Filipino, I use experiences and examples that are not inclusive. However, many of the concepts could be adapted for various cultures but to explicitly include other cultures would result in a book that would be much too long. Further, to use an inclusive title without changing content would mislead those who are considering my book. I am not an expert in other cultures. I needed a Filipino related culture book rooted in the U.S. context yet there was none. So, that is the book I wrote. According to UN census, 4 million Filipino Americans reside here. This book addresses their issues explicitly. Others can glean truth that will benefit all cultures.

In writing this book, I interviewed more than 200 participants over a span of almost four years through workshops, one-on-one interviews, focus groups, and surveys. Research and study of the subject for more than 20 years will be presented as a guide to help ease the tension that is often the result of culture clash between parent and child.

The methodology I employed in gathering the data is narrative inquiry. In other words, the content of this book is filled with stories I gathered from the respondents whose real identities remain anonymous, except for a few who did not mind being known. It is storytelling. Readers oriented to the scientific inquiry may dismiss the method as less authentic because the stories are not quantifiable, thus, not taken seriously. How honest are the subjects? Chances of being told what I wanted to hear may abound, too. But to avoid this occurrence, my interviews took place in group discussions, where participants knew each other intimately and during the Q&A session after each workshop. Comments were spontaneous and candid. Some participants also engaged in a deeper one-on-one interview.

The first time I heard about narrative inquiry was from my first Master of Arts chair of the thesis committee, Betty Jones, who is now a faculty emeritus at Pacific Oaks College in Pasadena, California. She encouraged storytelling of one's lived experience. It's a radical departure from scientific inquiry, but narrative inquiry is simply another way of knowing. I am not alone in my belief. Many before me have employed storytelling as their research methodology. One such person is Brené Brown, best-selling author, and TED speaker on *The Power of Vulnerability*, a topic that captured worldwide attention. Ms. Brown is a social worker and researcher who departed from the traditional method of performing research. She asked, "Is wisdom derived from experience more or less valuable than data produced by controlled research? What research should we allow into our professional journals and what should we reject?" She states, and I agree, "that the most useful knowledge is based on lived experience."[1]

In the United Nations survey of 2011, the report says an estimated four million immigrant and naturalized Filipinos reside in the U.S. What entails uprooting one's culture to live in another culture? Is it easy to live in the U.S. as Americans do? Can we transport the Filipino values easily into the new environment? As time goes by, like it or not, the impact of one's culture with the host culture and vice versa creates a transition in worldviews. This book addresses this shift and the struggles and triumphs that parents and their children experience in comprehending and surviving this evolution. I have written this book for the Filipino immigrant families because of my personal experience as a Filipino as well as coping with life in the U.S."

In my effort to capture the essence of my Filipino heritage, I encountered the work of Dr. Virgilio G. Enriquez, who wrote *From Colonial to Liberation Psychology* (2004). His work inspired me to rediscover my Filipino roots, our indigenous culture, the *katutubong kultura/kulturang lumad*. This second book, therefore, is clothed in the consciousness of my indigenous Filipino culture. Much of what is embedded in American culture is lost in translation because certain concepts do not exist in the Filipino society. In an attempt to translate themes and behaviors that are a part of American culture into the Filipino language, they do not make sense. For example, the term "self-esteem" is a beloved concept in the Western culture. However, once translated in Filipino, "*magpalagayang mahalaga sa sarili*," the term means

---

[1] Brené *Brown, Rising Strong: The Reckoning. The Rumble. The Revolution. (Spiegel & Grau: New York, 2015), xiii*

that a person is boasting. It gives a negative connotation to the listeners.

We inhabit an intercultural ability in the U.S. to seek our own kind whether it is intentional or not. While this book is geared for immigrant Filipino parents, the lessons can be far-reaching. We encounter images of diversity as we venture to the theaters, supermarkets, churches, train or bus stations, schools, etc., "Let us recognize the dynamic interaction, mutual influence, and interconnectedness with one another," according to Emmanuel Y. Lartey's book, *Pastoral Theology in an Intercultural World*. Therefore, why not be equipped with tools for better communication by becoming aware of the five causes of cultural clash in order to have meaningful interaction among those who bring a different perspective to the conversation?

Lutie Orteza Lee

CHAPTER 1

ORIENTATION OF THE SELF

"In the Philippine value system, kapwa (shared identity) is at the very foundation of human values. This core value then determines not only the person's personality but more so his personhood or pagkatao. Without kapwa, one ceases to be a Filipino. One also ceases to be human."[2]

—Dr. Virgilio G. Enriquez

I am intentionally approaching this discussion in the context of some highly prized Philippine values. I begin with **kapwa**, which is Filipino for shared humanity or shared identity. Hence, your *kapwa* is your fellow human being.

The Filipino's penchant for *pakikipagkapwa* (cultivating a shared humanity or identity) is the foundation of human values and is often exhibited to a fault. It becomes a fault carried to the nth degree when principles are sidelined for the sake of *pakikipagkapwa*. Such is the depth of the Filipino character, seeking unity with the other. The self is always seeking to merge with, not separate from, the other; this is the Filipino orientation of the self.

The everyday interaction of immigrant parents with their children is influenced by the self-orientation of each. The Western self-orientation differs from the Eastern self-orientation. The American self is a stark

---

[2] Virgilio G. Enriquez, *From Colonial to Liberation Psychology: The Philippine Experience* (Manila, Philippines: De La Salle University Press, Inc. 2004) 63

contrast to the Filipino self. The American center is the individual self with definite boundaries from others, including intimate partners, family, friends, and acquaintances. At times, especially for the young, the point of view of the individual self alone matters. The Filipino self, however, always considers others before making significant decisions.

Orientation of the self is not given prime attention because it is deeply lodged in our unconscious mind and remains unexplored. Therefore, we usually do not have an awareness of the fact that the unconscious mind dictates our behavior. However, scientific brain research today reveals that we have memories stored in our brains that we are unaware of. When they are triggered, whether it is pleasant or unpleasant, they dictate our behavior.[3] This brain research was a breakthrough. Thus, when our intentions, conscious and unconscious, synchronize with our behavior, the impact is extraordinary, be it positive or negative.

As an example, much has been made of the late Apple founder and CEO Steve Jobs' portrayed abandonment of his high school sweetheart and denial of paternity of their daughter. Yet, who can ignore the subliminal connection of his actions to Jobs' own painful abandonment as a young child by his biological father? Is it a mere coincidence that both men were alleged to have abandoned their children at the age of 23? We can no longer excuse ourselves by saying that it is not our conscious intention that dictates our behaviors and actions, especially if there is a familiar memory that may have triggered the behavior. The unconscious intention outside the realm of our consciousness dictates our behavior. No matter how painful or embarrassing, they

---

[3] Leonard Mlodinow, "How Your Unconscious Mind Rules Your Behavior." TED Talk, Bratislava, Slovakia, September 26, 2012. www.TED.com

become eye-openers to the seat of our beings, of who we really are in the present moment. Indeed, our "aha" moments teach us a lot! Own it, and you can be on your way to healing.

The quote introducing this chapter defines the Filipino individual self within the context of a culture free from the influence of Western-oriented analysis of the Filipino personality. The Filipino does not separate self from another, the *kapwa*. The more intimate your ties are with a person, the more integrated you two are and the closer you identify with each other—regardless of color, creed, or affiliation—the more you are the same; no separation. It should be noted, the closest English synonym of *kapwa* is "other." Yet, by its Filipino definition, *kapwa* does not acknowledge the concept embodied by the word other. In Filipino, *kapwa* is the unity of the self and the other. The English word 'other' is actually used in opposition to self and implies the recognition of self as a separate identity. In contrast, *kapwa* is a recognition of shared identity, an inner self shared with others. When *pakikipagkapwa* is the mode of interaction, it refers to humanness at its highest level. A person experiences *kapwa* not so much because of recognition of status given him or her by others, but more because of his or her awareness of shared identity. One is constantly expected to demonstrate a sense of being one with his or her *kapwa-tao* (fellow human being), which is considered the foundation of human values.

In Filipino culture, if one is *walang pakikisama* (inept at the level of adjustment), others might still say he would eventually learn or let him be that is his prerogative. If one is *walang hiya* (no sense of propriety or dignity), others say, his parents should teach him a thing or two. If one is *walang utang na loob,* (no appreciation of or solidarity with one's *kapwa*), others might advise to avoid him. But if one is *walang kapwa tao* (no shared self or identity with fellow Filipinos or human beings), people say he must have hit rock bottom. *Napakasama niya* (he is such a bad person). He is the worst.

To many Filipino readers, the above quote may come as a surprise because I did not use shame to translate *hiya*. In my research, I learned that shame is actually a direct translation from the Western perspective of understanding shame. Filipinos then bought into this analysis and concluded that *hiya* means shame. Filipino readers may also be puzzled as to my translation of *utang na loob*. We've always subscribed to the direct Western translation, a debt of gratitude.

Because of the Filipinos' constant show of *pakikipagkapwa*, we have gained global repute as a hospitable people. I agree! From the Filipino perspective, you are a human being if you have *pakikipagkapwa* toward others.

Let me end this section by sharing a story that has been circling the Philippine Islands. The joke is a living testament to our mindset of *pakikipagkapwa*. I will call it *hayahay* (carefree life). A teacher asks her third-grade students what they want to become when they grow up. Manuel answers, "I want to be a doctor so that I can help my *kapwa*." Rosa says, "I want to be a lawyer so that I can help my *kapwa*." Mario chimes in, "I want to be an engineer so that I can help my *kapwa*." Then Ernesto follows with, "I want to be a *kapwa* so that I will be *hayahay!*" For readers outside the Filipino culture, *hayahay* means a life with no cares and no woes; pleasurable, no worries. The humor in the answer is that the boy believes he doesn't have to work hard anymore because if you are a *kapwa*, then the doctor, the lawyer, and the engineer are there to help you! A closer translation of *kapwa* in English would be akin to a fellow human being. So, the boy is saying he wants to be a human being! This story has become so popular in the Philippines that there is now a new restaurant called, you guessed it, *HAYAHAY.*

Stories that highlight the American and Filipino orientation of self

I consider orientation of self to be the most important cause of intercultural conflicts. It is often the basis of unintended personal and professional "cross-fires" due to cultural differences. Here are some examples to which you may be able to relate.

Caution: Avoid judgment when reading these examples, as there is no right or wrong perception. Differences are differences, nothing more.

A. Food tasting

A few years ago, in New York, my adult daughter and I went out for a walk to see the city the day after Christmas. Several stores were open with beautiful holiday displays of discounted merchandise. In one of the stores, samples of oils were provided for customers to taste along with small chunks of bread. My hands were full, and I had winter gloves on, so I simply opened my mouth and waited for my daughter to shove a piece of dipped bread into my mouth. While she was doing this, I thought, "Oh, how loving my daughter is." To my surprise, she was giving me a dirty look! She said, "Mom, you are 65 years old, and you still want to be spoon-fed!" Oops, I thought. I let her comment pass. Then, we entered another store with a new food product to taste. This time I said, "I would have to be a moron if I don't do this myself." She chuckled, and we continued our walk. Later that night, after dinner, I approached her to have a heart-to-heart talk, and it was as if I was giving a one-on-one workshop about the orientation of the self.

My comment: The scenario above demonstrates the difference between my perception and my daughter's perception. She has lived in the United States since she was five. The impact of Western values contributes to her worldview of how an individual behaves. The American self encourages self-reliance and independence. Therefore, when I acted like a child, needing to be fed, she disapproved; hence, the dirty look. I explained to her that I could have gotten very angry and upset with her when she chided me. Children do not talk to their parents as if they're on the same level. The parent has authority over the child, at any age. However, I quietly chuckled because I understood her. Having awareness is the key! During our talk, she listened and explained her side. She said she thought I still had the remnants of my formative years, having been raised and spoon-fed by my *yaya* (nanny) in the Philippines. Her assessment and remarks were music to my ears. She said, "Mom, how I wish you would always explain and talk this way, very professional, and sure of what you are talking about! Thank you!" After that encounter, I felt that during the entire week, she was very attentive and always asked me what I wanted to eat. "Would you like this or that," she would ask me. It was an amazing experience.

Thirty-two years ago, there is no way I would have responded to her remark the way I did that day! Her comment would have been tantamount to having no respect for me, her mother. I would have thought, "How dare you talk this way to your mother!" I know she loves me, but her expression of love does not necessarily constitute oneness with me. I am an individual to her. She does not perceive me to be an extension of herself in the way that I see her as an extension of me. "Your joy is my joy; your sorrow is my sorrow," goes a popular saying in discussions of the Filipino self.

B. *Balikbayan* boxes

After one of my workshops on "Our Intercultural Lives," a mother came to me and shared an issue she had been having with her two young adult professional daughters over *balikbayan* boxes. *Balikbayan* is Filipino for homecoming; *balikbayan* box is like a care package. Under a government incentive launched in the 1970s, overseas Filipinos can send boxes full of goodies to their loved ones in the Philippines for a uniform price regardless of weight.

So the mother was so happy sending boxes to her loved ones, but her daughters resented it. Her U.S.-born girls did not understand why their mom would spend her meager pension to buy all sorts of food and other items to send to relatives on a regular basis, especially since the relatives were not in dire need of these items. The mother explained that she just wanted to share her blessings with her relatives. Unfortunately, her daughters did not understand this behavior, and it remained a thorny issue.

My comment: My daughter also did not understand why I sent *balikbayan* boxes. For her, it was an unnecessary expense, given my limited income. As a compromise, I promised her that I would only send one box on special occasions, like Christmas. Early one Saturday morning in Southern California, I got a call from her in New York. At the same time, a man from the cargo company was in my apartment to pick up the *balikbayan* box. Our conversation was going smoothly until she overheard the man asking me for more packing tape. She asked, who was that? I answered nothing, just the rustling of the leaves outside. But the man asked again for more tape!

This time, she exclaimed, "Mom, that is a man's voice. What's going on?" So I told her I was sending a *balikbayan* box. I had to tell her, lest she conclude I had a strange man in my apartment at seven in the morning!

To Americanized teens and young adults, the *balikbayan* box has become a source of resentment and misunderstanding. It's an all-too-frequent opening through which culture clash rears its ugly head again and again. Parents keep explaining, in vain, to their children that they just want to share the blessings they have in America with their less fortunate relatives, who are an extension of themselves!

Weighing both sides to even the keel

A deeper discussion is needed here to shed more light on the differing orientations of children born or raised in the United States and their immigrant parents from the Philippines. Immigrant parents will come to realize at some point that there is a concept of an individual self-operating within their Americanized children. The individual self stands alone and sees the world according to the point of view of the self. We must take to heart that our children, having been raised in the United States, have definite orientations/understandings of separate selves. It causes them anger and resentment toward us when we don't consider their individual point of view. It is not because they are cold-hearted, far from it. It is because they feel their time and effort in supporting us one way or another is not given value. Take, for instance, the story of one son who works hard and often reminded his mother to go slow with her donations to charities in the Philippines. His mother ignored his reminders and kept on giving. Then, when she emptied her pension, she came to her son expecting him to bail her out. This caused heated discussions. The mother was too stubborn to give due regard to her son's admonishment. In fact, this scenario commonly takes place in both the United States and the Philippines. From the children's perspective, if their parents do not listen and yet keep expecting a bailout, then it is the kids who are supporting the parent's charities.

Foregoing individual needs

A group-centered culture, for the most part, has little room for individual needs. The main focus is on what is good for the welfare of the group. The person who gives up his/her individual needs chooses to sacrifice to meet the family's needs. To reinforce this discussion, let me share what I sacrificed upon the sudden demise of my youngest brother. As soon as I learned of his passing, I knew I would have to give up the $500 that I had saved for Christmas shopping to contribute to his funeral expenses in the Philippines. Every individual in a group-centered culture gives up something to meet the group's needs. Are you appreciated for this gesture? Sadly, the answer is no, because as a family member, that is your duty and your obligation. Like it or not, fair or not, we are resigned to it. Every adult Filipino living in the United States has experienced his or her share of joys and hurts when helping their kin in the Philippines.

A mother's story

A young woman organized a birthday party for her daughter, who was turning three. The young woman's mother thought her daugter would appreciate it if she invited her American friend who had lavished the young woman with attention when she was little. Alas, when her daughter saw the American friend at the party, she cornered her mother in private and asked her, "Mom, what is she doing here? This is my party!" The mother was immensely hurt by this comment because she meant well. She thought her daughter would remember this friend who doted on her when she was small.

Now, this is where this story gets worse. I offended this mother when I explained that her daughter was simply expressing her self-orientation. "It is coming from nothing personal, nothing to do with love for you!" I said to her. "You did not inform her you were bringing an uninvited guest because you assumed she would be ecstatic. If she had been a daughter born and raised in the Philippines, she might have immediately understood what you did because you would have the same shared cultural values and assumptions." This mother, who shared her experience, expected support from me but did not feel supported because she felt I took her daughter's side! Of course, I did not. I only explained her daughter's behavior. Yet, the aggrieved mother could not hear me because she was dwelling on her own interpretation. She wanted me to support the notion that her daughter doesn't love her anymore. It is frustrating when we try but cannot unravel the cultural issues in a scenario like this one. My heart goes out to immigrant parents who are not quick to grasp such difficult scenarios that occur with their grown children.

C. Time-sharing

The American daughter-in-law was upset. It was their turn to vacation in the time-share condo in Acapulco, but her Filipino mother-in-law took it upon herself to invite her sister, the sister's husband, her brother, and the brother's wife. The daughter-in-law did not know how to address the issue. So, her husband did by explaining their definition of family. To his mother, family included her sisters and brothers and their spouses and children. Now that is extended family to the American daughter-in-law as her idea of the immediate family included only the parents-in-law and siblings-in-law, not their entire family.

My comment: There you have it: culture clash! To the American daughter-in-law, the extended family is not immediate family and is not customarily invited to family vacations, especially without prior discussion. The Filipino mother-in-law had a broader definition of family. Therefore she no qualms inviting her siblings' spouses to participate in the vacation. She will have to adjust because the self-orientation of her daughter-in-law is different from hers. The daughter-in-law can also adjust her expectations once she understands that the husband's definition of family is larger than hers. Ideally, it should work both ways.

D. A bowl of ice cream

While I was conducting a workshop on the topic of orientation of the self, one of the participants suddenly had an aha moment. She felt her behavior was vindicated by my explanation. She explained that her American husband and her Filipino daughters, both born and raised in the United States, would tell her that she is weird because she expects to be served a bowl of ice cream every time they have ice cream. They didn't understand why she sulked whenever it was not provided to her, she didn't ask them. She expected them to know she wanted ice cream, too. She protested that they were supposed to know! So, by their standard of behavior, she was weird because she expected them to read her mind. The American husband and daughter are shaped by the American worldview of the individual self. In their world, an independent person would ask, "May I have some ice cream, too?" This is a common example of how cultural conflict arises.

I interviewed a Filipino husband who spent most of his adult life in the United States. He complained that his wife, who was born and raised in the Philippines, was always accusing him of having an affair because he said, "I don't think of her needs all the time when I go shopping. She believes I must always buy something for her too. Even the simple task of fixing myself a bowl of ice cream while we watch TV, *nagtatampo na at hindi ko siya dinalhan na* ice cream *niya* [showing affective disappointment because I didn't bring her ice cream] brings up this issue. We always argue about this!"

E. What has food got to do with love?

This story, which comes from my first book, is a favorite of mine. The American father and Filipino mother were out shopping with their children. When it came time for lunch, the parents gave the children a choice, telling them they could either go with Dad or Mom to eat. Dad wanted pizza, and Mom wanted Chinese. But when all the children decided to go with Dad, Mom started walking alone toward Panda Express. Then she turned around and told her family, "If you love me, you would go where I want to eat!" Dad and kids did an about-face and followed Mom! Yet, the children couldn't stop thinking, "What has love got to do with the food I want to eat?" They could not reconcile their logic with that of their mom! They probably felt that their mom was weird. I wonder, haven't they ever heard the familiar saying, "the family that eats together stays together?"

My comment: Cross-cultural families and marriages experience culture clash in many ways other than personality differences. It is the wise parent who is aware of these issues and can explain this behavior to his or her children in a way that they can understand. If they can discern between their cultural selves (American and Filipino) they become culturally aware. Since much of the true face of a culture often lies deep beneath one's level of consciousness and is therefore not easy to recognize. Therefore, it becomes hidden and often results in culture clash. Yet, culture always surrounds us like the air we breathe. So, the more we are aware of how others perceive their world differently from ours, the better we can relate and connect to our humanness.

Living under the umbrella of the dominant culture, these differences in concepts of the self among Filipinos and Americans will cloud rather than clear the air if not understood and examined. As was commonly said in the ancient world from Persia to Egypt to Greece, "An unexamined life is not worth living." Because the Filipino strongly identifies with the family, it is of interest to point out that Filipinos are a small-group-centered people.

The Filipino tends to value the family very strongly, it is his small group. He has to have the approval of that small group for his every action and decision. One's self-worth is tightly woven into the group that the person cares about, be it family, friends, extended family, colleagues, church mates, or hobby club. The Filipino's self-worth is commonly referred to as self-esteem. It is felt when the Filipino achieves emotional integration into a group that shows him high regard or respect. In other words, one's need to belong is fulfilled. It does not bother a Filipino if he or she falls out of grace with an individual as long as he or she enjoys high esteem with the group, that is all he or she cares about.

In the American orientation, self-esteem is achieved when one accomplishes self-integration and is perceived to be a high functioning individual in whom heart, body, mind, and soul are fully integrated. A self-integrated American can remove himself from any group and still feel at home with himself. The more the person can transcend the influence and expectations of a group, the more this person is perceived as having high level of self-confidence. Such a perception of oneself is enough to boost one's self-esteem within the American culture context.

A WORD OF CAUTION

A culture clash occurs when our beliefs and behaviors come in direct contact with those of another person's beliefs and behaviors from another culture. But we seldom recognize this as cultural in nature. We often assume that the issue is linked to personality differences. However, this is culture clash! The stories mentioned above have differing assumptions and significant contrasts as to orientation, perception, and understanding of the American and Filipino individual self, and are examples of culture clash.

In as much as I am explaining our behavior culturally, we should not rest totally on the belief that all behavior is influenced by cultural orientation alone. We must leave room to consider the unique personality of the individual. There is always the overlap of personality with one's culture in the interaction.

A husband and wife that I know always butt heads because both have very strong personalities and come from different cultures. Not only do they deal with personality conflicts, but they tackle an additional layer of differing cultural orientation as well. Now that is a double whammy!

The orientation of the self on the collectivist point of view will not always have the automatic reaction of feeling one and the same with the other person in every situation. For example, just because you consider a person your best friend doesn't mean that in all circumstances this best friend would be included in your family circle. There may be one reason or another why the best friend is excluded in a particular situation. Therefore, we must be aware of not entirely blaming culture or personality alone but looking at the circumstances of a particular situation that could be influencing behavior.

In the underlying behavior of *pakikipagkapwa,* the individual is always looking into the collective experience of one's personhood or *pagkatao.* The Filipino is constantly seeking oneness with the other unless the other is perceived to be a *masamang tao,* a bad person. The Filipino self, therefore, is never separate from the other. On the surface, the Filipino individual seems agreeable all the time! The bluntness of speech in social interaction is uncalled for unless one is slighted or feels hurt, as in the above case of the mother who felt abandoned when her children chose to go with their father for pizza. Her situation gave her no choice but to use the love card. Whatever the situation may be, the chances are that most Filipinos, even when already slighted, will choose to remain quiet to keep the interactions harmonious. Maintaining good relationships is the highest priority and muzzling one's honest expression of feelings is the norm. In a way, it seems integrity has to be compromised to keep harmonious communication flowing. However, the Filipino has many levels of social interaction that allow him or her to be indirect in expressing his or her real feelings while avoiding offending others.

Individualists and Collectivists

In my first book, I focused on describing the American self as individualistic and the Filipino self as collectivistic. In other words, Americans are independent while Filipinos are dependent on the group.

In the groundbreaking book by Derald Sue and David Sue, *Counseling the Culturally Different,* the authors argue that among Asians, the self is defined within the identity of the family, whereas among Americans, it is defined as an individual who is independent of others, you are your own person, as is often said.[4]

Seeing through the lens of the Western culture

The previous analysis is missing the idea that the Filipino culture is its own expression of its indigenous concepts of human behavior. My consciousness in writing was to think in English concepts and translate them into the Filipino language instead of the other way around. For instance, within the context of Filipino culture, people are not occupied with self-esteem. They will ask what it means. I assumed that this was a universal expression! The teens and young adults who grew up in America would readily understand the term self-esteem, but not necessarily their immigrant parents. The closest Filipino equivalent would be *pagpapahalaga sa sarili.* In the Filipino culture, if you show and declare your *pagpapahalaga sa sarili* thinking you are expressing self-esteem, you are actually being perceived as haughty or arrogant, *mayabang,* as they derisively state in Filipino. Deference to the group is always the norm. The worth or *halaga* of a person is afforded in the form of respect to the person who has earned recognition from the group. In other words, the person has gained collective respect from the group.

---

[4] Derald Sue and David Sue, *Counseling the Culturally Different,* (New York, USA: Wiley & Sons, First Edition, 1980, Second Edition, 1990)

Another important cultural value is *pakikiramdam*. It is a common expression within the Filipino culture that if you have no *pakikiramdam*, then you are *manhid* (numb, tone-deaf, or dense). Once perceived to be astute in *pakikiramdam*, you will be admired and highly regarded by others. However, parents complain that their children, young or old, have become *manhid* living in the United States. They do not know how to read body language. One mother told me that if she stared at her teenager because of something negative she said, then the kid would stare back at her as if they were having a staring contest!

Since an estimated four million Filipino Americans live in the United States and the majority are naturalized U.S. citizens, I am not the only person who claims to have seen the effect of having been Americanized after more than 30 years of living in this country. In one way or another, we all have experienced the impact of American culture on our lives. We all walk around with altered lenses in varying degrees. In Harry Triandis' book, *Collectivism and Individualism,* the social psychologist explores the constructs of a collectivistic and individualistic society. As he points out in his book, "collectivists are closely linked individuals who view themselves as parts of a whole, be it a family, network of co-workers, tribe, or nation. Such people are mainly motivated by the norms and duties imposed by the collective entity. On the other hand, individualists are motivated by their own preferences, needs, and rights, giving priority to personal rather than to group goals." [5]

With this definition, Triandis establishes that, indeed, Filipinos are collectivists, parts of a whole. His individual self merges with the group he cares about.

---

[5] Harry Triandis, *Collectivism, and Individualism* (Boulder, USA: Westview Press, 1995)

What matters is meeting the needs or the goals of the group. He puts his own needs aside. The success of the group is also his success. Look at events like school graduations or job promotions. Families from collectivist-oriented cultures are visibly ecstatic at seeing their loved ones graduate or get promoted, feeling as if they are the ones walking across the stage to receive the diploma or get a handshake from the boss during a promotion ceremony. In a group-centered culture, the members act as collaborators, helping one another at any age of their lives. Members put aside their own individual needs for the good of the group. In psychological terms, such an individual's personality is characterized by an unindividuated ego. He has group-oriented personality characteristics. He values close emotional ties in public, defers to the group; prefers authoritarianism, dependency, and familiarity while dreading face-to-face interactions with strangers. Thus, Filipinos as a whole, prefer small-group values and do not have a strong individuated ego.

Individualists, on the other hand, have achieved a level of sophistication in cultivating the highly individuated ego. They have very good verbal skills and can discuss anything under the sun without becoming personal. Compare this with a Filipino who finds himself a stranger in a party or any social gathering. He or she will first look for some personal connection with the people around him before feeling comfortable enough to talk. Individualists are motivated in terms of their preferences, rights, and needs. Everything is seen from the point of view of the self. In fact, it is acceptable for individuals to leave their companies for higher-paying jobs. The priority is meeting personal goals rather than those of the company. Accomplishment is an individual effort.

In 1994, my grandmother was posthumously given the Golden Mother of the Year award on Mother's Day in the Philippines. On a special occasion such as this, naturally, there was a souvenir program featuring all the Golden Mother awardees in different categories. Their exemplary lives were highlighted. What's striking is that all of them included the college degrees their children earned and the names of the institution they attended. An American friend read the souvenir program and criticized the display of degrees. He thought this was irrelevant; after all, the awards and accompanying souvenir program were all about grandmothers. Doing the same in the United States, he said, would be seen as ridiculous. For him, earning his degree was an individual accomplishment. I asked him, "Who helped you earn your degree?" He replied, "No one but me." I asked him again, "Who paid your tuition?" Again, he replied, "No one but me. I took out a student loan. And I am still paying on the loan."

"That's where our differences lie," I told him. "You see, Filipino parents go out of their way to help pay the tuition of their children. Some sell their land, cattle, house, or jewelry. Thus, it is the parents' pride to list the names of their children side by side with the degrees they earned because they are the products of parental labor. You are an individualist, and we are collectivists. We have a different perspective, but that's okay."

"Immigrant parents fear the decisions their children, who have been raised in an individualistic American culture, will make." I continued, "They fear being sent to a nursing home when they become incapable of taking care of themselves. They fear the values placed on loyalty and care to one's parents and family members will be replaced with self-fulfillment and individual goals."

Lost status

There is a commercial center in West Covina, a suburb east of Los Angeles, that hosts a complex of Filipino businesses. Most prominent among them is a supermarket, Seafood City, which has become synonymous with the entire commercial center.

Seafood City has become a hub for elderly Filipino males, the *lolos* (grandfathers), who meet every week to hang out and talk about their life in the United States. They mainly grumble over their lost status in the family. They thought that when their professional sons and daughters petitioned them to come to the United States, it would elevate their station in life. To their dismay, they have been reduced to babysitting their *apo* (grandchildren). They even came up with a sardonic title for their new job: *apo*stolic mission. They find to their shock that some of their *apo* have no respect for them and even call them by their first names! Most disappointing of all, they find they are no longer part of significant family decisions and are only informed after the fact. "Our wise and tried ideas are no longer sought by our children," sighed one. In fact, some have expressed the hope of going back to the Philippines, where they would be revered for their wisdom.

A couple shared with me how hurt they were that their son and daughter-in-law decided on a preschool for their first *apo* and simply told them after the fact. The grandmother, who has a degree in Child Development, felt her expertise was devalued. When they brought the issue up, they were told that they did not grow up in the United States. Therefore, they would not know about the educational system.

Hurt feelings in the above scenario could have been avoided if both sides were aware of their worldviews when it comes to parenting. When I went to school to study Bicultural Development, I learned that the Western orientation has a **linear** outlook on life, whereas the Eastern orientation has a **circular** one. The linear worldview states that children are always the responsibility of their parents. When those children become adults and have their own children, then it's their turn. The focus is always forward and onward, creating a straight line, linear. Sending parents, when they become very old, to nursing homes is an example of the linear worldview because the thinking goes, parents are not the responsibility of their children. This linear outlook means that sending one's parents to nursing homes is a natural thing to do. Therefore, if a grandparent is not consulted in family decisions, like what preschool to send their grandchild, a linear worldview is present.

One of the most memorable movies of my youth was *Guess Who's Coming to Dinner*. Released in 1967, the plot centers on Joanna (played by Katharine Houghton), a young and charming white woman who falls in love with and decides to marry John Prentiss, a doctor who is African American (played by Sidney Poitier). While there are thought-provoking dialogues in the movie, what struck me most was this line John told his father, a retired mailman, "I owe you nothing because I did not ask to be born. I am your responsibility for as long as you live, in the same manner, that my future children will become my responsibility because I am responsible for bringing them into the world."

Here we see the linear (straight line) worldview. This statement is a stark contrast to the circular worldview in which parents will say to their children, "You owe your life to me because I brought you into this world."

The circular worldview sees life as a circle. The circle begins when the parents take care of their children and ends with parents growing old and weary and becoming the responsibility of the now-grown children.

In this worldview, parents are always part of the equation, including family decisions, even in their old age.

There are always exceptions to the rule. There are some American families whose senior parents still live with them. However, the importance of having an awareness of our differing worldviews on parenting cannot be understated.

Mother and son merging identities

A wedding took place recently, and during the reception, some members of the wedding party were asked to address the newlyweds. The groom's mother told her daughter-in-law in front of everyone that her son was still a virgin, and his wedding night was going to be his first time! Was this cool or cruel? Then, during the reception, when the time came to open the gift envelopes, mother and son raced to see who could get to the check inside!

Relatives and guests were perhaps amused or shocked at the pair's behavior. But to me, it was just a transparent demonstration of a mother and son operating as one; the son is his mother's extension and vice versa. I was not surprised to learn that the son had been living in the United States for only a year, compared to his bride who had lived here most of her life. I said to myself, *give him a year, and he will come around and discover his individual self.* Until then, get ready for some culture clash.

My own culture shock of self-orientation

My first definitive experience with the differences between my Filipino self and American self happened while I was teaching in a public school. One lunch break, my colleague (I will call her Susie) called me and three other teachers to a meeting: a Caucasian, an African American, a Latina, and myself, an Asian. Susie, who was Caucasian, was concerned over her upcoming evaluation, in which her performance in the classroom would be observed by the principal. Her evaluation was happening in two weeks. The reason for her concern was the seven disruptive boys in her classroom. Obviously, she didn't want her class to be disrupted by these seven students while the principal was evaluating her.

So, she called the meeting to ask us if we were willing to help her by trading her disruptive students with better-behaved students from our classes. All of us sincerely sympathized and considered her request— except the other Caucasian, who was adamantly against the trade. She said she didn't want to disrupt the established dynamics in her class in the middle of the year. Our jaws dropped because she was Susie's best friend. I was in culture shock! I could not reconcile the scenario taking place between these two best friends. Here we were, three minorities who all agreed to help Susie, a co-worker but nothing more, yet her best friend was ditching her. I silently concluded that this would break their friendship.

Boy, was I wrong. After we finalized the trade, I discovered to my shock that Susie and her best friend still remained the best of pals. They were able to separate their professional lives from their personal behavior. And that was my introduction to orientation of the self. But my question remained: How did they do it, separate their personal and professional relationships?

A year later, as I studied for a masters' degree in Bicultural Development, I found the answer. Perhaps, Susie respected her best friend for making an honest and strong stand for her principle. There's individualism for you. Juxtapose this with me and the other two teachers and where we were coming from. As African American,

Hispanic, and Asian, we considered our shared experiences of having disruptive students in the class. And take note, she had not one but seven! We had what Filipinos describe as *pakikiramay sa damdamin* (shared inner perception) of what Susie was going through every day. That's why we seriously considered her request. But Susie's best friend and fellow Caucasian, considered only her situation and had no qualms expressing herself.

Let me end this discussion with two timeless quotes representing these two polar opposites: the collectivist and individualist self-orientations.

One is an African proverb, "I am because we are and because we are, therefore, I am."

The other is by French philosopher Rene Descartes, "I think, therefore, I am."

Clash of individualism and collectivism

During my graduate studies, I became acquainted with a former Peace Corps Volunteer in the Philippines who shared one of her complaints about living among Filipinos. When she got married to her Filipino boyfriend, his relatives ran to her to ask for financial assistance. "Like what?" I asked. She replied, "Well, when so-and-so got sick and needed medicine or so-and-so needed money for surgery. I don't even know these relatives!" I felt then that I was becoming an "expert" in understanding the dynamics of collective culture, being a grad student in culture study. So, I explained to her that while she had the individual right to say no, her Filipino relatives would not understand because, in the big picture of the family, there is no one individual. Everyone is expected to contribute to the welfare of the group. And in her case, she had been designated financier of the family because of her access to U.S. dollars. I laughed while saying it, but it was true.

SPECIAL BENEFIT OF INDIVIDUALISM AND COLLECTIVISM

I want to give special attention to the significant benefits of individualism and collectivism. There are many benefits, but I will focus on those that top my list. Perceived to be an individual alone, expected to strive for the betterment of oneself, for reaching the stars by one's own effort, regardless of one's circumstances. Therefore, becoming one's own hero, you are provided the space and opportunity to actualize this potential. It is a tall order yet achievable with perseverance. When you have proven your potential with what you achieved to the nth degree, earning the respect of your peers and society-at-large, is the magic of individualism. You are given a chance to prove yourself.

This is where a collectivist society is slow in rewarding its people. As an example, Lea Salonga was already performing as a vocalist in her native Philippines. The powers that be in the music industry had not yet bestowed on her the crown in singing. Then, here comes Miss Saigon, a musical story. At age 18, Lea Salonga auditioned for the play and was selected for the role of Kim. She went to West End in the United Kingdom, and then on to Broadway in the USA, winning the Olivier and Theater World Awards and becoming the first Asian woman to win a Tony Award. Salonga returned to her motherland, the Philippines, and only then was she given a heroine's welcome. No Asian woman can claim the title she holds. Could she have gone as far in the Philippines if she had not demonstrated her talent to a Western audience that's constantly seeking individual accomplishment?

In a collectivist society, the drive to include everyone is carried almost to a fault. The end result is the Filipino core value of *pakikipagkapwa* (shared humanity). There is always enough food for all. There is always space or room for all. A Filipino stretches his/her humanity to accommodate all. It doesn't matter that we are like sardines in the bus so long as we all have fun together. We are going to be "floor leaders," a common expression Filipinos use to mean tonight we will spread our mats on the living room floor and have fun as we sleep, not minding how narrow our spaces will be. It's not necessarily comfort that matters but the camaraderie that takes place. There is no such thing as coming unannounced while the family is eating. There is always room for the uninvited guest. A classic example is the story of my friend, a Peace Corps Volunteer (PCV). On his exit interview after serving in the Philippines, he shared with me what he told the PCV coordinator when he visited me and my husband, James, in Taipei, Taiwan.

I went to the Philippines as an American volunteer, and I left as a world citizen. I am not ready to return to my country. So, I will hang out here in Taiwan for now. I learned to seek the people, the person first, not the comfort level of my accommodations. I used to find excuses when invited because I perceived my comfort would be compromised. As time went by, I began to be ashamed of my secret attitude. I've made adjustments, and now I can no longer go back to the old me. I went to the Philippines to conquer the Filipinos, but in the end, I was the one conquered.

Me and my daughter: An epiphany

Thirtiy-two years ago, in the wee hours of the morning, my 12 ½-year-old daughter snuck out of our apartment to hang out with friends. Had I given in to my anger, the consequences could have been disastrous. She said her friends were slapped, spanked, belted, and kicked out of the house by their parents. When they asked what I did to her, she just kept quiet. I did nothing.

I just showered her with love, following the example of the father, in Jesus' Parable of the Prodigal Son.

In the years that followed, as we navigated our relationship, I came to realize that my daughter just wanted an opportunity to be heard. So I tried my best to listen. It was a struggle to listen and not react because most of what she had to say, I didn't like.

Then one day, I had an epiphany. If I silenced my child, she would not grow up feeling empowered. Little did I know that, over time, we were both developing into our own individual selves as mother and daughter.

This is how it happened. One day, my daughter just blurted out, "Mom, are you just being Filipino when you go ballistic because I speak my mind?"

"Like what?" I retorted.

"Right now!" she responded, "Your hands are flailing up in the air! I think you are about to become violent with me!"

"No, that's just my way of expressing myself," I exclaimed. "But look at you. Are you being American when you talk this way to me because right now I am feeling you are disrespecting me, your mother!"

"Mom, no. I am only expressing my opinion, that's not disrespect!" she excitedly said.

This was it! As soon as she said OPINION, I suddenly got it. In the mind of our Americanized teens and young adults, they were only expressing their opinion. Quietly, I thought, disbelievingly asking myself, hers is expressing an opinion, but mine is my feeling? But because we, as parents born and raised in the Philippines, grew up without being given the chance to express our opinions, we only know to express feelings? As children, we were only seen and not heard in the family dynamics. Our teens and young adults in the United States are raised to be independent-minded.

As I continued to listen and allow her to freely express her opinion, little did we know that our tensions were gradually going away. Eventually, I learned to be aware of when to separate and when to be one with her. Being the mature adult in the relationship, I led the way, and my teenager followed. Indeed, it is the parent who must lead by example.

Lesson learned on my journey

Silence your child, your teenager, or your young adult, and a voice is lost forever. Let the family dynamics become their training ground by allowing them to speak up so they can one day face the world with gusto and confidence. In the long run, we want to train empowered kids. One day, our children will leave the comfort of our homes to make their mark in society. How will they fare if they have been silenced at home? In the workshops I have conducted with Filipino families, I often comment that teens and young adults simply listen but do not ask questions because they are in the presence of their parents. I always feel the tension in the air. No matter how much I encourage them to speak, they remain silent.

Impact of the American culture on me

Eventually, I came face to face with my own Americanized behavior as an individualist. I have been shaped by my 30-plus years of living in the United States, but also by the company I keep, including many close American friends here, in the Philippines, and in Taiwan. But the most significant part of becoming an individualist came out of my interaction with my American daughter. I became a pro in recognizing the individualist behavior of others. However, I often had no clue when I was exhibiting individualist behavior toward others!

I was visiting a dear friend who at that time was invited to a party. Since I was visiting her, I tagged along. I was well aware that the host and her family were only interested in bonding with my friend. I was a *saling-pusa*, the Filipino equivalent of the odd-man-out and behaved accordingly. I didn't socialize, kept my head low, and played with my new iPhone. Little did I realize that my friend was *sama na loob* (resentful) toward me because of my attitude. I made it worse when the family insisted I join them outside for a photoshoot. I was not cooperative. My friend could not understand my attitude. She thought I was *pakipot* (feigning unwillingness). She pulled me out of my comfortable chair and forced me to join the shoot. I insisted on standing at the extreme side because my friend was on the other side. I thought that when the picture was developed, it would have a nice presentation because the three sisters would be in the middle and the two friends would be on the outside. I was looking at the aesthetic effect. My friend didn't understand my intention, of course.

A few months later, when I was back in California, I had this big aha moment on my own Americanism while writing this book. I revisited this scenario with her, and only then did I catch my individualistic behavior. If I had been one and the same with her, I would have just gone along for the ride and experienced *pakikisama* (yielding to her lead). But I was stubborn, although ultimately, I obliged and joined the photoshoot. Revisiting this incident with her, she told me how *inis* (annoyed) she was with my behavior. Well, that's one individualized author for you.

Independence and dependence

Looking back at all of my experiences, I now realize that I have a mindset that results in independent and dependent behavior. Because the Filipino culture

34

values high collective thought, independent concepts have no place in the thought process and individualism has no place in the culture. The Filipino culture has no concept of having an individual self per se. The default setting is to always consider what is good for the group, especially the family. Often, when a family loses both parents at a young age, the eldest child will send his or her siblings to school and forego his or her personal happiness, i.e. marriage, family, etc.

The adherence to independent behavior, showing self-sufficiency, self-assertiveness, and self-reliance, has always been the foundation of the American character. This foundation becomes the breeding ground for individualism. One is always expected to develop his or her individuality, that is, the autonomous self, to have a unique self, develop one's own opinion, make one's own choices, solve one's own problems, have one's own things, and evaluate the world according to one's point of view. In a penetrating study of the American character called *Habits of the Heart,* the eminent sociologist Robert Bellah and his colleagues reported that the most important single characteristic of the American people is individualism. He said that American cultural traditions favor the individual, his personality, achievement, and purpose, over family.[6] Asked whether she is responsible for her husband, Margaret, one of those interviewed by the author, replied, "I'm not. He makes his own decisions." As for her children, she said, "I have legal responsibilities for them, but I think they are responsible for their own actions."

---

[6] Robert N. Bellah, et. al. *Habits of the Heart, Individualism And Commitment In American Life* (Berkeley, Los Angeles, London: University of California Press, 2008) 142-143

In the Philippines, however, the child is raised from birth to have a relational self. Desirable traits are those that develop closeness, respect, and devotion to others. This relational behavior translates into dependency. Actually, in the Filipino view, the child should not be rushed into growing up but is expected to develop gradually, gaining skills as necessary in the life of family activities and responsibilities. But viewed objectively, the values taught to children translate into dependency. Young Filipinos develop a relational self, finding their identity through their relationships with others. The Filipino child does not particularly aspire to be his or her own person and often seeks the help and cooperation of others in doing things that could be done individually. When viewed through American cultural thinking, which favors the individual over the family, such behavior is characterized as dependency and inadequacy. But for Filipinos, this is considered closeness, cooperation, respect, and duty, an essential part of how a Filipino child develops relationships with his elders. In the Philippine ideal, one is not an individual but a part of a family whose older members are the support and whose younger members a responsibility.

Immigrant parents in the United States, having been used to this parenting practice, are caught unprepared when their teenager begins to express independent behavior and develops a strong sense of self. Immigrant teenagers starting to assert their individual rights throw their parents off-balance. "They grew horns!" remarked one parent. From there, cross-cultural conflicts begin to emerge in the communication process.

Independence and self-reliance

I often wonder whether young Filipinos growing up in the United States are developing relational selves because all around them, their character is being shaped toward self-sufficiency, self-reliance, and independence. One time, I was a guest of a family and was surprised to see that the two sons prepared their own breakfast, dressed for school, and waited alone for the school bus. All the while, both parents were still fast asleep. You would not find this scenario in the Philippines. These sons are now on the way to becoming full-fledged, independent-minded individuals.

I interviewed a recent college graduate who just started her job. She spoke succinctly of her newly gained independence. "My parents were heartbroken after I declared my intention to move out of the house to join my boyfriend," she said. "It appeared my graduation present to them was my desire to live on my own with my boyfriend. I don't regret this decision a bit because I feel so free, and with freedom comes empowerment."

A Filipino parent's responsibility is to instill courage in their child, so they can try their wings. However, because parental self-concept always includes intimate others, the consciousness of nurturing their children into an independent adult does not come into focus, nor is there a deliberate intention to make them independent. Hear the words coming from the mouth of this single professional, "Mom, I'm already 46 years old, and you still baby me. I know you always put a blanket around me whenever I fall asleep on your sofa." Here is a Filipino mother who still sees her 46-year-old son as though he was five. "Oh my God, my baby is freezing! Here, baby, I'll cover you with this warm blanket." To Filipino parents, their children are their children, young or old, one with them, not separate selves.

Since our adult children in the United States are independent and self-reliant, we can benefit from their independent behavior as we learn more about their struggles, too. There is a growing ambivalence toward

American individualism today, as reported by Robert Bellah in his *Habits of the Heart* (2008) Bellah writes:

> Rather, we found all the classic polarities of American individualism still operating: the deep desire for autonomy and self-reliance combined with an equally deep conviction that life has no meaning unless shared with others in the context of community… while Americans strongly assert the value of self-reliance and autonomy, there is also the end result of feeling the emptiness of life without sustaining social commitments. Our young people growing up in the United States may be aware of this growing ambivalence toward traditional American individualism.

Life ought to be lived independently, but collectively as well. Life asks us to find the balance needed for a healthy, successful life, whether we live in the United States or the Philippines, or elsewhere. It is a good goal for all.

In-groups and out-groups

Unlike the ones who live in the Philippines, our teens and young adults in the United States do not have an understanding of multiple in-groups and out-groups. Filipinos live with layers and layers of in-groups and out-groups because we are a people centered with small group values. Perhaps, this is attributed to the fact that the Philippines are made up of scattered islands, over 7,000 of them, that were organized into tribes, each ruled by a chieftain. The typical social greeting of a Filipino is, "Where are you going?" rather than "How are you?" And the typical reply, "Over there," accompanied by a hand gesturing toward a certain direction, not naming a location, it's understood, is a testament to our country's archipelagic character. With such a background, our creation of in-groups and out-groups is inevitable. They can be confusing to our Americanized population. Let us, therefore, explore in-groups and out-groups.

It is important to understand the meanings of these two concepts. Failure to know what "in-group" and "out-group" mean has led to confusion, especially in instances where an ethnic group treats members of its own as outsiders, eliciting this common remark, "Those people cannot even get along with their own kind. They are no longer united as a nation."

An in-group is a group a person cares about, with whom he or she is willing to cooperate without demanding equitable returns, and separation from which leads to anxiety. An in-group is usually characterized by similarities among its members, who share a sense of common fate. Belonging to an in-group implies that each member has the right to get involved in the affairs of fellow members.

An out-group is a group with which one has differences or conflicts, disagrees about valued attributes, and is considered harmful in some way. Some groups are neither in- nor out-groups.

Here's another way of looking at it. Any Filipino social organization, from clans to neighborhood associations to chambers of commerce, inevitably break up into smaller groups or factions; these are the in-groups. Just look at any Filipino advertising directory, such as a phone book. There you can find all kinds of Filipino churches, professional groups, and regional associations.

Of course, this is not a particularly Filipino phenomenon. Each culture has its own important in-groups. The family is usually an in-group, but depending on the culture, other groups such as friends, in-laws, political parties, civic organizations, social classes, religious groups, educational, athletic, economic, artistic, racial, tribal, caste, language, or location collectives may function as in-groups. A member of the kin group can become an out-group member if there are insults, impropriety of behavior, or conflict.

How would you explain the concept of in-groups and out-groups as they appear in real-life situations? I am reminded of my first cousins. There are 47 of us. Yet, today, among first cousins, we have in-groups. Those who do not belong to the in-groups are given the treatment usually given to out-groups. Therefore, cousin in-laws who are members of the in-groups are treated better than those first cousins who belong to the out-group. Collectivists are extremely supportive of in-groups and in situations of conflict treat out-groups harshly. It makes no difference that we are related by blood. If you do not belong to my in-group, you are out.

Extending the analogy to another level, a religious group can be made up of people of different ethnicities who share the same theology. They become an in-group. Those outside their theology are given the out-group treatment. So as Filipinos keep changing groups, the dynamics of this behavior result in the forming of in-groups and out-groups. When conflicts occur within a group, cooperation dies. A new in-group is formed, and cooperation thrives again. Cooperation in collectivist cultures occurs only within the in-group; extreme competition characterizes relationships with out-groups. Those in the out-groups will also experience jealousy from some in-group members among them.

In an individualist culture like the United States, there are also in-groups and out-groups, but their ties to one another are loose. Members have liberal expectations of one another. If a member from an individualist in-group has failed the bar exam, other individualists can just shrug and say, try again, and the one who flunked the test won't be stigmatized.

Collectivists need to learn to expect individualists to be less attached to their in-group. If the relative of an individualist fails in school or is fired from a job, the collectivist will expect this event to be extremely traumatic; however, the individualist may not see it that way.

In this dichotomy of in-groups and out-groups, both individualists and collectivists have pluses and minuses. In terms of behavior, individualists have a higher tolerance toward those perceived as belonging to the out-group because they have looser expectations. Therefore, when it comes to marriage outside the race, there is more acceptance of the son- or daughter-in-law among individualists than collectivists. A friend of mine has sons who have wives outside of their own race, and they are wholeheartedly accepted and welcomed into the fold. The mother-in-law researches the native country of the daughter-in-law and learns food recipes and a few native phrases before her arrival. Contrast this to the behavior of another friend from Taiwan, whose parents were having anxiety attacks as they anticipated the arrival of their daughter's American husband. To them, he must prove his worth to be their son-in-law. He learned of their feelings in a hurry because the first thing he did upon arriving in Taipei was to look for a barbershop. His parents-in-law, upon seeing him at the airport, were horrified to see him sporting long hair and a beard.

However, among collectivist cultures, once the new son- or daughter-in-law officially becomes a member of the in-group, he or she will enjoy full acceptance into their fold. In fact, in-group members sometimes love their son- or daughter-in-law more than their son or daughter. An American Cambodian colleague remarked to me that her relatives love her American husband more than they love her. They lavish him with attention, food, and gifts. She feels dethroned. But in-groups and out-groups among collectivists and individualists certainly clarifies the seeming absence of consistency in behavior among their members.

We must not be misled by research done on collectivists and individualists that attribute their behavior only to ethnicity. Harry Triandis, a Greek American psychologist/sociologist, reminds us that collectivists and individualists could be attributes of religious groups. He states, "American Catholics are more collectivists than American Protestants, whereas all Americans are individualists relative to the world's population." Hsu (1983) noted, "The more individualistic Protestants are often the more prejudiced and discriminatory than the less individualistic Catholics."

True indeed. In the Philippines, Filipino Catholics are more collectivists than Filipino Protestants. Filipino Protestants appear to be more Americanized than Filipino Catholics. When Cardinal Jaime Sin, the iconic Archbishop of Manila during the rule of Ferdinand Marcos, gave directives to the Filipino Catholics, they obeyed collectively. "The 1986 People Power revolt that peacefully removed Marcos from power was partly attributed to the collective behavior of the Filipino people after they heard Cardinal Sin over the radio exhorting them to go out in the streets and support Defense Secretary, Juan Ponce Enrile, and Constabulary Chief, Fidel Ramos, whose open defiance of Marcos sparked the revolt."

A personal encounter with Harry Triandis
Personally, navigating around the in-group and out-group dichotomy felt like swimming through a

seaweed jungle. Therefore, I requested help. I was privileged to meet Harry Triandis when I attended the National Association of Foreign Student Advisors (NAFSA) conference in 1987 in Boston, Massachusetts. Triandis was among the speakers. After his presentation about cultures with high values of individualism and collectivism, I sought him to briefly discuss some of his intriguing claims. He confirmed that the Philippines is one of the countries with a high worldview of the collective experience.

I was intrigued by his statement that collectivist in-groups exhibit issues of prejudice and discrimination more than individualist in-groups. It is easier for outsiders to enter individualist in-groups because they have more tolerance for differences. What I found positive is his other statement, that as time goes by, once collectivist in-groups accept an outsider into their fold, that acceptance is permanent. It was an eye-opener for me. I would have never thought the same, due perhaps to my regrettably biased assumption that individualists have an attitude of superiority. Therefore, I felt, cannot possibly be open and welcoming toward those who belong to collectivist cultures. As Triandis explained, this is not necessarily true. I have since accepted his thesis.

It is, necessary to point out that Triandis' research focused on cultural attributes, not racial features of groups. Cultural attributes refer to the beliefs, values, behavior, symbols, language, and the overall way of life. They have nothing to do with physical features of the face, skin and hair color, and body type.

The Filipino style of social interaction (in-group and out-group)

The myriad of relationships that Filipinos are accustomed to is incredible. The in-group and out-group dichotomy that Triandis writes about is easy to navigate because Filipinos are highly relational people. There are five levels of social interaction that Filipinos can lean on as they move from in-groups to out-groups, depending on conflicting situations that arise. These five levels enable one to keep relating to others even though the latter belongs to the category of *ibang tao* (outsider).

The American who is used to only black and white relationships where there is nothing in between will be perplexed to witness the pleasant fluidity of Filipino social interactions, where no one seems to be at odds. An American researcher, Frank Lynch, observed, and concluded in his study, Filipinos avoid confrontation because they opt for smooth interpersonal relationships at all times. To which I say nothing could be farther from the truth. There is more than meets the eye.

Not being Filipino, the researcher missed seeing the many levels of Filipino social interaction: 1) *pakikitungo* (civility); 2) *pakikisalamuha* (mingling or mixing); 3) *pakikilahok* (participating); 4) *pakikibagay* (conforming); and 5) *pakikisama* (adjusting). The Filipino has many levels to choose from in dealing with the out-group. To illuminate further, here's an example. Recently, a friend of mine posted a link containing an unflattering view of a politician on his Facebook page. I posted a comment on his Timeline, which triggered an exchange of opposing views. If my friend and I were individualists or one of us was a collectivist, it's possible our friendship might have crumbled because of that exchange. But since we are both Filipinos and collectivists, we had options on how to deal with each other, the five levels described above, and hence preserve our friendship.

Here is another illustration of in-group and out-group behavior that doesn't exhibit animosity toward another group. I had a Filipino classmate during my masters' studies who confessed she felt used by her white neighbor. The neighbor was going to have a party and asked my classmate to teach her how to make *lumpia* (spring rolls). My classmate enthusiastically obliged. They rolled a hundred of them. During the evening of the party, my classmate waited for her white neighbor to call her to join the party. No call came. The only sound she heard from next door was laughter. She felt discriminated against because all the guests were white. After she told me her story, I asked about the group that came to the party. She said they were the neighbor's church friends. I asked her if she attended the same church, and she replied that she is Catholic, and the neighbor was Baptist. I sighed and explained to her that she was not discriminated against. Even if she helped her neighbor make the *lumpia* for the party, she wasn't invited for the simple reason that she just didn't belong to her neighbor's in-group.

Triandis' analysis also states that collectivist cultures can treat out-groups harshly with no apparent explanation, yet the person who is cast out knows why. Again, using the Filipino culture as an example, Filipinos use multiple levels of interaction in dealing with an out-group. They shield their in-group from any animosity the out-group may dish out. And how this works is not readily apparent.

Here is an example. Filipino Employee A seems to be favored more by the white employer than Filipino Employees B, C, and D. Because of this, Employee A is scratched off the in-group, and Employees B, C, and D are jealous of him or her. Employee A realizes soon enough because he or she is no longer invited to join the in-group for lunch. Employee A eats alone. But in other functions within the work environment, Employees B, C, and D still treat her cordially. The only time they will cease to be civil to Employee A is if they perceive her to be *masamang tao* (bad person).

These levels of interpersonal interaction are exclusive to the in-group or the *hindi ibang tao* (one of us) category: *pakikipalagayang-loob* (level of mutual trust and rapport); *pakikisangkot* (level of getting involved); and *pakikiisa* (level of deep solidarity, unity, and full trust). Never does one apply any of these levels to the out-group. In a nutshell, this is the highly sophisticated mode of relationships among Filipinos. If a Filipino has lived most of his or her adult life outside the mother culture, chances are that his or her Filipino cultural perspective might be muddled. And this I know from personal experience. As I write about my Filipino culture, I must constantly exercise awareness of my conscious and unconscious mind and trust that they operate as one. It has and remains a humbling experience.

At this point, a glossary of terms would be useful for non-Filipino readers:

Levels of social interaction for the *ibang-tao* or "outsider" category:
1) *Pakikitungo* (civility): Considered the most superficial. No personal involvement; mainly for dealing with strangers.
2) *Pakikisalamuha* (mingling or mixing): No personal involvement; mainly for acquaintances.
3) *Pakikilahok* (participating): No nitty-gritty personal involvement; mainly for close acquaintances.
4) *Pakikibagay* (conforming): There is personal involvement but no frank sharing of one's *kalooban* (state of mind or disposition)

5) *Pakikisama* (adjusting): There is deeper personal involvement leading to the next category of *hindi ibang tao* (one of us). *Pakikisama* is one building block among many in the development of a higher level of relationship."[26]

Levels of interpersonal interaction for the *hindi ibang tao or* **"one of us" category:**

1) *Pakikipagpalagayang-loob* (mutual trust and rapport)
2) *Pakikisangkot* (integral involvement)
3) *Pakikiisa* (solidarity, unity, and deep trust)

If all these building blocks are present, then the relationship can be said to have arrived at its highest plane: the category of *hindi ibang-tao* (one of us).

The Filipino who is keenly in tune with the push and pull of social and interpersonal interactions is aware of what is going on in any interaction. On the other hand, one who is disconnected from the mother culture will dismiss as shallow other Filipinos who have many best friends and can appear very close to a person without having any deep involvement. Such is the seeming paradox of the Filipino style of social interaction. My relationships vary in degrees, one would say. In fact, the many layers of social relationships, the Filipino version, keep one from being confrontational. Understand these layers for 'one of us and not one of us' categories and *pakikipagkapwa* continues.

Mangluod/Tampo (affective disappointment)

The Filipino concept of *mangluod* or *tampo* (affective disappointment) is an important element in this discussion. It happens all the time in an organization because of our in-group and out-group behavior. The larger the set of officers in an organization, the higher the probability that clashes over ideas will occur. Say there's a meeting. Officer A makes a suggestion. Officer B opposes it, and the discussion turns problematic because the disagreeing officers are good friends. I can hear Officer A saying to himself, "I thought you were my friend! Why are you disagreeing with me?" If neither one is culturally aware, B risks falling out of A's in-group.

Here is a classic example of how orientation of the self can generate clashes even when participants in a discussion belong to the same culture. My university alumni association has a long and proud history and its share of ups and downs. Association leaders and other officers clash over ideas, procedures, and strategies to keep the association going. *Mangluod/tampo* behavior is never far away during any disagreement, and officers privately worry about being kicked out of each other's in-group! A lot of anguish could have been avoided, if we were aware of this cultural pattern. The *mangluod* or *tampo* behavior toward a disagreeing friend is the result of unmet expectations (I thought you were my friend!). In-group and out-group behavior is activated, and this drives the dynamic of the discussion from bad to worse. *Mangluod* or *tampo* behavior takes place whenever officers in an organization disagree and each one perceives the other to be in his or her in-group. Not surprisingly, this behavior is characteristic in Filipino organizations without exception.

Democratic Club of Claremont

Outside the Filipino context, the rules are entirely different. Take the Democratic Club of Claremont; I am a member and attend its meetings. The dominant members are white, with a few African Americans and Asians. It was a culture shock for me when I attended my first meeting. When the floor was opened for discussion, sparks flew, and everyone was free to agree or disagree. They did so with passion, whether they were friends or not. After a considerable time, the moderator called for a motion to end discussions and take a vote even though an agreement had not been reached. The vote settled it for everyone. When my shock subsided, I said to myself, "well, I guess that's how they do it in the West." The unspoken rule, as you may have already guessed is, "we agree to disagree."

PARENTAL TIPS & GUIDELINES

Before culture clash occurs, a competent cultural detective must be alert, to understand what is going on. Accordingly, our cultural radar must be switched to high alert, and we must always be aware of possible occurrences in intercultural relationships. Here are my suggestions for strategies to prevent clashes from taking place.

Awareness

In seeking the perfect property in real estate, the mantra is "location, location, location." Likewise, when it comes to learning about a culture, the cardinal rule is "awareness, awareness, awareness." Why is this so? According to Elizabeth Conde-Frazier's book, *A Many-Colored Kingdom*, "In human social life, one's beliefs and behavior are constantly interacting with that of others. Not only do beliefs guide behavior, but also the reverse is true. Behavior shapes, orients, uproots, tears down, and raises the nexus of cognitive features that accompany and guide behavior in the long run. Human social life shapes culture and is profoundly shaped by culture."[7] Be aware of this truth.

---

[7] Elizabeth Conde-Frazier, *A Many-Colored Kingdom* (Grand Rapids, USA: Baker Academic, 2004)

It is important to establish your awareness and knowledge about the **orientation of the self** and our individualist and collectivist cultures or we will court disaster. In example A, if I had no awareness of our cultural self-orientation, there would have been a culture clash in the store!

Consider if it is individual or group point of view

Early on in your cultural interaction, become aware of the other person's point of view. Is the self (individualistic) or the group (collectivistic) considered? Once aware, you will know how to proceed to prevent clashes. If the other person is not aware, tell him or her what is being considered. Does the situation reflect the self or the collective experience?

Recently, I was invited to three events: two birthday parties and one discussion group. I knew exactly why I wanted to go to the two birthday parties because it would benefit me individually and collectively. I would have a chance to promote and sell tickets to the dinner dance that our nonprofit foundation was sponsoring. A win-win, as they say.

TED.com is a nonprofit organization devoted to spreading ideas in the form of short, often powerful talks. TED (Technology, Entertainment, Design) began in 1984 as a conference and now covers almost all topics, from science to business to global issues in more than 100 languages.

I watched a TED Talk speaker, Mark Bowden, an expert on human behavior, who claimed that each of the earth's seven billion inhabitants is programmed to be indifferent the moment he or she meets a stranger. On one level, it makes sense, "I don't know this guy, so I don't care about him." From my perspective, though, I thought of the Filipino's way of *pakikipagkapwa*, always thinking of the collective experience. No wonder

Filipinos are considered one of the most hospitable peoples in the world. They are welcoming to strangers.

Here are some popular quotes that encapsulate collectivist and individualist points of view:

"True freedom means you do not need the validation of others to be who you are." Greg Louganis (individualist)

"No man is an island, and no man stands alone. Each man's joy is joy to me; each man's grief is my own. We need one another, so, I will defend. Each man is my brother; each man is my friend." John Donne (collectivist)

"Cutting people out of your life doesn't mean you hate them; it simply means you respect yourself. Not everyone is meant to stay." Anonymous (individualist)

"I am because we are, and because we are, therefore, I am." African Philosophy of Ubuntu (collectivist)

"I think, therefore, I am." Rene Descartes (individualist)

"Don't walk in front of me, because I won't follow. Don't walk behind me, because I won't lead. Walk beside me and be my friend." Camus (collectivist)

Counting to a hundred

The oft-mentioned tip for dealing with anger comes in particularly handy for cultural interactions, which can often be frustrating. Start counting silently (before you use your acerbic tongue) and while you do, quietly process in your head what is going on to determine if a conflict is a personality issue or a cultural one. Chances are before you reach 100, you will be calm enough to talk reasonably.

But how do you distinguish personality from cultural differences? What is the clue? Personality triggers your emotions because it is a style of being that is in collision. For instance, put two headstrong personalities together, and bam! Explosion! Culture issues are rooted around differences in practices, traditions, beliefs, values, communication, working styles, family practices, etc., not personality per se.

Be intentional in earning **respect** in your communication style. Pay attention at all times to your tone of voice. Teens and young adults often comment that their parents raise their voices and are quick to get angry. Here's why. Parents perceive their children as disrespecting their authority.

I confess to having an impulsive tongue, which is why a friend suggested I count to 100 and not 10, to calm down my thoughts and feelings. So, one day, when I was about to explode at my daughter, I started counting and thinking about what was going on with the conflict. Before I reached 100, I knew the answer. Counting helped my emotions dissipate and allowed me to think clearly.

The Filipino's penchant for *pakikipagkapwa* (shared humanity and identity) is the foundation of human values that is sometimes, if not always, upheld to a fault. Such is the depth of the Filipino character seeking unity with the other. The self is always seeking to merge with the other; the two are not separate.

It is important that teens and young adults along with their immigrant parents feel that they are heard and that their perspectives are honored and accepted.

REFLECTION

"Culture is dictatorial, if not understood and examined."
—Edward T. Hall

CHAPTER 2

HIGHLY VERBAL AND NON-VERBAL CULTURES

*"Pahiwatig...operates as an instrument
of verbal and nonverbal expressiveness in
a culture that is at once accessible and
inscrutable to an outside observer, artful
indirection in communicating wants
or feelings.[8]*
—*Melba P. Maggay*

Pahiwatig, as defined by Dr. Melba P. Maggay, is a ploy that Filipinos are adept at applying in communication patterns. It is an artful "hint" to communicate what is really in one's heart regarding wants and feelings. And it "takes a great deal of *pakikiramdam* or discernment to accurately determine which *pahiwatig* is going on.

What is *pakiramdam*? *Pakikiramdam* is defined in Dr. Virgilio Enriquez' book, *From Colonial to Liberation Psychology, The Philippine Experience,* as a shared inner perception, a feeling for the other, and a sensitivity to signals that are not readily apparent. *Pakikiramdam* is the capacity to read another person's nonverbal language. It is a silent virtue nurtured in the Filipino culture. If you lack this trait, you are called *manhid* (numb, tone-deaf, or dense). You are supposed

---

[8] Melba P. Maggay, Understanding Ambiguity in Filipino Communication Patterns (Quezon City, Philippines: Institute for Studies in Asian Church and Culture, ISACC, 1999) p. 14, 20.

to be astute in reading what is going on by observing how everyone is behaving. There are no words needed because you let your actions tell the other person you "get it." You simply know. Practicing *pakikiramdam* sharpens one's awareness and sensitivity to perceive the meaning of the behavior of others. Dr. Rita Mataragnon characterizes *pakikiramdam* as an "emotional *a priori* judgment," one that is supported neither by fact nor experience. Yet how one arrives at that judgment involves a myriad of mental and emotional processes: deductive reasoning and inference; gathering and processing information; drawing conclusions or assumptions; and trusting a hunch, among others, a heightened awareness and sensitivity.

Pakikiramdam is not unique to Filipino society. It exists in varying degrees among various Asian and North American cultures, including Native American tribes. Modern American society prizes the opposite behavior: speaking clearly and concisely. And yet, *pakikiramdam* has made inroads in America's management and academic circles. A bestseller in the 1980s, *The Secrets of Japanese Management*, discusses how to win in business through ambiguity, vagueness, and indirection. At the center of their discussion is the art of reading subtle clues in a business transaction, an art that, if mastered, can lead to more profit. SAVVY, a magazine for business executives in the 1980s, lends support to this book. The authors note that the best managers in any organization are successful because they have acquired finely tuned perceptual powers. "Our culture does not make much of subtlety. But those who excel in organizations are masters at reading subtle signals." So indeed, some form of *pakikiramdam* does exist in American culture.

This *pakikiramdam* behavior was first brought to my attention by my friends who were Peace Corps volunteers in the Philippines during the late 1960s. They complained that Filipinos do not speak in complete sentences. They tend to stop midway and then nothing leaving the puzzled Americans to figure out the complete message. Another habit they found frustrating: Filipinos give noncommittal replies. My friends are often dumbfounded when given answers such as: "*sinabi mo*" (so you say), "*ikaw ang bahala*" (you're the boss), "*nasa sa iyo yan*" (it's up to you), or "*kung yan ang gusto mo*" (if that's what you want). I would have advised them to give up trying to understand the Filipinos' verbal language and instead use their *pakikiramdam*—that's the name of the game, folks. Malba Maggay would describe this as ambiguity in Filipino communication patterns.

An excerpt from my first book states, "The Filipino language is 60 percent body language and 40 percent verbal. Filipinos intuit to know or understand something because of what they feel or sense rather than because of evidence. When talking to one another, frequently [a person] senses what the other person is going to say next. In the process, sentences are left unfinished, no need to proceed because the listener has already read the speaker's body language."

In reading this chapter, Filipino children need to acknowledge and recognize the value of *pakikiramdam,* a behavior that is vital to their immigrant parents' way of being. By doing so, the children may answer one perennial question: Why do their parents expect them to know what's on their parents' minds? That's so unfair, isn't it? Yes, it is unfair of the parents to expect their Americanized children, who grew up in a culture where everything is verbalized and spelled out clearly to understand a message that isn't spoken. But they should take comfort in the fact that understanding this behavior can lead to more successful communication and a happier relationship with their parents.

THE HIGHLY-VERBAL CULTURE

It is interested to note what happens to one who is oriented to a different culture, a culture that values speaking skills and demands attention to the speaker's words more than his body language. Filipino teens and young adults who have been born and raised in the United States have naturally developed skills in speaking the English language. As a public-school teacher, I followed the teacher's manual, which instructed me to teach my elementary students to speak and write in clear and concise English. The teacher's manual had no instruction to teach children to pay close attention to body language. In fact, it did not mention the concept of body language. I was trained to teach students how to express their opinion and to give convincing details that support the opinion. I took pains to explain the difference between fact and opinion to my class. What I ignored in my classroom instruction is that immigrant children go home and start applying what they have been taught at school. However, at home in Filipino culture, children are not encouraged to express their opinions openly and frankly, because it amounts to showing disrespect to the parents, who have authoritarian status in the family. Boom! Culture clash!

One parent told me that she doesn't win arguments with her son because he is very good with words and the spoken argument. So, to keep peace in the family, she just keeps agreeing with him even though she doesn't understand what she is agreeing to most of the time! *"Oo na lang ako nang oo (I just keep saying 'yes'),"* she sighed in defeat. And she continued, *"Naloloko na ako sa anak ko, ako'y pinagsabihan mag go to counseling.* (I was going crazy with my child. I was told to go to counseling.)

A few days ago, a hilarious interaction occurred among my friends and me. Kaila is African American, Big Bear is Native American, and Shelly is Caucasian. We were together for a few days. Shelly had just returned from a trip to Hawaii and brought some jewelry as gifts. She gave a pair of earrings to Kaila. The following day, Kaila, wore them and went straight to Shelly, expecting her to notice the earrings through her body language. She didn't say a word. Big Bear and I immediately noticed her earrings. Shelly did not realize that she wasn't reading Kaila's nonverbal cues. We laughed. She kept asking, "Whaaat?" We laughed some more. Shelly was oriented and trained to hear words, not read body language. Before the poor girl got frustrated, we finally told her!

Below are stories to illustrate further differences in communication between verbal and nonverbal behavior orientations.

Nonverbal stories

The following stories illustrate *pakikiramdam:*

A. **Where is the measuring cup?**

I was renting a room in a house. Another room was rented by a Filipino husband and wife. One day, the house's owner, a Caucasian woman, asked the husband, "Where is the measuring cup, Rudy?" She was standing in the middle of the kitchen asking for the measuring cup. I was sitting at the kitchen table working on my laptop. Rudy replied from his room: "It's there." "Where's there?" answered the owner. "It's there," was the repeated reply. "I am standing right here in the kitchen, and I don't know where 'there' is?" the owner replied in an annoyed tone. Meanwhile, I knew exactly where the measuring cup could be when I heard Rudy say "there." The owner asked one more time in a voice slightly raised, hardly able to contain her anger: "Where?" Stomping, Rudy came out of his room, went straight to the cupboard, opened it, and got out the measuring cup. He put the cup on the table and returned to his room without saying a word to which the owner said, "if it was in the cupboard, why didn't you just say so?"

Since Rudy was at this point, obviously, not interested in engaging the owner in a conversation, I answered her question. I told her I knew immediately where to find the cup. She asked, "How?" I replied, "My goodness, would you place the measuring cup in the refrigerator? Would you find it under the sink or inside a microwave? I would look in two places, the cupboard or the drawers. It would be in one or the other.

My comment: "You see," I explained, "You are oriented to hear explicit instructions. "You belong to the 'everything must be spelled out' culture." I continued, "Whereas in our culture, we are expected to practice *pakikiramdam* automatically. We do it all the time!"

B. The house of "that one."

In February 2015, I gave a workshop at a Filipino church titled "Our Intercultural Lives." During the Q&A portion, a young adult daughter said that every time her mom asked her to get something, she didn't say exactly what to get. She only says, "that one!" She wanted the key, the bag, the book, but they were all "that one!" the young woman complained. "Why can't she be more specific? Why can't my mother spell out that one?"

My comment: So, there I was in that familiar place, trying to explain to her the Filipino's nonverbal orientation, how we are expected to practice *pakikiramdam,* shared inner perception, with one another. I addressed the parents in the audience saying, if we are aware of our Filipino behavior, we ought to be just as aware of the fact that our children grew up in the United States. It is likely they have not been exposed to this behavior often enough to adopt it. So, how could they possibly know that they are expected to read what is on our minds? They have been oriented to receive explicit verbal instructions.

A son shared his experience: His mom would ask for her earrings saying, "Can you get my earrings from my bedroom?" She expected her son to find them. "But earrings are so small, how can I find them?" complained the son. Well, I joked, if you were a daughter, you would probably have a better idea.

C. *Pakikiramdam* applied and reciprocated

I was staying at the house of my friend, who was Caucasian. She was hosting a meeting. I took it upon myself to ask her if she needed me to do something for her. She did. She asked if I could slice the bagels in half and place them in the oven to toast while she ran out to buy some juice? I complied.

But why did I ask her in the first place? I did because I was aware of the verbal communication patterns of her culture. She would not assume that I would automatically help her, and she would not want to impose. So, I offered to help. And she was very appreciative that I asked!

After the meeting ended, the attendees left, and we were alone. I told her, if it had been a Filipino meeting, I would have just jumped in to help without waiting to be asked. The following morning, my friend was preparing toast for herself and her boyfriend. I said out loud that I would make one for myself later. We continued the previous evening's conversation. When she finished preparing the toast, I was surprised to see she included me in her count! My friend said that she "filled in the blanks." Since she was preparing toast and I said I'd make my own later, why not make one for me too? How nice: She picked up *pakikiramdam* fast. We had a good laugh out of that situation.

My comment: In one of my workshops, a mother who is a nurse, shared her experiences as a leader of the care team in a nursing home. The Caucasian nurses on her team would always ask what kind of help she needed. Their Filipino counterparts didn't bother. They sensed what she needed and began helping. I gave her my opinion: The comfort level of the Caucasians, based on their verbal orientation, is to ask for instructions. The Filipinos' comfort level is different based on their nonverbal orientation. They understand and proceed to do what needs to be done without saying a word.

D. **"Honey, how will you survive if I'm not here?"**

The Filipino wife comes home from grocery shopping and left lots of groceries in the car. Her Caucasian husband was home. She thought he would get up and follow her to the car to help bring the grocery bags inside. Instead, he continued to watch TV as if he did not notice her arrival. Finally, she asked him to help. To her surprise, her husband said, "Honey, how will you survive if I'm not here?"

My comment: What is going on here? It is simple. The Caucasian husband's cultural orientation dictates that men and women are expected to be self-reliant and independent. Therefore, he assumed that his wife would carry all the groceries inside without asking for help as he would do, since she is not old and frail.

The Filipino wife's cultural orientation is different. Men and boys are always expected to help women and the elderly carry things and do heavy physical work. She expected her husband to be similarly oriented and therefore, help her bring the groceries inside without being asked.

E. Wrapping dumplings

Last Christmas, my daughter, her husband, and I spent holidays with my best friend's family, which included her grandchildren, daughter-in-law, and son-in-law. While preparing dinner, friends of her children came to visit. Naturally showing *pakikipagkapwa* (shared humanity) to all, my friend invited the kids to join us for dinner. But that required more food and more time to cook it. Now, dinner would have been ready faster, not to mention less stressful for the cooks, if one or two kids would have offered to help us. But to my dismay, no one did.

So, there I was, doing everything—cooking, wrapping, steaming. My friend was cooking *pancit* (noodles) at the same time. We were the only ones working while the others just watched. The adult children were at the table, so I thought of wrapping the dumplings I made in front of them, hoping they'd get the cue and help out. To me, it was apparent that I needed help. Instead, the kids marveled at how quickly I worked wrapping the dumplings! Nobody got our body language, not even as we were looking at them as if our eyeballs were ready to pop from the stress!

My comment: We, on the other hand, did not ask for help either. I wish I would have said something instead of steaming in quiet resentment. It would have saved us a lot of time and work. I went back to the kitchen to laugh at how hilarious our situation was at this point! What an experience! This is also an indication of the strong influence of one's cultural orientation becoming automatic on one's behavior. It was only in retrospect that I realized we ought to have spoken up and asked them to help us because they had no clue what our body language meant. They lacked a keen sensitivity to our verbal and nonverbal cues.

PAKIKIRAMDAM DISSECTED

The *pakikiramdam* norm of behavior is deeply entrenched in the psyche of the Filipino culture. It leads to nonverbal language resulting in one-way communication instead of dialogue because *pakikiramdam* carries a **deep interpersonal connection**. But what if such a deep interpersonal relationship is absent? Let me mention the positive and negative attributes of this behavior in the context of Filipino culture. Research conducted by Raj Mansukhani succinctly specifies these attributes. Briefly, the positive attributes are as follows:

1) *Pakikiramdam* is the ability to sense nonverbal cues from others.
2) *Pakikiramdam* is a way of reconstructing another person's state of feeling or being.
3) *Pakikiramdam* is a right-brain activity or skill.
4) *Pakikiramdam* is an activity or skill that has a hesitating, tentative quality to it.
5) *Pakikiramdam* is an improvisational skill.
6) *Pakikiramdam* is attentiveness to contexts.
7) *Pakikiramdam* is a skill used to maintain smooth and harmonious interpersonal relationships.
8) *Pakikiramdam* is a covert mode of communication.
9) *Pakikiramdam* is a sensitivity that is expected of another.
10) *Pakikiramdam* is part of a larger cultural expectation to be verbally indirect and ambiguous. Indirect communication is the norm.

11) *Pakikiramdam* is a deep interpersonal connection.

The negative features are:
1) *Pakikiramdam* may encourage hypocrisy.
2) *Pakikiramdam* may make communication more tedious since people who engage in it are not willing to get straight to the point.
3) *Pakikiramdam* may encourage gossip.
4) P*akikiramdam* could result in intuitions that may be incorrect, especially if one is not adept at the skill.
5) *Pakikiramdam* may generate outlandish expectations that could not humanly be met, especially if persons who engage in the indirect methods of communication expect that their implied messages will always be understood.
6) P*akikiramdam* could lead to communication patterns that are confusing, particularly for foreigners who want to interact with Filipinos.
7) *Pakikiramdam* may actually give persons in authority more power than they deserve. Since Filipinos will allow themselves to be direct towards such persons: priests, doctors, public officials. These persons will, therefore, have direct access to what others can only guess.
8) *Pakikiramdam* may encourage conformity because people will not want to make others think that they are different or superior.
9) P*akikiramdam* is pervasive, so Filipinos might get the impression that someone who is trying to be frank is being manipulative and harsh even if that is the kind of language required in a particular situation.
10) P*akikiramdam* is a right-brain activity, so it discourages criticisms.

11) *Pakikiramdam,* social interactions will always run the risk of degenerating into game-playing.

The very common remark one hears because of *pakikiramdam* is **"I just know."** The Number 11 positive feature listed above states that *pakikiramdam* is a deep interpersonal connection. It is, but if there is no deep interpersonal connection with the other party or the openness for dialogue is diminishing, how can one proceed to communicate one's heart? Chances are it might "degenerate to game-playing" according to negative feature Number 11. The claim, "I just know," thus remains unexpressed to the party involved. So. the person claiming, "I just know" will then behave quietly according to what "one knows." Words are no longer necessary, nor is there any need to communicate because "I just know." Therefore, we simply move on. Ultimately, *pakikiramdam* is a form of one-way quiet communication with the self.

I understand how *pakikiramdam* behavior is frustrating to our Americanized children. These poor kids only know verbal communication, but their immigrant parents do not verbalize clearly, they just give vague insinuations and suggestions, but expect them to understand. They seldom hear clear, specific statements from their parents. So, misunderstanding inevitably ensues. Both parties expect the other to communicate the same way they do. It creates a frustratingly crazy scenario! One parent in my workshop exclaimed, "How can I have a decent conversation with my Americanized 26-year-old daughter without getting into a shouting match?"

The nature of the *pakikiramdam* concept requires two-way communication, but it is always done nonverbally! This is exemplified best in driving, an arena in which verbal communication is useless for obvious reasons. Nonverbal skills, especially reading other drivers' intentions, is vital. If you're a driver in the Philippines, you practice a lot of *pakikiramdam* to avoid accidents that happen a lot on the busy streets of Metro Manila and other major cities. A deeper interpersonal connection is going on here, folks, and paradoxically, it takes place among strangers. Foreigners riding jeepneys (the iconic Philippine public jeep) and buses often freeze in terror as they watch two vehicles about to collide head-on. Yet they evade each other in the nick of time as if they tacitly predicted the other's next move. This happens all the time on Manila's busy streets. A lot of two-way *pakikiramdam* occurs among drivers!

The importance of cultural awareness

I want to stress the deep importance of cultural awareness, a gift for reading the big picture right away without saying a word. And for me, a hallmark of a highly functioning individual. I found the most rewarding experiences in my workshops were during the Q&A sessions when the participants had an "aha" moment. It is a tremendous joy to watch because it is the breakthrough moment when awareness is captured. I rate the success of my workshops through the energy levels generated in the exchange of questions and answers. Parents often are perplexed over their Americanized children's inability to understand them by merely observing their behavior. Why? The answer is simple: Their kids have been socialized to pay more attention to the spoken word than behavior. For the Americanized child, body language has a supporting role to speech. Native-born Filipinos are socialized to be most sensitive to cues in the person's behavior, not the words he is saying. Body language is secondary to Americanized adult children. They wait to be spoken to, to be given directions, or instructions in words rather than looking for independent meaning in body language.

Here is a familiar situation. The mother gives instructions, in her usual Filipino style, to her two teenage sons who are watching TV. She tells them, "I'm going out on an errand. When you hear the dryer buzz, get the clothes out." She goes out. When she returns, imagine her anger to find the dry clothes lying in a pile on the couch! She asks her sons: "Why didn't you fold and hang them?" The sons' replied, "You didn't tell us to! You only told us to get them out of the dryer." Obviously, the mother assumed her sons would have the common sense not to leave the clothes lying in a pile. Well, Mom, you may not be aware of the fact that common sense is often "culturally biased." Our Americanized children grow up thinking that everything must be verbalized; nothing is left to assumption or expectation.

Another example: Parents in a church community lament that, as senior citizens, they should no longer be expected to do heavy work like hauling tables and chairs. Usually, after the Sunday service and potluck lunch, they are left to clean up while the younger church members fiddle with their phones or tablets. "Where is their respect?" one of the parents grumbles to me. "Can't they see my back is already hurting? We told them once to help out. They can't expect us to keep asking them every Sunday! What is wrong with them?" To help, I offered to hold a workshop for the young members.

Autonomy and self-reliance

Immigrant Filipinos need to be aware that their Americanized children have been socialized to perceive them as capable parents in every way, including lifting tables and chairs. I often hear complaints from parents who carry grocery bags inside their homes, and their children do not rush to help them. Sometimes their kids ask them if they need help, but only when they see their parents visibly struggling. I explained this scenario in my previous book:

> For Americanized teenagers, body language is a foreign language that is difficult to master. For instance, an immigrant father struggling with a bundle of groceries is understandably irate with a child who asks him if he needs help. Both parties misread each other's behavior. The parents expected their teenager to read their behavior, but the latter was socialized to wait for verbal instruction from the parents. For the teen asking, "Do you need help, Dad?" was the ideal way of demonstrating respect for a parent, not going ahead to pick up the grocery bags without saying anything. Part of the Americanized teenagers' socialization is to be self-reliant. He would hesitate to go ahead and pick up the grocery bags without asking because Dad might feel insulted for being perceived as incapable. If Americanized teenagers and their parents continue to fail to understand each other's style of communication, more conflict will break out in their efforts to be heard.

Therefore, immigrant parents take heed and remember: Like it or not, your children have already embedded in the seat of their consciousness the highly prized trait of self-reliance. This mentality is sealed forever. It is important to be constantly aware of this fact. The following story should help you remember:

"A Filipino caregiver friend of mine recently related her experience while caring for an affluent 103-year-old woman. The client had just returned from the hospital, so her mail had piled up. Apparently, she wasn't able to rest well during her hospital stay because she was constantly falling asleep now that she was back at home. My friend, wanting to be helpful, thought she would open the envelopes for her client, as previous clients asked her do. To her surprise, when the client awoke, she asked, why her mail had been opened. She felt her privacy had been violated. She threatened to sue my friend, who had to apologize repeatedly while explaining why she did it. But her explanation added insult to injury because it implied that the client was incapable of opening her mail! Lesson: Never assume. Ask first. Never underestimate the self-reliant mindset of Americans—not even a 103-year-old!

One of Robert Bellah's interviewees for his book *Habits of the Heart* (2008) answered the question, "Why did he work so hard to support his wife and child?" The interviewee, corporate executive Brian Palmer answered, "I guess self-reliance is one of the characteristics I have pretty high in my value system." Self-reliance is a popular and valued trait among Americans. My friend's nonverbal behavior of opening her client's mail without even asking, even though she intended to make life easier for the client, violated the cardinal rule of self-reliance. My friend's *pakikiramdam* behavior, an "emotional a priori," as Mataragnon would say, suffered a head-on culture clash.

Our Americanized children who have become young adults have completely absorbed the values of American individualism, contrary to their parents' home-grown values learned in the Philippines.

Naturally, they wear this American individualism as a badge honor in their interactions and their relationships with their parents. Yet, unbeknownst to them, this tradition of American autonomy has in recent years come to be viewed with ambivalence. Bellah's *Habits of the Heart* (2008) discussed this ambivalence extensively and suggested that the values of collectivism are as important as individualism. We need both to survive not just in the United States but wherever we live. "The inner tension of American individualism adds up to a classic case of contradiction. We strongly assert the value of our self-reliance and autonomy. Yet, we deeply feel the emptiness of a life without sustaining social commitments. We are hesitant to articulate our sense that we need one another as much as we need to stand alone, for fear that if we did, we would lose our independence altogether. The tensions of our lives would be even greater if we did not, in fact, engage in practices that constantly limit the effects of an isolating individualism, even though we cannot articulate those practices nearly as well as we can the quest for autonomy."

HIGH CONTEXT AND LOW CONTEXT CULTURES

In my book, *Teaching Cultural Diversity Through Children's Literature: Applying the Kluckhohn Model* (2001) I discuss high and low context cultures as originally formulated by Edward T. Hall. It is relevant to mention this theory because it lends support to my discussion of verbal and nonverbal cultures. Cultures operate in contexts. "Without context, the linguistic code in the language carries no meaning because the code only carries one part of the message. Some cultures are high context, and others are low context. High context cultures look at physical context such as events and situations, with low explicit coding, whereas low context cultures look at ideas, systems, organizations, theories and principles, with high explicit coding." Let me quote more explanations of this theory, "A high context (HC) communication or message is one in which most of the information is either in the physical context or internalized in the person, while very little is in the coded, explicit, transmitted part of the message. A low context (LC) communication is just the opposite. The mass of the information is vested in the explicit code. Twins who have grown up together can and do communicate more economically (HC) than two lawyers in a courtroom during a trial." What does it mean in simple language? Because the twins growing up together know their nonverbal behavior so well, words are not necessary to communicate; a lot of *pakikiramdam* is going on. This is the high context (HC) culture. Whereas two lawyers who only meet in the courtroom during a trial will rely more on their exchange of words for information and less on body language to communicate. This is the low context (LC) culture.

To be more precise about high context culture, let us seek the assistance of the work of Melba P. Maggay, who specializes in Filipino communication patterns and intercultural communication, for help in clarifying high context culture. "Being high context, the culture has a high degree of meaning shared by all participants. Verbal input, therefore, functions as a kind of shorthand; much is suggested, and much is assumed. *Pahiwatig,* for instance, has a verbal component, which while plain to insiders is almost always ambiguous to outsiders; what is heard is rarely what it is below the surface. Through *pakiramdaman,* one reads its subtle meanings in the various combinations of context and nonverbal cues that accompany the speech."

The verbal component of *pahiwatig* has evocative ways to express the need or want for something that might be easily misunderstood outside of the context in which it is meant to be expressed. They are *paglalambing* to do sweet talk or acts of kindness or love, sometimes even to pretend to have *tampo*, a kind of affective resentment so that you are noticed. *Paglalangis* is another type of expression, by embellishing one's statement to get the desired response. *Paala-ala* is an indirect reminder of promise or favor that one anticipates you would do. *Pwede bang awitan,* an expression said half-jokingly because you are eyeing something someone else owns but it is valuable to you. It starts with a compliment, which in turn elicits the reply, *"Oh, talaga...gusto mo?"* (Really...Would you like to have it?). Well, readers, you have just been exposed to one Filipino style of discourse called *pahiwatig*!

Our Americanized youth and young adults living in the United States belong to a low context culture while their immigrant parents, born and raised in the Philippines, live in a high context culture. A lot of the code has been internalized by the parents, and they expect their Americanized children to be able to read them through body language. But how can this be possible? No wonder culture clash occurs!

THE YIN-YANG OF THE VERBAL AND NONVERBAL CULTURES

I propose that verbal and nonverbal cultures explore each other's strengths and weaknesses. Both cultures are important. One can't be a successful communicator by just knowing one or the other. In the American child, everything must be expressed verbally, openly, and as calmly as possible. In fact, when an argument ensues, many Americans believe it should be conducted in calm, moderate tones with a minimum of gestures. Loud voices, vigorous gesturing, more than one person talking at a time are signs to many Americans that a physical fight or at least an unproductive shouting match is about to occur. In other words, it is a prelude to violence!

The yin-yang polarity

Instead of introducing these opposing styles of communicating as potential "enemies," let's apply the yin-yang polarity of verbal and nonverbal cultures. Alan Watts, the British philosopher, writer, and speaker, discussed this polarity:

At the very roots of Chinese thinking and feeling lies the principle of polarity, which is not to be confused with the ideas of opposition or conflict. In the metaphors of other cultures, light is at war with darkness, life with death, good with evil, and the positive with the negative, and thus an idealism to cultivate the former and be rid of the latter flourishes throughout much of the world. To the traditional way of Chinese thinking, this is as incomprehensible as an electric current without both positive and negative poles. Or polarity is the principle that + and -, north and south, are different aspects of the same system, and that the disappearance of either one of them would be the disappearance of the system. Introducing this yin-yang principle, both immigrant parents and their Americanized children may reach a place where when differences surface, applying this principle may alleviate potential miscommunication.

Some of you may silently comment, "Yeah, right, easier said than done!" I hear you! This principle runs opposite of or conflicts with the either/or logic of the Western world. The world of light (good) and the world of darkness (bad) are always at war, and we are conditioned to think that good must prevail over evil with nothing in-between! "The either/or way is predominant in the Western way of thinking and is closely linked with the Aristotelian logic of the excluded middle. According to this exclusive way of thinking, things have to be either this way or that, either good or bad, either true or false. There are no alternatives between them." Among Asian cultures, especially the Chinese culture, logical thinking is not either/or but both/and or yin-yang. Both/and thinking does not look at two sides as opposites in a conflict but as complementary. "In conflicting dualism, we must fight our opposite and win by eliminating it. This kind of dualistic thinking is a pervasive form of either/or thinking that represents the Western mind. The either/or way of thinking splits the opposites as if they have nothing to do with each other. The both/and way of thinking recognizes not only the coexistence of opposites but also their complementarity nature." I am reminded of the saying, "one person's trash is another's treasure." The crucial question to ask is how popular is the both/and way of thinking in the conscious mind of the U.S. population? What we are oriented to when conflict occurs is, one must be right and the other wrong; the opposition view is dominant. There must be only one winner! Who has time to think yin-yang but only those deeply rooted in this principle? Next time you go to the cinema, observe the logic in the dialogue of the actors! Either/or? Both/and? Or is the logic of each character considered equally valid?

Finding the good in the bad-and-good in verbal and nonverbal cultures

A verbally oriented society rallies around clarity, certainty, and perfection. Yet human relationships are riddled with ambiguity, uncertainty, and imperfection. How can one achieve perfect verbal skills if this is the case? Developing nonverbal skills may help. Applying *pakikiramdam* in your relationships could help. Becoming astute in reading unspoken behavior may provide a key and strike a balance between verbal and nonverbal behavior. Now, let us turn the table around to nonverbal language and ask what is the good in the bad-and-good in nonverbal orientation? The valued behavior of *pakikiramdam* may sharpen perceptual power. But what's the bad part? The emotional character of *pakikiramdam* is laden with unproven facts or experiences because it takes place in the realm of perception. Sharpening one's speaking skills may help express yourself. Finding the polarity of verbal and nonverbal orientation may enable us to have a positive attitude toward these two orientations among cultures. If we get rid of one, the system of communication limps along ineffectively because verbal and nonverbal expressions are different aspects of the communication system. We need to apply *pakikiramdam* and express words each time. Therefore, think of ways to marry verbal and nonverbal cultures, to develop both *pakikiramdam*, and the use your words.

The benefit of *pakikiramdam*, verbal skills, and yin-yang polarity

A very poignant example of this discussion about the benefit of *pakikiramdam* is something my nine-year-old daughter did when I became a single mom. With my meager salary as a public-school teacher, it was difficult to make both ends meet. I rarely expressed my struggles to her out of maternal instinct, yet she learned to read my nonverbal behavior, she practiced *pakikiramdam*. After a day of work, I took her grocery shopping. It was already getting late. As I was about to get out of the car, she volunteered to do our breakfast grocery shopping. She must have observed that I was tired and looking haggard. So, my not even ten-year-old child went out to buy groceries for the first time. I was speechless at her gesture. Thirty minutes later, she came back looking triumphant! She just did it! She learned to apply *pakikiramdam*!

As a member of a non-profit foundation, I noticed that a colleague had excellent speaking skills and was an astute observer. No wonder she holds a key paid position in a for-profit organization. Not a United States native, she arrived in this country as an adult, yet has mastered both verbal and nonverbal skills. I think of her as a model to both immigrant parents and Americanized teens and young adults. Her success proves that it is never too late to acquire skills in verbal and nonverbal language. Anytime is a good time to learn.

Discussing further the yin-yang polarity, our orientation to bad vs. good is so deep that we are convinced there can be only one winner. We don't realize that if we look deeper, there may be good in bad and bad in good! This may be illustrated by the Taoist fable of the farmer whose horse ran away. As the story goes, following the loss, the neighbors came to the farmer to commiserate, since losing a horse was considered bad luck. "What misfortune you have suffered," they said. He replied, "maybe." The next day, the horse returned and brought with it six wild horses, and the neighbors came by again, exclaiming, "what good fortune you have." He said, "maybe." Then the following day, his son tried to ride one of the wild horses and was thrown off and broke his leg. Again, the neighbors came, this time to offer their sympathy. "Oh, what misfortune you have suffered," they said. Again, he replied, "maybe." The day after that, conscription officers came to the village to seize young men for the army, but because of his broken leg, the farmer's son was rejected. When the neighbors came by to say, "what good fortune you have," again he replied: "maybe."

The point of this fable is one never really knows if an event is either good or bad. Sometimes it's both. Put another way, no matter how badly events unfold, sometimes something good can come out of them. Bad news can turn into good. There's something to be learned in the yin-yang worldview, which embraces the good, the bad, and the ugly.

According to Watts (1975) the yin-yang world is self-sufficient. The universe has checks and balances of operation, such as, fortune and misfortune, life and death, good and bad, the wheels of change evolve keeping the universal order, thus we say in the yin-yang world, this is the good in the good-and-bad." Perhaps you've heard the expression, "just go with the flow." This statement is characteristic of Chinese philosophy, yet it has come to be universally accepted, and we are all better off for it.

BOTH/AND THINKING

The increasingly common use of the yin-yang principle, translated as both/and thinking, in the West, which has been dominated by the Aristotelian thinking of either/or, is indeed an interesting and heartening development. Here is an excerpt from my first *Culture Clash* book (2001):

I teach TED 667, also known as Cultural Diversity and Reform: A Critical Pedagogy, at National University in San Bernardino Academic Center in San

Bernardino, California for graduate students in the Teacher Education Development program. The course is designed to communicate the dynamics and challenges of educating our increasingly diverse population. The course leads educators to explore and exchange ideas of what is important in the lives of students and teachers, the school community and society, as they move toward transformative education. One of the course textbooks is Peter McLaren's *Life in Schools* that encourages a dialectical approach in teaching. This style of teaching moves away from the traditional mindset of either/or thinking. McLaren writes:

It is crucial not to mistake "turn-taking" for genuine dialogue, or to believe that getting all the opposing positions out on the table is the same thing as being able to make a coherent argument that supports your position, while at the same time considering other positions. You can't simply have a "pick and mix" approach, but need to genuinely hear the opposing positions, and consider them in light of their coherence, their contradictions or lack thereof, and their ability to hold up to rational challenge. We should allow students to acquire a dialectical consideration of social life.

To apply this dialectical method of thinking means to give up the either/or way of thinking. Hence, students in my class are introduced to the both/and way of thinking. They, receive handouts about yin-yang philosophy, which are readings chosen to elicit both/and discussion and argument. I advise them to suspend the either/or logic for an academic exercise. The first two nights of discussions were difficult because the traditional either/or mindset got in the way. As students began to apply themselves to the both/and exercises of arguing and processing, they learned that in the both/and way of thinking or arguing, both sides of the argument are affirmed, and no one seeks to destroy an idea by proving it wrong. Instead, students explore what affirmation they can find on both sides. At one class meeting, I challenged them with the topic of affirmative action. Instead of proving it as only a bad thing, the class was asked to show both its good and bad aspects, and that these can be both friend and foe. My students could then see that the both/and way of thinking or arguing seeks the complementary dualism, rather than the conflicting dualism of the opposite. As they began thinking in both/and terms, we used the topics in McLaren's book for discussion. The students did not realize that, as they got deeper into their discussion, the genuine dialogue was taking place. Even late in the night, my students did not show signs of being tired or sleepy. On the contrary, as the center assistant commented later, they were fired up and not letting up in their arguments.

Hess writes in *Caretakers of Our Common House*, "Hard dialogue does not mean that we argue until one side wins an argument or demolishes another's viewpoint. It aims to probe the depths of an issue. There are no winners or losers in genuine conversation; there are participants who are together seeking and constructing truth." The both/and way of arguing seeks harmony and cooperation, and the class discussions encouraged creativity and critical thinking as they sought a win-win solution. One requirement of the course was a scholarly paper using both/and way of arguing logic and writing it was a cultural experience for the students. It sharpened their critical thinking while challenging others who said they were not used to the kind of logic it uses. Each TED 667 class I taught allowed my students to experience the both/and way of thinking in the classroom.

Don't get the impression that I am saying the either/or way of thinking does not count. Quite the contrary, the either/or and both/and way of thinking are badly needed in the world. We need to be able to incorporate this approach into life. Most laws that regulate our social functions are based on an either/or approach. We must say 'yes' or 'no' to a child who needs discipline. In other words, the dualistic either/or way of thinking has its place in our social functions and critical judgments. I firmly believe that when problems become too complex to solve, applying both/and thinking and logic is the road to take because giving answers of plain "yes" or "no" is too simplistic. Start practicing the yin-yang principle!

FAILURE OF INCLUDING BOTH/AND LOGIC IN

Amy Chua's book, *Battle Hymn of the Tiger Mother* (2011)

This book was originally intended to be a memoir that traces the author's transformation from a strict Chinese American raising two mixed-race daughters (her husband is Jewish) into one who reluctantly concedes to some Western ways because of her defiant second daughter. It triggered a bitter clash of cultures over childrearing practices of Chinese parents and their Western counterparts.

The book generated a firestorm of reactions from readers and critics. After reading the book, I am not surprised! First of all, take the author's professional background: she's a lawyer. Second, naturally, she demonstrated in her language the "lawyerly" approach to her argument in proving her points. Third, she argued her either/or logic with gusto, throwing out the yin-yang way of thinking, to prove that Chinese childrearing practices are superior to Western ones, and that hit a collective nerve in the consciousness of parents with their Western-oriented childrearing philosophy. She recently wrote on her blog of receiving a package from California that contained shredded pieces of her entire book. Talk about a strong opinion!

Chua condemned established beliefs about Western childrearing practices. She applied the either/or worldview, meaning, one is better than the other. In this book I am leaning toward the both/and logic to prevent culture clash. On the other hand, Amy Chua, takes pride in her Chinese heritage, yet has no qualms in arguing in a Western-Aristotelian either/or mentality in her book. What a shame that she did not embrace the yin-yang philosophy that is at the center of the Chinese culture she is so proud of. Nowhere did her book concede cognizance of the yin-yang polarity in a positive sense (finding the good in the bad-and-good). If she did, perhaps, the majority of the average American reading population would have been more receptive to her book and its message. However, if you can read her argument objectively, you may find a grain of truth. I did because I sincerely get the issues she raised, particularly certain Western-oriented childrearing practices which she believes are lax. After all, I juggled two childrearing practices: the Filipino way I grew up with, and the Western approach that I learned here. For instance, the Western obsession with self-esteem in America has become so paramount it defeated the Asian philosophy of developing obedient and respectful children through authoritarian rule. I find myself see-sawing on these two opposing practices. Given that, reading Chua's no-holds-barred book was a jaw-dropping experience.

Chua's daughters are now college-age. One is at Harvard, the other at Yale; they are on their way to developing academic skills to add to their other "marketable and impressive" skills in piano, violin, tennis, and fluent Mandarin. Chua ensured that her children were taught useful skills. Read the book for details on how Tiger Mom trained her daughters in these skills. I believe that this book would have been more highly regarded by the majority of her readers if Chua tried to find the good in the bad. If she had found the good in childrearing practices that marry Chinese culture and Western ways, the yin-yang polarity instead of strongly proclaiming that Chinese ways are better than Western ways when it comes to childrearing. Even as this book was met with disapproval, Amy Chua was named one of Time Magazine's Influential Persons in 2011.

THE CHALLENGE

The challenge for you, my readers, is can you adopt the yin-yang principle? Parents are you able to find the good in the bad-and-good behavior of your highly verbal American children. Children are you able to find the good in the bad-and-good behavior of your immigrant parents using nonverbal gestures? What is important for us to understand is why our immigrant parents "go bananas" when their children address them as equals, "I am not a mind reader!" If both sides can try to gain a better understanding of the other's behavior, tensions will gradually go away.

PARENTAL TIPS and GUIDELINES

Below are three measures that can keep us from coming to a culture clash when we fail to apply the yin-yang of verbal and nonverbal behavior. The first strategy is the Iceberg Model for Awareness, Second, is Connecting Dots, and the third is the Diamond Rule.

THE ICEBERG MODEL FOR AWARENESS

When culture clash is occurring, think iceberg. An iceberg floating in the wintery ocean eludes us if we only see its comparatively small top that rises above sea level. Because what we fail to see is the massive iceberg beneath the surface. The visual iceberg represents the attributes of cultures that are primarily oriented in visual awareness: food, flags, festivals, fashions, music, games, literature, and the arts. Fortunately, this visual awareness is not as likely to generate a culture clash. It is the hidden aspects of the culture, the massive iceberg beneath the surface that causes the most conflict because they are not readily seen. They are out of our cultural awareness. When we relate cross-culturally, we are not aware if we are clashing with another person's culture because much of it is hidden: modesty; concept of beauty; child-rearing ideals; rules of decency; definition of sin; courtship practices; superior/subordinate relationships; concept of justice; incentive to work; notions of leadership; tempo of work; facial expressions; roles in relation to status, age, sex, class, occupation, kinship, etc.; proximity of space; nature of friendship; expressing of emotion; group decision-making; orientation of self; health/illness practices; eye behavior; definition of insanity; patterns of visual perception; logic for the either/or thinker; logic for the both/and thinker; handling emotions; orientation to past or future; arrangements of physical space; preference for competition or cooperation; being vs. doing orientation; harmony vs. mastery of nature; human rights orientation; authoritarian orientation; egalitarian orientation; verbal vs. nonverbal orientation; (See Iceberg Model Appendix A).

These are some examples of cultural beliefs and values that are beneath the surface. Those who share common cultural values and assumptions would be the ones most familiar with these attributes. But if you are an outsider to the culture, chances are you won't know if you are violating rules of conduct. That can lead to culture clash. The diagram in the index will help visualize this iceberg model of awareness. Refer to this model from time to time. Before a culture clash conflict escalates, be reminded that the issue at hand can be the massive unseen iceberg under the water.

CONNECTING THE DOTS

In 2005, Steve Jobs was the commencement speaker for the graduating class at Stanford University. He talked about many life lessons, include one of them that highlighted the wisdom of reflection so you could connect the dots in your life. He said that when it comes to the dot-to-dot connection, it happens at one particular moment, after events have occurred because you can't connect the dots thinking forward. It is only in retrospect that you make these connections. I, too, have connected the dots. One day, I suddenly realized that as the mother, the parent, I hold the power to silence or to empower the voice of my child. Having experienced this dot connection, I am always striving to allow my child's voice to be heard and helping her be comfortable in speaking her mind. In the chapters that follow, among my discussions, I remind parents that we don't need to silence our children to hold power. We are the parents. Practice dot-to-dot connection in parenting and let us raise empowered children.

THE GOLDEN RULE VS. THE DIAMOND RULE

Do you focus on your needs or the needs of others? While the answer admittedly varies from person to person, the Golden Rule, "Do unto others as you would have them do unto you," is an ancient and universally accepted rule. It is expounded in many faith traditions, implying reciprocity. Agreed, this is a tried-and-true rule, **but** the rule only works within the context of cultures sharing the same values and assumptions unless participants are aware of others' values. It comes up short of achieving success in intercultural relations or cross-cultural communication as it is generally applied. People in different cultures don't necessarily appreciate the same behavior. Some compliments become insults when they are applied to another culture. Many behaviors have different meanings to other cultural groups. Thumbs up in one culture is not always a positive sign in another culture, so be aware. Success in communication with others requires connecting to their values, their shared assumptions, their memories, their desires. This can be a new Golden Rule. Let's call it the **Diamond Rule**. It goes like this:

Diamond Rule = Do unto others as they would have you do unto them.

Golden Rule = Do unto others as you would have them do unto you.

The new rule focuses on the goal of connecting with the other through a win-win attitude with them for the intercultural living experience. To apply the Diamond Rule, one needs to focus on connecting with the needs of those outside your own culture. For example, after the 9/11 attacks, one of my friends wanted to connect with Muslims as a sign of solidarity. What did she do? To be able to accompany her Muslim friend to her mosque to pray, she dressed like her so that she could be respectful and thus gain entrance into the house of worship. If we are aware that other cultures have different values, we are more likely to accept them. The Diamond Rule can be used to avoid culture clash because you are willing to connect outside your culture. Immigrant parents and American teens and young adults, take this lesson to heart. It may improve your parent-child communication. Parents can put aside their Filipino perspective to hear their American child. Teens and young adults can do likewise to achieve harmony in family relationships. Above the Diamond Rule though, let us follow Jesus' take on the Golden Rule. "Love your neighbor as yourself." Even if we fail to adhere to Golden and Diamond Rules in crossing cultures to achieve better relationships, Jesus' words might yet be our saving grace to avoid culture clash.

I am not about to leave this most important guideline to prevent culture clash from careening down the road without putting the personal stamp on how the Diamond Rule came to being.

My culture clash experience with my American daughter gave birth to the Diamond Rule. My daughter raised my awareness of our conflicting cultural values and assumptions. As I stared at the Golden Rule, "Do unto others as you would have them do unto you," an AHA moment came to me. While it implies consideration of needs, we do not share the same culture. I discovered that changing a couple of pronouns could produce the opposite effect, forcing my focus on the intent of the Golden Rule that is so often missed. PRESTO! This was what I was looking for, and I named it the Diamond Rule. Do unto others as they would have you do unto them. The Golden Rule allows the focus to be self-centered – "what would I want in the situation." Whereas the Diamond Rule forces me to focus on others' perspective. It is easy to miss the intent of the rule: "What would I want if I were in their shoes." The Golden Rule from a cross-cultural perspective becomes the Diamond Rule which states explicitly that it should be what the other person wants. Therefore, the Diamond Rule becomes our guidepost in keeping us alert to a potential culture clash.

THE COMPARISON BOARD

This is best applied in church settings, among the youth and parents. (See Appendix B) The facilitator must be well-familiarized with this concept. The Comparison Board has been designed to facilitate games that compare and contrast two concepts or cultural values or opposing ideas. The game helps participants visualize the ideas and values of others.

REFLECTION

"In other words, a true human, is not a model of righteousness, a prig or prude, but recognizes that some failings are as necessary to genuine human nature as salt to stew."

—Alan Watts

CHAPTER 3

AUTHORITARIAN and EGALITARIAN ORIENTATIONS

"Your children are not your children. They are the sons and daughters of Life's longing for itself. They come through you, yet they belong not to you. You may give them your love, but not your thoughts, for they have their own thoughts."[9]

—Khalil Gibran

With the above quote, the Lebanese poet reminds us that our children are entrusted to us by our Creator for care. We are their temporary custodians. We hold them only for a little while because one day they leave to make their mark on society. We don't own them, but we have the responsibility to nurture and love them before they mature no matter what the odds we face. I want to believe that the above passage, written in 1923, was intended to be a prophetic message to parents.

Authoritarian upbringing, Philippine context

When I embarked on writing this book, I wanted to include new research, new experiences, and fresh viewpoints from workshops and interviews with parents, teens, and young adults. The Philippine and American childrearing styles each include the challenges. There are many parenting options. Diane Baumrind proposes an authoritative parenting style popular in some American

---

[9] Khalil Gibran, *The Prophet* (New York: Alfred A. Knopf, 1923) 17

families.[10] Amy Chua, author of *Battle Hymn of the Tiger Mom* (2011), shares her Chinese-influenced parenting style with the strict yet successful method she applied in raising her own daughters.

Filipino immigrant parents residing in the United States frequently face the dilemma of how to respond when children defy the parent's high expectation of absolute obedience to their authority. I attended an event sponsored by SIPA (Search to Involve Pilipino Americans) on September 25, 2015, in the Historic Filipinotown neighborhood of Los Angeles. One of the event's speakers said, "A growing number of Filipino parents complain that they have lost touch with their children, or it seems that the single biggest complaint from Filipino parents about their children is, *"nakalimutan na nila ang kaugalian natin...walang respeto dito* (they have forgotten our ways; here, children have no respect)."[11] If this is true indeed, we must search our hearts as we ask ourselves: What has gone wrong and why? Who initiated the conflict, the parent or the children? Why is there conflict instead of harmony in the parent-child dynamic?

We should begin by focusing on the childrearing practices of Filipinos who have been born and raised in the Philippines and have come to adopt North America

---

[10] "The authoritative parenting style: Warmth, rationality, and high standards," posted in the World Wide Web, 11/27/2015: http://www.parentingscience.com/authoritative-parenting-style.html

[11] Talk given, "Encouraging Togetherness and Better Communication in the Filipino Family," SIPA (Search to Involve Pilipino Americans) event on July 25, 2015, in Historic Filipinotown, Los Angeles, CA

as their second home. Since time immemorial, we have adhered to parental authority as the absolute in raising our children. One does not need a degree in child psychology to know that we have been raised under authoritarian rule in our homes. We came to accept parental authority as absolute when we were children growing up. When we became parents, we expected to continue in that style.

But alas, in America, some parents base childrearing practices on equality and democratic rule, which are at odds with our rigid authoritarian orientation. Here lies our parental dilemma, one that we are often unprepared to face. We are surprised when our children flirt with the rigid boundary between parents and children, start questioning our parental admonitions, and worse, escalate into challenging our parental opinion and authority. As children, we grew up with our individual voices having been silenced, with no mechanism for expressing our opinions. We conducted ourselves from a passive stance, compliant, respectful, and obedient to the authority of our parents and elders. This is the outcome of an authoritarian upbringing. Here are some stories illustrating defiance of parental authority, of parents asserting that authority, and the perspective of U.S.-born children that speaks of having equal status with their parents and/or grandparents.

Authoritarian/egalitarian oriented stories
A. "Hi, dude."

A father was entertaining a friend in his living room when his 17-year-old son entered and greeted him, "Hi, dude!" "*Pumanting ang tenga ko* [my ears burned in anger)!" the father explained to me. So, he pointed his finger at his son as he angrily replied, "Don't 'dude-dude' me! I'm your father!" The son was startled by what he thought was unexpected anger from his dad.

My comment: The informality in the American speech and conduct, a product of the overarching egalitarian culture, informs his son's attitude. Therefore, he can address his father casually by calling him "dude." Of course, as far as the son was concerned, he was not being consciously disrespectful to his father. But by calling his dad "dude," the son is actually putting his father on equal footing with himself, and for his father, this is a no-no. Treating one's parents as an equal and addressing them as if they were one's friends often generates anger or hurt among parents, who see such treatment as disrespectful and insulting. When I was in seminary, during the first day of class, the international students didn't know what to answer when some professors announced that they could be called by their first names if students preferred.

Sometimes this egalitarian orientation can also be perceived as an expression of upper-class entitlement. Witness the high school student, who comes from a wealthy family and who tells his teacher, "Do you have a problem with me?" after he is reprimanded for noisy behavior in class. There is definitely no culture clash if both teacher and student were born and raised in the United States. The student might not even be aware he is exhibiting a rather entitled attitude; he may think he was showing natural behavior. This is not a cultural issue; it can, however, be a class issue. The teacher can rightly call out the student for his haughty attitude, and wise is the parent who uses this opportunity for a dialogue with his or her child to let it be known his or her place in a teacher-student relationship. My advice to this parent is don't blame your child because he may just be projecting his egalitarian orientation. The son, in this case, didn't know any better. That's one weakness of the egalitarian orientation. It does not teach children to know their place when it comes to the hierarchical context of relationships.

B. "I got married."

I joined some friends watching the fight of the century boxing match in Las Vegas. As friends began to arrive, a married couple greeted us with voices that barely contained a mix of anger and sadness. It turns out their daughter had just called them to say that she just gotten married to her boss, who was a lot older than she was. She was their only child in her mid-20s.

My comment: This is a heavy-duty one for me. I cannot imagine how I'd feel if this were my daughter. I have to say, no matter how much the parents insist on their traditional Filipino role as the absolute authority, the daughter has the last say on this one. I was not privy to this family's particular dynamic concerning traditional Filipino childrearing. There may have been other incidents in their family dynamic that warranted the daughter's independent decision-making without consulting her parents. In any case, the parents have to choose to adopt a positive or negative attitude toward their daughter and son-in-law, because what's done is done. I am happy to report that recently, I learned the parents have forgiven their daughter, and accepted her decision, welcoming the husband into the family. Isn't it prophetic what Kahil Gibran said? One day our children will leave us. We hold them only for a little while, but do we hold their heart? Pay attention to this one, authoritarian parents.

C. "I'm your father."

An Ecuadorian dad, married to a half-Filipino-half American wife, was arguing with his son one early morning before he drove him to school. "I don't want to wear this t-shirt. I don't like it," the son pleaded with his father. "But this is brand new, and I want you to wear it," answered the father, annoyed. "Dad, I don't like the design," the son explained. "I am your father, and I want you to wear it or else I won't fix your breakfast!" the father replied sternly. Mother intervened. "Son, don't wear it if you don't like it, and I will fix your breakfast," she assured her son. Mother turned to her husband and said, "How dare you say that! You will ruin his self-esteem!" The father snapped back, "You Americans always say self-esteem, self-esteem! But look how many crazies live in this country!"

My comment: Whoa, this is a big show of parental authority. As you can obviously glean from the father's statements, parental authoritarianism is true not only in the Philippines but in other group-centered cultures as well. On the contrary, many in American culture focus on self-esteem almost to a fault. And while it is true that mental illness is on the rise in the United States, I wouldn't go as far as attributing it to the so-called "self-esteem culture."

D. A daughter's suicide

On May 25, 2015, a 13-year-old Filipino American girl committed suicide by jumping off a bridge on a busy interstate highway in Tacoma, Washington, reportedly due to online shaming by her father. The father reportedly cut off the teen's long flowing black hair, videotaped the act, and posted it online, deciding it was the proper punishment for an offense, which was never disclosed. The video shows the girl with her newly chopped-off hair as she stands next to a pile of her beautiful black locks on the floor. However, the public humiliation and punishment apparently took an enormous toll on the child, who committed suicide just days after the video was uploaded online. She exited the passenger seat of her grandmother's vehicle, climbed over the bridge railing, and jumped "without hesitation," landing on a car below.[12]

My comment: For Filipinos, this is not a first! It happens in the Philippines too many times. Unfortunately, the blame lies solely on our authoritarian style of parenting. There are so many stories of families and marriages destroyed because of parents' insistence on blind obedience to their authority, which they believe is absolute. Tragically, there is acceptance of even such a morbid result for such a rigid childrearing practice. We grieve, accept, and ultimately, we move on. Authoritarian rule is our way of being.

E. A dream is gone forever

Upon graduating from high school, a young professional shared a dream she had of owning a beauty salon complete with all the offerings: manicure, pedicure, spa treatment, haircut, styling, coloring, eyebrow waxing, threading, hair dyeing, etc. Her ambition was to go into cosmetology. But her parents would not hear of it. If she wanted to be financially supported, she had to attend a four-year college and earn her degree. So, to college she went and wasted three years hopping from one major to another, not knowing what she wanted. Today, she is a physical fitness professional.

---

[12] "Fil-Am girl kills self, apparently after online shaming by her father," posted 9/6/2015 at http://globalnation.inquirer.net/124209/fil-am-girl-kills-self-apparently-after-online-shaming-father

My comment: Here is another example of killing one's dream or one's passion because of parents' authoritarian rule and thinking they know what is best for their children. Instead of helping the child to reach for the stars, they are encouraging her to be content working at a 9-to-5 job; and living life as an employee instead of becoming an entrepreneur.

THE FILIPINO WAY OF BEING: AUTHORITARIAN RULE

Authoritarian rule in childrearing practices in the Philippines means parental authority over children is absolute. "Filipino children are likewise expected to obey parental authority and sacrifice individual interests to prioritize familial obligations (Medina, 2001; Peterson, 1993; Wolf, 1997)"[13] A high premium is placed on children to be **compliant and obedient** to the parents' authority out of **respect**. Parental authority, obedience, and respect are the legs of the stool. Observance of respect out of obedience to parental authority dominates the interaction of the child with his or her parent. One does not retort or answer back but quietly complies. The child has no opinion, which is in contrast to the egalitarian orientation of many American parents, who see their children as self-directing and hence should be allowed to assert and express themselves (Schaefer & Edgerton, 1985).

A penchant for authoritarian leaders

In my previous book, *Culture Clash (2006),* I wrote: "A leader with a charisma and authoritarian

---

[13] "Attributions and Attitudes of Mothers and Fathers in the Philippines," 2 posted 8/21/2015 on http://www.ncbi.nlm.nih.gov/pmc/articles/PMC3150789/

presence enthralls the heart, mind, and soul of Filipinos, making them feel proud. They tolerated the government of Ferdinand Marcos' presidency for 20 years despite the well-documented corruption because to them his rule boiled down to exuding authority. Marcos fulfilled the Filipinos' need for an authoritarian figure in their lives."

The recent Philippine presidential election has once again borne out this need in the person of Rodrigo Duterte. Duterte is a charismatic leader and avowed authoritarian. He was elected president by an overwhelming majority of the vote. Who is Rodrigo Duterte? He was the mayor of Davao City who ran undefeated for seven terms. He is believed to have rid his city of corruption and drugs, the latter through controversial *death squads* that assassinated suspected dealers and users.

Davao residents expressed a feeling of security, and the city's population exploded as countless Filipinos arrived to relocate in the city. Duterte has now implemented his Davao solution for the entire country, earning him international criticism for apparently directing or inspiring summary killings of drug suspects without observing due process. Google his name to find more facts about this man.

Why the penchant for authoritarian rule? How a person is raised as a child determines what type of public leader he or she wants. Filipinos are the products of authoritarian parenting practices. Adherence to authoritarian rule comes at an early age. When one exudes an authoritarian character, he or she is held in high respect and regard. The dictator Marcos, despite the corruption that characterized much of his 21-year rule, was once placed on a pedestal of respect and admiration. Now the same appears to be happening with the rule of President Duterte.

On the other hand, the many American children are socialized to question authority, because what is being developed is a strong expression of the individual self. A high tolerance for freedom of expression is the rule in America. Simply log on to any internet chatroom, message board, or social media site, and you can read all sorts of opinions for and against any issue. American presidents are defended and attacked. In America, respect for authority is predicated on it being earned.

Following are samples of statements revealing parents' and teenagers' reactions to authoritarian parenting.

- "I give you food, shelter, clothes, and education. What I say goes!"
- "My threat works because I tell my teenagers, if they really test my authority, I am willing to go to jail in my effort to discipline them. Who will take care of them once I am in jail?"
- "I cannot change anymore. This is me. My child must listen to me. I am her mother."
- "My mom cut my Halloween costume to pieces because she said it belongs to the devil. I went out with my friends without a costume."
- "I told my parents, don't hit me again, I'll call the police!"

The interviews I've conducted with parents yielded many statements that implied adherence to and insistence on authoritarian rule and children's obedience to it. We tend to pass on to our children the parenting we received. The problem here, however, is that our children were born and grew up in an environment that does not support such philosophy and practices. The dominant U.S. culture stresses the offering of choices to the child while he is growing up. It is a highly democratic society. As parents, we can choose to pass on to our children the authoritarian style of parenting we received and suffer the consequences, or we can revise our parenting style to become compatible with their environment. When our Americanized young adults do not feel heard when an argument occurs, deep-seated resentment may develop toward the mother or father. Then tolerance for mistakes has a short circuit. Tempers flare, easily. One college student said that all he wanted was to hear his parents say "I'm sorry" sometimes. It would make a difference, he sighed. Sadly, he said his parents always justify their behavior as right, and he is wrong. Parents, how many of you could really bring yourself to say, "I am sorry" to a son or daughter? Perhaps, if we practice listening with our hearts, we may hear their moans and groans. And if they do likewise, they will also hear yours. It is a humbling act to listen with the heart because I have done it. What's magical is that the need to be right does not matter anymore. It seems to imply that humility is to the heart what arrogance is to the mind. Why? The mind is protective of its ego; the ego must be right all the time. The ego does not know how to say, "I am sorry." The mind is knowledgeable and hates to be wrong.

Have you ever thought that one day there might be a role reversal in the family dynamic? Your young adult becomes a bona fide professional, and one day you are old and weary living on your pension, and it is not enough to support your needs. To some, a life-debilitating incident may occur. Would they desire to support or help you in any way if there is deep resentment? Exercising your authority over them will no longer be easy. There will be more culture clash, or the grown children will decide to keep biting their tongues to have peace in the house.

Some parents retire "rich" and do not need the financial support of their children. Some grow old with fat bank accounts and stay on their high horse because they are financially able, yet no meaningful communication exists with their American children, who are now young parents. Their children come and go, visiting them with their grandkids, but it is done in an empty ritual fashion. After the exchange of "hellos," the children are in a hurry to leave for two reasons: there is nothing to talk about, or they are avoiding culture clash.

Obedience

Obedience and respect are the byproducts of authoritarian childrearing practices. The absence of obedience and respect in relating to parents and the elderly is considered a transgression in a collectivist culture, such as the Philippines.[14] The biblical edict, "Honor thy father and mother and thy days will be long," runs deep in the hearts of Filipinos. Disobedience to the teachings of elders will bring destruction and misfortune, *gaba* in the Filipino language. (The closest English word is "comeuppance," meaning retribution or divine punishment.) The Filipino child grows up having to constantly face demands of obedience to elders, starting with the grandparents. The child must contend with the three aspects of what obedience entails. First, since his or her parents, particularly the mother brought the child into the world, there is submission and a debt of gratitude owed. Second, he or she is expected to obey those who are older. Third, misfortune will be visited upon a disobedient and disrespectful child throughout his or her life.

---

[14] "Attributions and Attitudes of Mothers and Fathers in the Philippines," (paraphrased from p.3) posted 8/21/2015 at http://www.ncbi.nlm.nih.gov/pmc/articles/PMC3150789/

From the very beginning, gratitude, respect, obedience, and fear are held out before the child, insistently and as one package, to secure his or her compliance. Therefore, it's not hard to imagine how immigrant parents and their American teenagers are constantly at odds over each other's words, attitudes, and behavior because, quite simply, they were socialized in two opposing cultures. The American culture tends to produce defiant children who express their individual rights, whereas the Filipino culture tends to produce compliant and obedient children who live up to parental expectations. A gross act of disobedience occurs when Americanized teenagers answer back to their parents or grandparents. In the Filipino culture, the youth show respect by simply being quiet. Out of respect for one's elders, one has no right to express any opinion at home. Disobeying and disrespecting parents is tantamount to committing a mortal sin, and it will likely incite anger.

This expectation of compliance and obedience, if observed to the nth degree, ties the child to his or her parents in obligation and duty throughout adult life. Following are examples of statements from my interviews with teenagers expressing the pressure they feel to "obey" their parents:

- My parents say, "stay at home," that's all they say. I can do anything as long as I stay at home. I can listen to iTunes, play on my iPad, talk to my friends on my iPhone, read, eat, just "be" at home after school hours and during the weekend.
- Are you kidding? I will get in trouble if I speak my mind!
- My parents always compare me to them when they were my age in the Philippines:

good, obedient, honor students. Why do
they say that?!

Filipino parents proudly show off their compliant
and obedient children. One example is a self-assured,
confident teenager whose father is a popular pastor of his
church in Southern California. The father insisted his
daughter promise not to have a boyfriend until she was
in college. Consequently, the daughter lives a lie; her
boyfriend is one of the young people in her father's
church. The entire youth congregation is aware of it. The
situation looks ridiculous because the parents constantly
promote their daughter as a model of purity who is
postponing romantic relationships until college. The
young members look sideways, downward, and upward
to avoid eye contact with the pastor. It is all they can do
to keep from giggling or blurting out the truth. I asked
the daughter if she was worried her parents might
discover her deception. She laughed it off and said, "By
September, I will be in college. I will be free!" The youth
laugh in the dark, too.[15] As parents, sometimes we see
our children, especially in their teens and young
adulthood, as our trophies, not realizing that holding
them up that way may boomerang.

Respect
Respect is an important value among Filipino
parents, and the same is expected of their children. One
grows up learning that respect comes with age,
experience, and position in society. You earn respect by
virtue of your age. In America, if respect can be placed

---

[15] Lutie Orteza Lee, *Culture Clash: The Americanized
Teenagers, Implications for Parenting, Teaching, and
Mentoring* (New York, USA: Valor Circle Books/Arbor
Books, 2006), 16-18, 20

in a barometer, it goes up and down the scale, as you earn or lose it. You are constantly proving yourself worthy of it. In the Philippines, senior citizens are held in high esteem because it is presumed that wisdom comes with age. There is no pressure to prove you have self-worth.

The Filipino culture produces respectful people. For example, the national language of the country, which is now called Pilipino, but is popularly called Tagalog, contains words denoting respect when addressing persons perceived to be older than the speaker.

"Respect and submissiveness toward those who are older and have higher social rank is mirrored in the Tagalog dialect, which contains terms of politeness and deference like *"po"* or *"ho"* inserted into a conversation with an older person, something akin to the use of "sir" and "ma'am" in English."[16]

"While "sir" and "ma'am" are used sparingly, "po" and "ho" are uttered automatically at the end of every sentence, as if to assure its listener that respect is always maintained. While seldom used in English, it is natural to Filipinos, for whom respect is a highly prized trait, a virtue that must be inculcated in every child.

I would consider Filipino immigrants as the cultural group that places the highest premium on respect of anyone regardless of one's socioeconomic status. Parents introduce their friends to their children as *"Tito"* (Uncle) or *"Tita"* (Aunt), and henceforth, it is presumed that this is how their friends will be addressed by their children. This privilege of attaching titles of respect is shown only to in-groups.

Excessive concern for respect sometimes has humorous consequences. The above parental custom has become so pervasive that some American teenagers say

---

[16] Alfredo and Grace Roces, *Culture Shock* (Portland, OR: Graphic Arts Center Publishing Co, 2003) 27-28

that whatever attraction they have for the children of their parents' friends fizzles out the moment they remember that they are related, otherwise, why call them "Auntie" and "Uncle?"

The other extreme is that children may automatically call the parents of their American friends "Tito" and "Tita." In fact, a teenage girl thought it was "cool" to call her boyfriend's parents "Auntie" and "Uncle" even though they were not her parents' friends. Respect is good but can get out of hand when applied in the American context.

In the American context, showing respect to someone is not predicated on filial or political authority or socioeconomic status, but on performance. Often, to be respected, one must achieve something of greater proportion than others and maintain it to continue earning that respect. In contrast, here are some examples from my interviews of Filipino parents and their teenage children:

- When my teenager answers back, my ears literally turn red and feel hot. If not for the child abuse laws here, I would have slapped her a long time ago."
- My mom was surprised when she learned that I call my boyfriend's parents "auntie" and "uncle." What was I to do? She trained me to call all her friends that.

The mother in the above quote was naturally surprised to find her daughter had been calling "Uncle" and "Auntie" people not considered in their in-group.

Filipinos' adherence to respect also extends to the poor, which borders on patronizing behavior. It is internalized in the Filipino psyche that the lowliest in society are given public consideration in language.

Confronted with a filthy, ragged, and persistently annoying beggar, one is never justified to exclaim, "beat it, you bum!" but expected to address him in the Filipino way: *"Patawad po,"* literally, "forgive me, sir"— forgiveness for not being able to give him alms. A person of high status who demonstrates an obliging and gentle behavior with someone of lower status (employer to employee, housewife to the servant, elder to younger) is highly esteemed.

A respectful person is considered a virtuous person. To Filipino parents, having an outspoken child is a sign of failure for not being able to raise an obedient and respectful person.[17]

Style of communication

Because of the authoritarian practice in the family dynamics, this style of communicating has proven to be one of the starting points wherein parents go into a flying rage because children question their authority.

In the Philippines, the child grows up without his opinion ever being valued or acknowledged, so he learns not to express it. He is taught to suppress unpleasant feelings and never to question his or her parents' authority over any issue. Parents have the last word, period. Not standing up to them is a sign of respect. Such an upbringing develops in the child excellent skills in sensing the nonverbal cues of the parents. A Filipino will watch the listener carefully for any postural or intonational cues, body language, that would enable the child to learn what the other is feeling. One Filipino

---

[17] Lutie Orteza Lee, *Culture Clash: The Americanized Teenagers, Implications to Parenting, Teaching and Mentoring* (New York, USA: Valor Circle Books/Arbor Books, 2006) 21-23

summed it up by saying he never asked a question before knowing what the answer would be. The nonverbal communication is enhanced by the use of euphemism and indirect expressions, which are part of Philippine languages.

Making matters worse for the parents is the fact that Americanized teenagers have been oriented to be frank and calm in expressing themselves, to the dismay of their parents. Oftentimes, they come across as their parents' equals. They have no awareness that this behavior is immediately translated as disrespecting the authority of their parents. What they perceive as natural, normal behavior of talking is interpreted as otherwise, the cue is missed. Naturally, their parents become agitated with such disrespect and make it very clear, often with a raised voice. Another cue missed. Such a strong reaction is interpreted by American teenagers as the first step toward their parents becoming violent and even abusive. Again, another cue missed: being agitated is simply another style of communication among Filipinos, a means of driving a point home emphatically.

Filipino immigrant parents' communication style of being animated, passionate, emphatic, and emotional is guaranteed to be misinterpreted by anyone who assumes that the American standard of talking is the right way in the world. It is a losing battle for immigrants who will go through life laboring under a negative perception. Those who feel they are victims of injustice will likely exhibit heavy emotions as they express their plight. On the other hand, those who caused the injustices are often unaware of the pain they have inflicted and thus sound calmer many times over than their victims when two parties discuss the matter. This behavior from parents is sometimes perceived by their Americanized adult children to be perplexing because to them, frankness is normal talk.

The parents' sentiment is summed up by a mother who said, "it is always painful for me because my daughter hates it when I cover up instead of telling the truth. *Ang sakit niyang mag salita* (her truth-telling hurts), but she speaks the truth. Truth hurts *kasi eh* (that's why)!"

A new system of parenting

In my research, I found a proverbial light at the end of the tunnel, an alternative to the outright authoritarian style of parenting in the Philippines. It is a system of classifying parenting styles proposed by Diane Baumrind, an approach that has been tested throughout the world and has been linked to the most successful child outcomes.[18] This approach is common to middle-class settings around the world and has been very helpful for struggling parents.

Baumrind's idea was to describe how parents control their kids, and she defined three major approaches to parental control. **Permissive parents** are reluctant to impose rules and standards, preferring to let kids regulate themselves. **Authoritarian parents** demand blind obedience from their children, which resonates with Filipino parents; no ifs and buts, just outright obedience. **Authoritative parents** take a different, more moderate approach that emphasizes setting high standards, nurturing, and responsiveness, and showing respect for the children as independent,

---

[18] "The authoritative parenting style: Warmth, rationality, and high standards" (paraphrased), p. 2, http://www.parentingscience.com/authoritative-parenting-style.html

105

rational beings. The authoritative parent expects maturity and cooperation while offering children lots of emotional support.

Our Filipino American teens and young adults would perhaps, respond positively to authoritative parenting because it mirrors respect for the individuality of the child and gives them space to reason. Alas, it will surely prove to be a challenge for Filipino parents to adopt this approach. A Philippine study by Liane Pena Alampay and Rosanne M. Jocson, found that in sociocultural values, the Filipino culture fosters traditional attitudes favoring parental authority and child obedience. The compliant child gets all the attention and love from parents. Retorting and answering back is a big no-no and all hell will break loose when Americanized children question the authoritarian voice of their parents.[19]

In the summer of 2009, I was the invited speaker of a church's family camp. For me, it was a dream fulfilled, to preside over the bridging of the generational gap between immigrant parents and their Americanized teens and young adult children. In one session, I gathered both sides to share their misgivings in a dialogue. The dialogue was going smoothly with me as the go-between making sure that both sides felt heard. At one point, the children began to feel they hit a breakthrough as they aired their family's so-called "dirty laundry" (past grievances of parenting behavior) and from thereon became more and more emboldened to express their opinions while their parents sat in silence and visible discomfort. Finally, one parent suddenly suggested we

---

[19] "Attributions and Attitudes of Mothers and Fathers in the Philippines," (paraphrased) 1, posted 8/21/2015: http://www.ncbi.nlm.nih.gov/pmc/articles/PMC3150789/

stop because it was time for choir practice and suggested that we continue the session tomorrow. Well, that was the end of it. The youth and I felt as we were hanging in the middle. What happened here? It was a rare scenario. The cardinal rule of not questioning the parents' wisdom was broken, and to the parents, this was unacceptable and had to stop. So they stopped it. I left the dialogue with the unpleasant impression that somehow the parents felt I sided with the youth.

In retrospect, it may have been difficult for parents to hear their teen and young adult children expressing themselves with gusto as if they were their equals. As I said in my previous book, this conflict is often dramatized when two parties communicate. Teenagers in American society are accustomed to addressing their parents as equals because they are encouraged to express their opinions by their peer group and teachers. Filipino parents find such behavior obnoxious when practiced at home."

"Children in Asia are not seen as people who have their own views; if they do, they have no right to express them. They are left out of family conversations and decisions, even those concerning their very lives. Unaccustomed to making their own choices and decisions, Asian children often reluctantly let their parents make decisions for them."[20]

Contrast this upbringing to that of immigrant teens growing up in the United States. Immigrant parents have to deal with children who demand to be heard at the family table, who express themselves candidly as if they were talking to their friends. How do you break the cultural impasse?

---

[20] Eun Y. Kim, *The Yin and Yang of American Culture: A Paradox* (Yarmouth, Maine: Intercultural Press, 2001) 80

The following are remarks from parents and teenagers from my interviews:

- My teenagers do not ask my permission. They just tell me, for instance, what they are going to do and where they are going on Friday. Then they have the nerve to ask me to drive them there!
- I correct my teachers when they mispronounce my Filipino name. I ask them, "what's wrong with my name that you can't pronounce it correctly. I have no problem pronouncing yours.
- My parents are cool. They give me room to breathe. I'm friends with my mom.

Many teenagers growing up in America do not realize that not all forms of relationships thrive on equality. The only relationship I know that thrives on equality is friendship and, in some instances, business partnerships. You are friends because you have a mutual admiration. In marriage, that is debatable. Outside of friendship, all relationships follow a hierarchical order: parent-child; boss-subordinate; military officers-soldiers; teacher-student; principal-teacher; executive-assistant; landlord-tenant; eldest sibling-youngest sibling; etc. The list is endless. In America, we live with the notion that we are all equals. Yet, one feels this is not the reality, only an illusion that we like very much to be true.

We cannot undo our formative years. It would take many years of therapy to renounce our cultural upbringing consistently. The following is a story about what happens when two people relate to each other according to their cultural orientation, one relates under the notion of equality, the other is socialized into a hierarchical organization. An American Peace Corps volunteer hired a Filipino maid during her stint in the Philippines. The maid did all the cooking and washing for her. As time went by, their rapport deepened, and was even envied by some of the American's friends. When she had problems, she ran to her maid and shared them with her, sometimes crying to her. Her maid tried to help her the best way she knew how. When her assignment in the Philippines was over, saying goodbye proved to be heartbreaking. During one of their goodbye talks, both said something that, surprisingly, underlined their true feelings about the relationship. The maid said, "I tried to be the best maid anyone could ever have," while her boss said, "I tried to be the best friend any person could ever have." The Filipino's statement, seeing herself as a maid despite her American boss treating her as a friend, shows how impossibly difficult it is for the maid to escape her cultural orientation.

Unpacking Amy Chua's Childrearing Discipline

My first reading of *Battle Hymn of the Tiger Mom* by Amy Chua left me speechless, especially over the strict discipline with which she raised her daughters; it came across as bullying, demanding, and threatening. On the second reading, however, I began to "hear" her as a mother bent on instilling hard work and future skills into her daughters. By the third reading, I began to see that her style does not belong under authoritarian parenting. Rather, she fit Diane Baumrind's description of authoritative parenting. That being said, I am ready for some backlash from Chua's critics. This is my takeaway. Amy did not withhold or withdraw love from her daughters. The daughters know that they are loved by their mother who is driven to perfection. The daughters were allowed to reason with and express their minds, although the mom didn't give in to their demands.

There is a verbal give-and-take between mother and daughters in which the mother explains the consequences of good and bad behavior. To me, this is not authoritarian but authoritative parenting. Authoritarian parenting does not include explaining the reasoning behind consequences. In fact, at one point, Amy's willfully defiant 13-year-old made her get down on her knees in humiliation, and she got a dose of her own medicine.

I have 25 Post-It Notes marking pages of Chua's book that resonated with me. I wholeheartedly agree with the points she makes in the chapter, "On Generational Decline" (pp. 20-24). My maternal and paternal grandmothers ruled their households with the proverbial iron fist. My parents, uncles, and aunts were subjected to harsh discipline. But my paternal grandma was worse than the maternal grandma. She assigned professions to each of her nine children, with a stern warning to pursue them or else. On my father's side, one aunt was a pharmacist, the other a professor of philosophy, and the last a medical pathologist. Among my uncles, two were lawyers, one a surgeon, one an accountant, and one an agriculturist (who was assigned to manage the farmland). Of the nine, only my father did not complete his assigned profession. World War II interrupted his law studies, and he went to seminary and became an ordained minister. His mother accepted this decision. However, she was not happy with his choice to marry my mother. For many years, my father was disowned, yet what was ironic was grandma accepted us, her grandchildren. So, my uncles and aunts followed their parents' desire for careers, but when it came to their children, a sort of rebellion took hold, and they were lax with us. Interestingly, now and then my cousins and I would exhibit parental behavior reminiscent of our grandparents. When we compare notes, we make the same connection. It must have something to do with what our *Lola* (grandma) told our parents.

For instance, growing up, my siblings and I noticed that when we went to public places, we could eat food bought from street vendors if we were with our mother, but not with our father. The most he gave us was White Rabbit candy. He would tell us to let it melt in our mouths until we reached our destination. White Rabbit is a hard candy. Dad's rule was no chewing in public because it was unseemly. Even when I rode in the company of friends, later on, I turned down offers of food, although I have since eased up.

And even though she doted on us, her grandkids, *Lola* laid out one harsh rule: stay away from the kitchen. Anyone caught in the kitchen was punished. My two cousins were made to kneel on the floor for hours because they were caught eating leftovers in the kitchen. It is the servants' domain, *Lola* said. Working with one's hands is inferior to using the mind. In retrospect, I often wondered how this rule was drilled so deeply into our unconscious. I and most of my cousins chose careers that make use of our minds. So, on that note, I admire the parenting style of Amy Chua for instilling in her daughters a love of physical labor while at the same time encouraging them to develop and exercise their minds to perfection.

My Anchor, Kristi

For any parent anywhere in the world, the defiance of our authority is a very painful price for raising children. The experience can be profoundly life-changing too, as what happened to me 32 years ago, in the dead of Easter morning when I encountered the rebellion of my teenage daughter. My discomfort and panic in those few minutes of discovery are as raw as ever:

"It is so hot...I'm perspiring...Better turn off the heater...I wonder if my daughter is sweating too from this heat...let me check her room...Oh, my God, she is not in her bed! It is 4 am. Where is she? Where is she? What shall I do? Somebody help me!"

Thus began my journey as an immigrant Filipino American parent, joining millions of others who were trying to cope with their American teenagers. Heart-wrenching arguments became our daily state of affairs. It became my passion to learn how to relate to her. I did not believe she was entirely to blame for what she did.

Being a single mom with no family or partner, I naturally turned to my fellow teacher and closest friend, Kristi, for help and comfort. I called her, hysterically breaking the news. She lived 40 minutes away by car and understandably couldn't run to my side. Instead, she suggested I call the police. Kristi became my anchor in those difficult days, for which my sheltered life in the Philippines did not prepare me to deal with appropriately. I was a first-grade teacher with zero skills in dealing with U.S. teens. I didn't know where to begin and what to do. Kristi's words were a big comfort, "Lutie, I have been there, done that. Brace yourself; this is what some teenagers do. I drove my parents crazy when I was a teenager. Trust me; I will talk to her. I am not worried."

My daughter came back before 6 a.m. "If she intended to run away, she would not be back," I was assured by the police officer I talked with that morning. Now that I was aware of her tendencies, sneaking out of the house when I was asleep, sleep was out of the question. I had to watch her all night. Kristi and I decided that the only way for me to get some rest and write my lesson plans was for my daughter to sleep at her house. Little did I know of the ordeal that was to follow.

At that time, we had less than two months left before the school year ended. I decided it was time for us to visit the Philippines. Kristi decided to make the same trip with her two daughters. In the days leading up to our flight, I was gripped with fear that my daughter's friends might prevent her from leaving the country. We stuck to our plan of my daughter sleeping at Kristi's house until the day of our flight.

We followed the same schedule for two months. Monday to Thursday, my daughter and I would have a quick dinner, followed by a 40-minute drive to Kristi's house in Northridge, California. There, I would leave my daughter, then drive back to our house in Pasadena. In the mornings, Kristi would drop my daughter off at school on her way to work. After school, my daughter and I would go home, and the cycle began again. I told my daughter not to tell a soul where she was at night. Kristi used authoritative behaviors with my daughter, and I want to believe that kept my daughter in line, to my relief and gratitude.

Kristi and I met as primary school teachers and then became best friends after our marriages crumbled almost at the same time. Little did I know that I would become her anchor after her 19-year-old son was fatally shot during a robbery at the sandwich shop where he worked. For me, it was truly a triumph of her deep humanity when she openly supported Barack Obama for President transcending the pain of losing her son to violence committed by an African American. In 2013, Kristi lost her battle to cancer and went home to the loving embrace of our Creator who, I imagine saying, "Well done my good and faithful servant."

I dedicate this book to her, Kristi:
into the darkness and warmth of the earth,
into the sadness, the smiles, the memories,
into the cycle of living, dying, and rising again,

113

Rest in peace, in love. Amen.

Successful Parenting Stories

Look for the common denominator of the following stories.

Marion

A mother with five children and one on the way, Marion lost her husband during emergency surgery. Overnight she became a widow of six! With their savings, she bought a house. They had been missionaries in Nigeria. She was a nurse, and he was a doctor. They stopped by California on their way to the Philippines for their annual vacation. Her husband checked into a hospital because of unbearable headaches. It turned out he had a tumor on his brain as big as his fist. It had to be removed at once. He did not survive the operation. Because her husband died in her hands, Marion vowed never to return to work as a nurse again. She changed careers and became a postal worker, and a single mom supporting four boys and two girls. As a single mom living on a meager budget, she came up with a strategy to keep her children from making unreasonable financial requests. "From now on," she said, "before you ask for money to buy this and that, you must tell me if it is a need. If it is really a need, I will give you the money. But if this is just a want, figure out your own way to have it." So early on, Marion trained her children to differentiate needs from wants. Today, all of them are doing well, married with children, gainfully employed and thriving in their careers. All shower their mother with much love and appreciation for how she raised them. She is the queen of their hearts and the proud grandma to 12 kids! On her birthday this year, they sent her to New York City for a reunion with her high school classmates. Upon her return to California, there was a birthday celebration for her each day of that week.

CJ and his brothers

This is a story of how one family made a collective sacrifice for the higher goal of cultural balance. A mother and her three teenage sons left the United States to live in the Philippines for ten months out of the year for six years, so the boys would be immersed in the Philippine culture. The wife and sons lived apart from the husband and father for ten months, reuniting briefly during Christmas and summer break. I wrote about their experience in my first book:

> A family I will call Cruz decided to send their three boys to finish high school and go to college in the Philippines. Seeing their children [becoming] too Americanized, this couple thought the time has come to give them the foundation to become Filipinos again. For ten months, Mom stayed with her sons while Dad worked in the United States. During Christmas and the summer months, they came back to America. This arrangement went on for six years. At first, their sons resented the plan, but now they love it. They have come to appreciate their culture and now speak Tagalog, albeit with an American accent. More power to these parents who are raising bicultural and bilingual children!

Since then, all three sons have finished college in the Philippines and are now back in the United States. I recently interviewed them, and this is what the eldest, CJ had to say, "I salute my parents for the sacrifices they made to introduce us to Philippine culture. I could have stayed in the Philippines and pursued a career in the entertainment industry, having become a mini-celebrity of sorts, but in the end, I opted to return to the United States." I asked why and he was quick to explain that he could see leading a decadent lifestyle down the road and losing the right perspective. To date, CJ has decided to enter the priesthood. I talked to his two brothers, and they chorused that life in the Philippines taught them to be **humble** and **respectful toward elders**. I ask, why humble? Their reply, "We saw poverty all around us. We knew our stay was only temporary and we would be back in the United States, the land of plenty and opportunity. Our friends could only dream of coming here, and we were humbled over our good fortune." I also talked to their mother, who spoke of how the sacrifice was well worth it. Her heart went out to her friends in the United States who are at a loss as to what to do with their Americanized young adult children who no longer observe cherished Filipino traditions. She suggested that we start an association for Filipino mothers to lend support to the plight of those raising Americanized children.

Ofelia

Ofelia worked as a nurse in a prestigious hospital for many years and was close to retirement. Her three children are all professionals. Her husband died when her children were still in high school. I asked her how she managed to keep her children from getting into trouble, realizing that high school is a challenging time for parents. She said she made it a point to have a close relationship and open communication with her kids. As soon as she sensed a problem, she was the first to ask them. In her very loving affectionate way, she encouraged her children to share their burdens with her.

"*Ang tono na ating boses ay napakaimportante* [the tone of our voices as parents is very important when we talk to our children]," she explained.

Marilyn

This mother did not waste time in making sure that her son Joel's musical talent did not go unnoticed. Despite limited resources, she managed to give her son all the love and support she felt he needed to fulfill their dreams of a musical career for him. She researched voice teachers and scholarships. Her hard work paid off, and today Marilyn is a proud mom to a son who has a fulfilling career as an entertainer performing on cruise ships and in Las Vegas. And Joel has not forgotten to show gratitude to his mother for all her sacrifices. I asked her if she would do it all over again, making all the phone calls and visits to find places for her son to develop his talent. "I would do it again and again because my son loves singing and playing musical instruments," she proudly exclaims. Accolades to this mom.

Daisy

In spite of the authoritarian stance of her husband toward their children, Daisy created an atmosphere of openness for her children to make them feel that they could always come to her to share their problems no matter how shameful they may seem. Her heart was always a refuge for them. It seemed to have paid off because her children are now professionals doing well in their careers. The successful children thrived by having a meaningful relationship with Mom while they learned skills to relate to Dad.

Ben and Josie

Ben and Josie were troubled by the signs that betrayed their son's gender orientation. The denial came first before the eventual, painful acceptance. However, after they read a love letter he wrote and left in his bedroom, perhaps on purpose, they were left with no choice but to confront him. They did, and he came out to them. Ben and Josie faced a dilemma. They recognized the fact that denying their son's sexuality would be devastating to him, but they grappled with their feelings over the issue. In the end, they decided their relationship with their son would suffer if they did not accept his choice. When their son found love, they went out of their way to support him. The son felt extremely fortunate to have parents like Ben and Josie. Not only that, Ben and Josie were instrumental in helping the parents of their son's partner to accept their son's sexuality. It is not often that we find Filipino parents who support a gay child's life choices. Every parent faced with this must decide how to navigate their beliefs and their relationship with their child. In parenting, we must often make difficult choices. In this situation, there are no easy answers. Today, Ben and Josie's son and his partner are thriving in their chosen careers.

Amy

When Amy Chua's book came out, one of the critical comments published for all to read was, "To consider parenting to have ended when a child turns 15 seems premature." Well, Chua may have proved her critics wrong. Her two daughters appear to be thriving as college-bound students, one going to Harvard and the other to Yale.

COMMONALITY

What did you notice? **Marion** persevered in raising six children ranging in age from a few months to 12 years. She showed tenacity and a pragmatic outlook on her "need versus want" contract with her children, one that was forged in reason and love. **CJ and his brothers** returned to the United States transformed into respectful and humble young men due to the sacrifice of their parents. **Ofelia's** forgiving and conciliatory spirit as she recounted her relationship with her children came through strong and clear in my interview with her. What would have happened to Joel if **Marilyn** did not shower him with the love and support she did to provide for developing his talent? **Daisy** provided an emotional sanctuary where her children felt safe to unburden themselves. **Ben and Josie** provided unconditional love and support for their gay son. **Amy,** whose parenting style I have discussed here, demonstrates that love and a strict upbringing are not at odds.

In summary, all the stories demonstrated **love** from the parent and **cooperation** from the children are essential ingredients in a successful parent-child relationship. **When parents succeed in loving their children for who they are, and children, in turn, feel and think that their parents love them, there is no reason to rebel. It boils down to how parents make their children feel about themselves.**

PARENTAL TIPS and GUIDANCE

The passages below are suggested to help prevent culture clash from exploding and wreaking havoc in your families. They are excerpts from my first book that are aimed to guide and teach:

1) **Authoritarianism**: Imposing our authority over our teenage and young adult children is first on the list. Let's face it, our upbringing in the Philippines was not democratic but rather authoritarian. In the authoritarian household, children have no opinion in the family. Parents

brandish force (sometimes using it) in dealing with teenagers to enforce obedience. Some of us separate our teenagers from their friends if necessary. We strictly monitor their schedule of activities. In my interview with one teenager, she mentioned that one of her friends was practically a prisoner in her own home after school hours. Her dad continually watches her like a hawk. Even when she goes to the bathroom at night, he stands outside waiting for her. Every hour her mom and dad take turns going up to her bedroom to check to see if she is there. Such parental behavior can become a breeding ground for adolescent rebellion.

We try to use shame-inducing statements, but to our surprise, our statements turn out to be all bark, no bite. A teenager growing up in the American culture is not motivated to change behavior by shame. Shaming them does not work. A daughter of a friend's friend became pregnant. The family wanted to send her to the Philippines to have the child born there. The daughter was determined to stay in California and continue schooling. She walked proudly as her body was enlarging with motherhood, while her parents were dying of shame. To the American teenage daughter, every day that she could face the world was another step toward empowerment.

My critique of authoritarian rule is that it discourages young people from thinking for themselves and engaging in critical self-reflection. We would turn them into robots. Allowing our children some room to reflect helps them name their feelings. This process is empowering to the individual allowing them to know who they are and who they want to become. The pregnant daughter cited above obviously knows what she wants. As Filipino parents, we must allow room to let our teenagers express their views once in a while, and to respect these views; al parent we must strive practice authoritative, not authoritarian, parenting.

2) **Education**: Parents with more formal education will resort to reading books about authoritative parenting strategies, having by now realized that the Filipino style does not work. Some parents will attend seminars or workshops. I attended one and learned something important. The facilitator told us to close our eyes and think back to the time when we were teenagers. He asked us who our heroes or mentors were. With our eyes closed, we were told just to say out loud who they were without necessarily mentioning their given name, but just describing who they were. These were the names we heard blurted out: coach, aunt, uncle, maid, mom, dad, teacher, neighbor, grandpa, grandma, godmother, etc.

We opened our eyes and were asked what we could say about these people. What do we notice with these names? "None of you said my best friend," noted the facilitator. We spend most of our waking hours with our friends, and yet we don't perceive them as our heroes and mentors. The same thing is happening to our teenagers. They are with their buddies most of the time, not with their heroes or mentors. **As parents, we must pave the way for our children so that they will have mentors as they navigate their lives into adulthood.** We must be intentional in guiding our children toward friends and relatives who we think are good candidates to be their mentors. We must create opportunities for the two to make connections and hope these connections take root and grow.

Looking back, I think this became the case with my daughter and my best friend Kristi because the two had plenty of time together when I sent the former to sleep in the latter's house for almost two months. My daughter revealed this bond later on when she told me that Kristi missed their online Scrabble for three days in a row, which led her to worry that Kristi's cancer might have turned worse. True enough, she was right. Kristi died soon afterward. The day she died, my daughter canceled her flight to attend a wedding so she could be at Kristi's memorial service that weekend.

3) **Church and in-group**: Some parents who are active in their local church will seek the help and support of their brethren, while those who do not attend church will approach their in-group. Church spiritual mentors may even encourage spiritual practices for teenagers. However, this approach may boomerang. The youth may link themselves to a support network among their peers who they naturally gravitate to, not the adults in the congregation. The absence of intergenerational togetherness in the church encourages division, as members fall in with their age groups. We must be intentional, to consciously encourage our youth to connect with spiritual mentors beyond our in-group friends. Let's make our youth's multi-generational involvement an active goal.

4) **Guilt feelings**: Some parents go through feelings of abject failure in raising their children. I know some of these parents, and I see the pain etched on their faces. I am often at a loss for words when I hear folks despair over their parental shortcoming.

   One couple's daughter fell in love with a boy, not to their liking. She was 19. So they issued her an ultimatum: parents or boy. The daughter chose the boy. Her parents banished her from the family, confident she would come to her senses and return to them. Soon after, their daughter's boyfriend got seriously ill and needed money for medicines. The daughter approached her parents for help but was rejected. A few months later, the boy died. The daughter was pregnant with his child, unbeknownst to her parents. Three months after she gave birth, the baby died. One day, she was walking down the street and met her father. But she did not recognize him. Instead, she asked him if he had seen her baby. Alarmed at the sight of his daughter, the father called his wife. They looked for their daughter and brought her home when they found her. They are now giving her the best care they can to restore her to health. What lesson can we learn? Parents, pay attention to this one story. Check your parenting style. Is it authoritative or authoritarian?

5) **Blame nature over nurture**: *"Ewan ko ba, talagang matigas ang ulo na anak ko* (I don't know, but I think my child is really stubborn.) This is her nature, there's nothing I can do. I already did my best."* At the height of my problem with my teenager, I often heard this remark from other parents who faced the same problem. They were blaming their teenagers. The statements implied that this is their nature, and one couldn't go against it. It is futile. But I kept asking myself, where is the room for nurture? How can one decide so soon that the teenager is already demonstrating full

nature? Deep inside me, I refused to agree. I have the responsibility to nurture my teenager, to direct the "unfolding nature" toward healthier ground.

When I informed my daughter's Dad that I was left with no choice but to relocate to upstate New York (where a distant relative lives) to keep our daughter away from friends who were falling into bad behavior, his reply hit like a spear to my heart. It kept echoing in my mind, "But if this is the nature of our daughter, moving to New York would be a waste of your time and money. It will hurt you more if the same thing happens again." I recalled answering, upset, "If I accept your idea, what is my reason for getting a higher education if I cannot apply what I studied? No, this is where nature ends, and nurture comes in!" I guess he realized that I had already made up my mind because he said, "Okay, I don't agree with what you want to do, but I will financially help you move. His reply was a soothing balm to my wounded heart. The move paid off within six months. In the course of our four-year stay in upstate New York, our mother-daughter communication and relationship became better and better as we slowly learned how to read each other, culturally speaking. I now realize that I was still more fortunate than most parents. I received financial support from my former husband. I was grateful to my distant relative and her husband for opening their home for us to stay in while we were getting situated. Other parents with fewer resources and options would have to seek other avenues. My decision was also based on deep faith and countless hours of prayer. We nurture toward the right direction the unfolding nature of our children.

6) **Tough love:** To this day, the scenario below is still tops in my book as the longest agonizing night a mother can experience because of her tough love approach toward her daughter. In our lives as parents, we face a thousand moments when our parenting is challenged to the core. We do all we can in our own human power to solve the problems we face with our teenage children. Out of our frustration of feeling we have done all we can do and still encounter the stubborn will of our children; we surrender to them out of exasperation. One young mother mentioned what she told her son, "What else do you want me to do? I have done everything!" My advice to parents is as follows. Avoid expressing this feeling to your children because they are not yet mature enough to take life into their own hands. **Don't fall into this trap, surrender to God, not to your teen.** And continue to communicate with your teen in an authoritative way about why you do what you are doing.

On the evening that my teen daughter realized our trip to upstate New York was not really a 10-day break in the middle of October but something more permanent, all hell broke loose. She had to be restrained by my cousin and her husband to keep her from attacking me! So much drama took place that night. She has no memory of that long night or the expletives she hurled at me. She was crying, and I was too as I told her, "I am doing this because of my tough love for you!" At one point during this ordeal, I stepped outside while my cousin and her husband tried to calm her down. In the darkness of the night, I shouted at the top of my lungs and surrendered her to my Creator. "She's all yours dear God, I have used all the strength I can muster," I cried. I went back inside and saw that she had calmed down. She rocked herself to sleep. Six months later, she gave me a birthday card that was music to my soul. (See Appendix D.)

7. **Humor**: Do not underestimate the power of humor! It is the best medicine when the going gets tough. This is precisely what happened to my daughter and me. When we learned to joke and to catch the moment when we are simply being "Filipino and American," we learned to laugh. And the strangest thing, the tension went away on its own course.

REFLECTION

> *In coming to know a second or a third culture, one discovers how much that was taken to be reality is actually an interpretation of realities that are seen in part and known in part; one begins to understand that many things assumed to be universal are local, thought to be absolute are relative, seen as simple are complex; one finds that culture shapes what we perceive; how we perceive it and which perceptions will be retained and utilized.*
>
> David W. Augsburger

CHAPTER 4

CONSIDERING PROPRIETY BEHAVIOR (*HIYA*)

Hiya is bandied about as shame or embarrassment, utang na loob got to be known as reciprocity. But no one really got carried away except when pakikisama was elevated to the status of a value and passed off as a Filipino goal, purpose, and objective.
    —Dr. Virgilio G. Enriquez

What pushed me to write this chapter is the lost understanding among our Americanized teens and young adults of "*hiya*" behavior in the Filipino context. They would probably even say, what does that word mean anyway? In the indigenous concept of the Filipino culture, *hiya,* first and foremost, is all about preserving what is considered propriety behavior, courtesy, decorum, and good manners. A decent human being behaves with propriety, he or she has *hiya.* And when it doesn't exist, there is no *hiya,* shameful, as we would probably say. *Hiya* feeling or behavior has both moral and social dimensions. It has both positive and negative connotations. But a lot was lost in the English translation, which simply equates *hiya* to shame.

This is why our American children are puzzled because the American interpretation of *hiya* only describes the moral dimension. To them, the only meaning of hiya is a wrongful act or scandal that brings shame or embarrassment to the family or individual. A recent example is American swimmer Ryan Lochte. Lochte has won 12 Olympic medals and enjoyed worldwide respect and adulation. He was brought down in shame after he lied to the media about what happened to him and his teammates during the early hours of August 14, 2016, in Rio de Janeiro. Lochte said they were robbed at gunpoint on the way back to their hotel from a post-Olympics party. However, Brazilian police later uncovered what actually happened: they vandalized a gas station toilet.[21]

Filipino parents expressed dismay as they watched the news, *"nakakahiya* [shameful]," they said. Their U.S.-born children observed their parents' reaction and wonder, "what's the big deal?" Of course, the kids believe their parents are handing down moral judgment, when the parents are just noting a departure from propriety behavior in a specific situation. You see, Filipinos raised in the native culture have been taught to maintain propriety behavior, to maintain one's dignity at all times. So, American kids, take note, it doesn't take a scandal to have *hiya*. Any kind of behavior has a *hiya* factor. According to Enriquez, to have *hiya* is to consider what is propriety behavior in any situation. Doing the decent thing at all times is paramount. The object of having *hiya* is not the self—it is always the other. To have *hiya* is to maintain a good relationship with the group. It means holding one's tongue instead of speaking the truth and thus threatening to harm the relationships. This is the expected behavior, the default setting. But to our U.S.-born or raised children, who are oriented toward the self, the default setting is to speak straight, speak one's mind, and without a thought of the other. A mother expresses her frustration as she tries to tell an unpleasant truth to a friend: "I try to be vague about what really happened, but my daughters scold me for hiding

---

[21] Ryan Lochte, "Dancing Saved Me" (NY, NY: US Weekly Issue 1133, October 31, 2016)

the truth!" Now, before anyone gets the wrong idea, let me be clear: *hiya* has a moral dimension. But it is intertwined with a social dimension. Observing propriety behavior and retaining one's dignity is very important.

Dr. Virgilio G. Enriquez, the Father of Filipino Psychology

In my effort to capture the essence of my Filipino heritage, I studied the work of Dr. Virgilio G. Enriquez, who wrote *From Colonial to Liberation Psychology* in 1994. His breakthrough in redefining who we are as a people earned him the title, "Father of Filipino Psychology." His work reconnected me to my Filipino roots, our indigenous culture, and the ways of the *"katutubo/lumad* (natives)." From that moment, I began to think and write in the consciousness of my cultural heritage. Enriquez's monumental research uncovered a Filipino indigenous culture that remains pristine in the face of centuries of Western colonization. While his pioneering work was cut short due to an untimely death in 1995, Enriquez left a legacy so robust it inspired others to build on it.

One of Enriquez's seminal accomplishments was constructing our Filipino personality core values—*hiya, utang na loob,* and *pakikisama*—as a triad. In doing so, he fashioned more accurate definitions of this fundamental triad: *hiya* is "propriety/dignity;" *utang na loob* is "gratitude/solidarity;" and *pakikisama* is "companionship/esteem."[22] Thus, he rescues this triad of core values from the Western shortcuts that have led to misunderstanding: "shame" for *hiya*, "reciprocity" for *utang na loob*, and "smooth interpersonal relations" for

---

[22] Enriquez, Virgilio G. From Colonial to Liberation Psychology: The Philippine Experience. Manila, Philippines: De La Salle University Press, 2004, p. 66.

pakikisama. In his more organic construction, the three core values are interconnected and interdependent in their functions. They are like the three legs of a stool holding up the very identity of the Filipino itself. If one leg is removed, the identity does not work, it is not Filipino. We need to understand each value independently to fully grasp the unity.

Hiya

Our surface everyday *hiya* (propriety/dignity) behavior has **no moral dimension** (however, it could describe scandalous behavior) but is **social in character.** Because it is social, *hiya* naturally folds in with *utang na loob* and *pakikisama*—the three operate as one and therefore cannot be treated as separate, disconnected behaviors. Enriquez calls this our "accommodative surface values" which function primarily to maintain the status quo either on an individual or group basis. Over the years, American-oriented researchers have seized on this category to such an extent that all other values have been pushed to the sidelines. Because of the high visibility of studies, translation labels for each of them has seeped into popular usage and have been taken as appropriate. In other words, the labels that Westerners created for the Filipino behaviors they studied evolved into the norm. Thus, *hiya* became "shame" and was treated as an independent behavior that acts on its own without affecting or being affected by *utang na loob* and *pakikisama*. Enriquez has since corrected this flawed Western analysis that stood unchallenged for 50 years. The three values are inseparable, and they operate as one. To understand *hiya,* one must understand *utang na loob* and *pakikisama.* Of course, this is not an easy task. How great it would be if I could make you emotionally accept and understand the triad with just one stroke of my pen. Unfortunately, we have 50 years of misunderstanding to contend with; a misunderstanding so entrenched it is considered the norm. And the norm is that *hiya, utang na loob,* and *pakikisama* are three separate independent behaviors. Well, nothing could be farther from the truth.

Pakikisama

Pakikisama, enjoys the highest status in the hierarchy of interpersonal behaviors according to previous Western-oriented studies, that all but ignored other levels of interpersonal relations. Enriquez clarifies, "Of the three surface values, *pakikisama* (companionship/esteem) has received the most extensive treatment in the Western-oriented social science literature in the Philippines. It was used by Lynch (1961, 1973) as a primary basis for the construct of 'smooth interpersonal relations' or SIR. Again, the analysis suffered from the lack of attention to related Filipino concepts. In fact, the most valued form of relationship goes beyond *pakikisama.* [It is *pakikipagkapwa* (shared humanity)].

"The construct of smooth interpersonal relations as proposed by Lynch (1964) is supposed to be acquired and perceived through *pakikisama,* using euphemisms in the language and utilizing a go-between. He was successful in penetrating the highest level of interpersonal relationships in the *ibang-iba* category (not one of us), leading him to believe that *pakikisama* is a value. However, he did not take cognizance of the importance of the other levels of interpersonal relations beyond *pakikisama,* making his observation valid only to a certain point, and therefore inadequate. Lynch unwittingly reduced *kapwa* from the deep solidarity found in a shared inner self to superficial smooth interpersonal relations."[23]

---

[23] Ibid, 70.

For so long, we have been trying to understand ourselves, our identity, our character, through the lens of Western sociologists, and we didn't even realize it. Worse, this perspective has led us to develop an ambivalent, even disdainful attitude toward our core values. We have been taught to view them as a tiresome burden, not a virtue. One mother I interviewed just blurted out in exasperation, "I hate this *hiya*! I hate this *utang na loob*! I hate this *pakikisama*!"

The following example strengthens Enriquez' point. A woman threw a party to celebrate her birthday. For the big day, she made *ube* (purple yam) cake and *pancit* (noodles) that she had cooked using her special recipe. The party site was far from her house, so she needed to leave early in order to be the first one to arrive. In her haste, she forgot to bring the *pancit*. Her husband dropped her off at the party, then grudgingly drove back home to get the *pancit*. When he returned with the *pancit*, the party was almost over and most of the guests had already left. "This is all because of my wife's *pakikisama*," he sighed. I can hear Enriquez' vigorously disagreeing as he says, "your wife's behavior goes beyond *pakikisama*. She values *pakikipagkapwa* (having shared humanity) more." But see, *pakikisama* and the SIR imperative have been burned into our consciousness as the end-all and be-all, so much that we fail to recognize that a higher, more noble behavior is actually at work here: *pakikipagkapwa* (shared humanity).

Utang na loob

How about *utang na loob*? This is another Filipino value that has long been mislabeled and incorrectly defined as "reciprocity," akin to exchanging gifts or trading favors, to such an extent that some of us have grown to hate it. Isn't it annoying to be reminded about one's *utang na loob,* because it implies an obligation? And yet, we did not realize until recently that our notion of *utang na loob* is wrong, a distortion foisted upon our consciousness by Western anthropologists and authors. Enriquez said:

The problems with the token use of Filipino psychological concepts in the context of a Western analysis that relies on the English language and English categories of analysis are many. It no doubt can lead to the distortion of Philippine social reality and the furtherance of the miseducation of the Filipinos. It is no coincidence that Kaut (1961) hit upon *utang na loob* (debt of gratitude) as a key concept for the analysis of Tagalog interpersonal relations, considering that *utang na loob* is just one among many psycho-social concepts that relate to the theoretically fertile concept of *loob*. [Kaut] admitted that 'debt of gratitude' is not altogether unknown in Washington, D.C. Even Americans recognize *utang na loob;* they just happen to prefer *kaliwaan* or immediate payoffs whenever possible. To argue that *utang na loob* is a Filipino value is therefore misleading, to say the least, and dangerous at best. *Utang na loob* would be convenient in perpetuating the colonial status of the Filipino mind. Perhaps, it is not a coincidence that out of a long list of *loob*-related concepts [*sama na loob* (resentment), *kusang loob* (initiative), *lakas na loob* (guts)], *utang na loob* was singled out and perpetuated as an important aspect of the Filipino national self-image. In addition, the English-language interpretations of *utang na loob* as reciprocity happen to be useful in promoting the image of the colonizer as a benefactor.[24]

So, suddenly we are told that we've been living with the wrong notion of *utang na loob,* a gross distortion of the original indigenous concept. We've been led to believe that *utang na loob* is a transactional, mercantilist concept. This concept focused only on the *utang,* which literally means "debt" and ignored the *loob,* the interior part that speaks to the intensity of feeling the giver and receiver have for each other. But the *loob* is important. It is the source of the energy that drives this behavior, the glue that fuses the giver and receiver in a sacred bond.

Loob has no material or monetary value—you can't put a price on something that resides at the center of one's being and essence. Unfortunately, *utang na loob* as we know it today denotes "a direct exchange of goods and favors" or reciprocity of favors. Focusing on the *utang* and ignoring the *loob* strips this behavior of its profound motivation, gratitude for and solidarity with our *kapwa-tao* (shared humanity). Under this mercantilist definition, one who is displeased with the other's behavior is quick to remind the other of favors done. A relationship is now reduced to a shallow transaction: I scratch your back, you scratch mine. The translation of *utang na loob* into "debt of gratitude" is attributed to Charles Kaut, an American anthropologist who coined it in the mid-1950s while the studying rural communities in the Tagalog-speaking regions. Intentional or not, Dr. Kaut's translation weighed the behavior with a negative mercantilist connotation that

---

[24] Ibid

persisted for decades. It is often equated with another transactional definition: "reciprocity." Therefore, the behavior no longer emanates from the depth of one's being. It is not considered a sincere act because payback is presumed or expected. Worse, because it has been reduced to an "exchange of goods and favors" or "reciprocity," *utang na loob* has been distorted into a form of moral judgment. For instance, if A helps B and then later on A comes to B for help and B does not help A, then B is called an ingrate. The person has no *utang na loob;* a harsh label reserved only for the lowest of the low.

Let us be clear. The profound and correct meaning of *utang na loob* is a behavior that acts out of a deep, long standing bond. We do what we do out of that deep bond, not because we owe a favor or expect one in return. Nor do we speak about what we do, because speaking about it reduces it to a material good with a price tag—and when you put a tag price on something, it is cheapened. If a deep bond exists between giver and receiver, they have what is called a "shared inner perception" wherein the acts they do for each other need not be spoken about or referred to, one just "knows" what the other is feeling. If the receiver is grateful, the giver will feel that gratitude. No "thank you" is necessary. Conversely, the giver does not have to remind the receiver of what has been done, and to do so would cheapen the deed.

"*Utang na loob* is, therefore, a value which moves to recognize, respect, promote, and at times defend the basic dignity of each person," said Enriquez. To drive this point home, let me cite an act of human kindness given to my daughter and me. When it became apparent that I had to leave my husband, my friends were afraid to welcome us to stay temporarily with them, except for Eric and Meg. Eric said that we were free to stay with him and his wife until we found a permanent place. Without this offer, we would have been sleeping on the street that night! This is what *loob* speaks of, "defending the basic dignity of the person," a priceless act of humanity to the other.

Can we still reclaim the original indigenous definition of *utang na loob?* Can we apply the correct Filipino language that restores its true meaning?

An important question

Why did I construct this chapter's title, "Considering What is Propriety Behavior (*Hiya*)" in such a way as to equate "Propriety Behavior" with *"Hiya* (Propriety/Dignity)?" Why didn't I add *utang na loob* (debt of gratitude) into the mix, especially since Enriquez argues that *hiya* and *utang na loob* are considered one category. The answer is simple. *Hiya* exerts a deeper and more powerful motivation in our basic personality and carries both positive and negative meanings. Sadly, however, *hiya* has increasingly come to be perceived negatively, a moral virtue whose lack thereof relegates its owner to the depths of humanity, when in fact it is a sort of social auto-checker to help one maintain good relationships. Here, I want to discuss both the positive and negative implications of *hiya*.

The definition and concept of *hiya* that we embraced starting in the 1960s was the "clinical" description of this behavior. It all arose out of a clinical case involving a person who experienced a loss of shame. In fact, I wrote about this case in my initial book. The case created such an impact that its findings, particularly the negative connotation of *hiya,* seeped into our collective subconscious. From there, it engendered a Filipino character trait that is now popularly labeled "*hiya* personality." Filipinos accepted that they were a *hiya*-oriented people. As all this was developing, I was a college student reading about the negative implications of *hiya* in my sociology class. I accepted the negative implications, a presumption that a bad deed has been done. We must have done something bad, we must feel shame. It created a collective feeling of inferiority that we would stew in for three decades. Then Virgilio G. Enriquez came along and changed the definition and flipped the inferiority and negativity into a beautiful portrayal of who we really are, based on his research into our indigenous culture. In his 1994 book, *From Colonial to Liberation Psychology*, Enriquez introduced new language in describing our *hiya*. This time, in a positive light. He provided the correct context: We are a people who are constantly considering the question, "What is propriety behavior?" That's it! Enriquez singlehandedly turned our cultural narrative into the right direction as we struggled to find our collective identity, who we are as a people.

Fractured personalities

No wonder we are where we are as a culture. Our accommodative surface values—*hiya, utang na loob*, and *pakikisama*—have been "hacked" to pieces by cultural outsiders. Do we accept being labeled as having "fractured personalities," as implied by James Fallows in his famous article, "A Damaged Culture: A New Philippines," written 29 years ago for *Atlantic Monthly?*[25] The article erroneously exposed a dichotomy in our Filipino personality, a fractured personality, or at least that is what I surmised Fallows wanted to express. Let us dissect this so-called "damaged culture" in the light of the ongoing discussion of our three core values.

---

[25] James Fallows, "A Damaged Culture, A New Philippines" (New York: Atlantic Monthly, November 1987).

Fallows wrote: "If the problem in the Philippines does not lie in the people themselves or, it would seem, in their choice between capitalism and socialism, what is the problem? I think it is, and that it should be considered a failure of nationalism" (p.18). While there is some grain of truth in it, this analysis of Filipino behavior is flawed.

Stories about propriety behavior and the moral dimension of *hiya*

A. Limited budget

A son in his late teens was often left puzzled and bewildered by his parents' behavior. On one particular summer vacation, his parents reminded him and his brother that they could not rack up exorbitant expenses because of a limited budget. For this reason, the parents accepted the invitation of their *tita* and *tito* (aunt and uncle) to stay with them instead of in the customary hotel. But lo and behold, according to the son, every day they would stop at the fruit stand or bakery and buy almost all the fruits and pastries to give to *tita* and *tito*. "I already passed up on stuff I wanted to buy, and yet my parents splurge on so much food, the kitchen is overflowing," he groaned. "I don't get it! My mom says it's *nakakahiya* (shameful) not to do so. What have we done wrong in the first place?" The son could not understand why the behavior of not buying the food is shameful.

My comment: If his mother had explained the essence of *"nakakahiya"* to him, he may have understood. "Son, when I say *nakakahiya*, it doesn't mean we did something to be ashamed of. What I mean is your father and I do not want our family to be perceived as taking advantage of your *tito*'s and *tita*'s generosity because it

140

is not proper behavior." So, she is explaining that the least she could do to show them that they were not freeloaders was to bring them food. If his mom explained it to him in this way, the son would stop associating *hiya* with shame, which is the language of the Western perspective and how he was raised. Unfortunately, Filipino parents lack the correct language and struggle to explain to their American children the concept of *hiya* in the context of our indigenous culture's concern for propriety behavior.

That leaves the poor kids knowing only half of the definition of *hiya* they learned through the Western point of view. The moralistic half that looks dimly at bad behavior uncovered. That's *nakakahiya,* shameful. However, as we have already discussed, *hiya* in the original indigenous concept relates only to propriety behavior. It has none of the moral dimension that the Western perspective has unfortunately ascribed to it.

B. Lost in translation

A teenage son prevents his father from mingling with his friends whenever they hang out at his house. Naturally, Dad is offended. I asked the son about his behavior. He replied, "*Tita*, I have been embarrassed several times because when my dad starts to tell stories, he keeps switching his pronouns—he to she and vice versa. So, he starts his story with a boy, then in the middle of it he becomes a girl, then at some point, she is a boy again. My friends get confused listening to him because he keeps doing 'sex change operations' on his characters! I know that Filipinos talk like that. I am used to it, but my friends are not, so it's confusing to them and embarrassing to me."

My comment: Awareness is key to understanding this particular Filipino speech oddity. Both father and son meant well. The propriety response would be to make the son's friends understand that this is a habit of older Filipinos, and they unconsciously fall into this gender pronoun trap. That said, the father must be made aware of the confusion he's causing despite his sincere efforts to connect with the son's friends. If nothing is done, Dad may start perceiving his son's behavior as disrespectful. Culture clash may ensue.

In many Asian countries, there is no specific pronoun for "he" and "she." The Philippines is no exception. There is only one pronoun: "*siya*," meaning "he and/or she!" Gender identification has never been a problem in Filipino language conversations, that is until one switches to English. Filipinos raised in the native culture do not internalize the English grammatical concept of gender pronouns because they are oriented to the pan-gender pronoun *siya*. But if the listeners are native English speakers, oriented toward specific gender pronouns ("he" and "she"), it can really be confusing for them to listen to a native-born Filipino telling stories!

C. Unique Filipino nicknames

During her first visit to the Philippines, my daughter could not contain her culture shock upon being introduced to my mother's sister. "Hello dear, meet your *Lola* (Grandma) Fatty." "Like, what?!" my daughter blurted out. "That's mean!" I explained to her that when her grandma was a child, she was the chubbiest among the siblings, hence the name, Fatty, which stuck throughout her life. The following day, she met other relatives who had nicknames said twice: Klingkling, Dokdok, Lovelove, Ruthruth, and Junjun. As I expected, she was puzzled by this naming practice. Why say the name twice when once would do? I also told her that she has a cousin named Junto, which was taken from June 2, her birthday. To which she replied, "So, Mom, do you mean if I lived here, my nickname would be July 18?" Being an outsider to native Filipino culture, she felt embarrassed to call her relatives by their nicknames, especially her Lola Fatty—she still thinks it's a mean thing to call one's grandmother.

My comment: Well, is there a cultural explanation? Of course, there is! It is rooted in the heart of Filipino culture. Every culture has a habit, a practice, a tradition that goes back so long, no one even knows where it started. But it's there, and it's vital. Social scientists have a term for it: value orientation. Here's another social science term, which describes this Filipino habit, which is naming the "ascriptive effect," or how one comes across to the other. Filipinos habitually express comments about one's physical characteristics plainly and without judgment. So, when one nicknames a person "Fatty," they are not judging the person's character, just describing his or her most prominent physical feature. I learned that Dokdok got his nickname because when he was a baby, he threw tantrums and would bang his head against the wall. In this case, the nickname, which mimics the sound of the headbanging, takes an onomatopoeic twist, "dok-dok." Therefore, for Filipinos, it's the person's ascriptive effect on others that would cause them to respond in kind by giving the person the appropriate nickname. In this case, what would be considered propriety behavior is accepting what others perceive you to be based on striking physical characteristics.

Here is an example: A friend of mine, looking at her recent photos, was aghast at how much weight she gained after her two-week European cruise. She posted the photos on her Facebook page with this comment, "I noticed that my nose flattened as my face stretched to become fatter and rounder. Well, well, well, I have to accept the consequence of becoming fat!" She nailed it succinctly! Some people who are not oriented to "ascriptive status" but are into "achievement" would feel shame to publicly admit to becoming overweight and would be insulted if someone commented in the affirmative: "Yes, I agree." Culture clash would surely occur!

In studying for my first master's degree, I was introduced to the Kluckhohn Model developed by Fred Strodbeck and Florence Kluckhohn in 1961. According to this model, Western cultures tend to be oriented to a Doing value, whereas those in the East gravitate toward a Being value. In the Being value orientation, "the preference is for the kind of activity which is a spontaneous expression of what is conceived to be 'given' in the human personality. The orientation is not into the development of the personality. The personality is oriented toward expressing WHAT IS at the moment. The personality simply expresses what *is*. This activity orientation is also prone to looking at or describing the phenomena just as they are, implying no bad or good interpretation. There is no evaluation. It is just stated as it is. This personality has the habit of accepting just what is. There is a tendency for self-expression of the emotion at the moment whether it is pleasant or unpleasant." It is enough just to be!

In a Doing value orientation, "the preference is for the kind of activity that results in accomplishments which are measurable by standards conceived to be external to the acting individual. The aspect of self-judgment or judgment by others, which relates to the name of the activity is based mainly upon a measurable accomplishment achieved by acting upon persons, things, or situations. What the individual can do or accomplish is often the question of a Doing-oriented person. The Doing-oriented individuals prefer to get things done. They are solution-oriented toward the fix-it mentality."[26] Applying this to the example of the woman who posted her "overweight" photos on Facebook, the propriety behavior is as follows. If the woman is a Doing-oriented person, a commenter should not mention how her "affect" strikes the commenter. But if the commenter is a Being-orientation person who won't hesitate to ask, "why have you become fat?" expect a culture clash.

Here is another example. I was visiting a friend who shared that she had accepted the fact that her daughter-in-law had become her "arch-enemy," her *bête noire.* As she talked about their conflict, I spotted the trigger. It was a culture clash, but my friend did not recognize it as such. Instead attributed it to their personality differences. I told her, "Well, it's possibly a combination of both. If you are fond of making comments about her direction, and she is a Being-orientation person, she won't mind. But if she's a Doing-orientation person, she will interpret your comments as judgments. Suddenly, my friend comprehended my explanation and said her Americanized son does not like to mingle with Filipinos because they always call him *"taba* (fat)." Apparently, the son is assuming he is being judged by them. My friend explained to her son that when Filipinos make this comment, they are really just greeting him. Now that she has been acquainted with the Doing-versus-Being value orientations, she has a more credible explanation to offer to her son.

Another difficult challenge we face is one of discernment, who among the Filipinos residing in the

---

[26]Lutie Orteza Lee, Teaching Cultural Diversity Through Children's Literature: Applying the Kluckhohn Model (Quezon City, Philippines: New Day Publishers, 2001), 50-51

United States are already deep into the Doing-orientation mindset and who are still Filipinos at heart and don't mind being called nicknames describing their physical attributes—those of the Being-orientation. Culture clash could be lurking in the corner! Be discerning before you launch a comment.

D. 'My youngest daughter is pregnant!'

All parents dread the news of an unwanted pregnancy of their teenage children. It's a universal reaction among parents. Unwanted pregnancy and what to do about it causes Filipino parents considerable heartache, mainly rooted in the sense of *hiya* that has entered the intimate family circle. This particular *hiya* feeling resonates with the Western notion of shame. There is now a moral dimension: getting pregnant at a very early age is not acceptable. Propriety behavior has been violated, and social status is damaged. The daughter or son has broken the rules of the culture. The family does not have the resolve or courage to face the community. Here is an excerpt from my first book that tells of how one family handled the news:

> We were considered the ideal family in the Filipino community. But how do you hide a pregnant teenage daughter? I want to tell my story to the world, that it is our human need to have a perfect family, free of blemish. But I tell you, no matter how well we raise our children to be 'perfect,' they will make mistakes. I was devastated when my youngest child, my 'baby' broke the news that she was pregnant. I had just arrived from abroad as a conference speaker and was surprised that my 'baby' was the only family member who was not at the airport

to greet me. When I asked where she was, there was silence. I learned the truth when we reached home.

My world turned upside down. I thought I would collapse with sorrow. I had to drink a glass of water. I didn't waste time. Think, think: Should we stay in the community or go elsewhere where mother and daughter could live incognito for the next nine months? The family opted for the latter option. I took a leave of absence from my job. My daughter and I lived in a rented condo for the next nine months. We were complete strangers to the other residents. We returned to our community after the baby was born.

Why did I move away? I wanted to spare myself from having to answer questions about my daughter (and the pregnancy). I wanted to focus on my daughter and the baby. My husband and the rest of our kids stayed in our old neighborhood.

I learned humility firsthand from this experience. We were up on a pedestal as one of the admired families in our community, and then we fell down, hard. Does that make us an 'abnormal' family? For me, what mattered, in the end, is that the family was intact, and the bonds of love were strengthened during the ordeal. All families have skeletons in the closet. Some of us are not able to keep them in the closet forever because of the nature of the problem. How do you hide a pregnancy? In the end, LOVE is what sustains you.

Our collective consciousness in the Filipino culture drives us to have *hiya* (shame) because we have lost control of the pride and dignity we present to the community we care about. We failed as parents in safeguarding our minor child. We want to keep the unwanted pregnancy within the family as much as we can. Contrast this attitude, however, to the Americanized teenager who insists on facing the world and continuing school despite her growing body. Here is another excerpt from my first book:

> A daughter of a friend's friend became pregnant. The family wanted to send her to the Philippines to have the child born there. But the daughter was determined to stay in California and continue her schooling. She walked proudly as her body enlarged with motherhood, while her parents were dying of shame (*hiya*). To the Americanized teenage daughter, every day that she could face the world was another step toward empowerment.

My comment: Here we have a daughter who thinks her individual self matters more than her parents' concern over what the community would say? She exhibited no shame, just a resolve to face the world. But in the first example, the mother's sense of pride has been shattered. Her recourse is to remain incognito by moving to a place where no one knows her and the daughter. It's driven by a resolve to keep her sanity. Depending on where one leans—the self or the group—one moves toward that direction. The choice is yours.

The collectivist's self-esteem is tied to the other's validation of the collectivist's behavior. The dictum of collectivist cultures, "we are because I am," plays a significant role, a boost of self-esteem to collectivists. It is of paramount importance to the collectivist to feel valued by the group he or she cares about. What is earth-shattering to them is the loss of *hiya*, the self has become a nonperson. The *hiya* feeling in this instance literally becomes the English equivalent of shame because, by that definition, *hiya* is a moral issue. On the contrary, *hiya* by the original indigenous definition is not about maintaining the status quo, according to Enriquez.

In my first book, I explained, *"Hiya* is central to the molding of a Filipino child's behavior. It is difficult to understand *hiya* in English language terms because it involves two opposing concepts: shame (loss of face) and pride (saving face). Worse, *hiya* affects not only the wrongdoer but also his family. Under *hiya*, the child endures intense feelings of inferiority, humiliation, and loss of self-esteem, and learns a pattern of defenses to avoid them." (ibid., 31) This particular *hiya* has a moral dimension in which the child has committed a horrendous act, not behavior that preserves the status quo.[27]

"Hiya is a mixture of pride, dignity, self-control, and shame. [Enriquez offered essentially the same definition: *Hiya* is a mixture of *utang na loob* (gratitude/solidarity) and *pakikisama* (companion/esteem).] To be *"walang hiya"* (without *hiya*) is to be without modesty or character—it is one of the worst things one can be called."[28]

"The implications of *hiya* could be soul-shattering because it is directed at the core of one's

---

27

28ibid., 31

being. To be without *hiya* is to be stripped of your clothes for the public to view, rendering you a nonperson, a nothing." (ibid., 31) This is the Western analysis of shame attached to my explanation. Shame has a moral dimension. The Filipino individual has done something immoral.[29]

"A person or family will go out of their way to hide an embarrassing incident from public knowledge. However, some things cannot be kept from the public view, such as a daughter getting pregnant or a son getting arrested if it's making the news. While such incidents are also embarrassing in Western cultures, they can be catastrophic to Asians. Thus, a sense of shame as a deterrent to scandal presumes that Asian American communities have low rates of mental or juvenile problems compared to blacks and Latinos. Don't be fooled by the statistics"[30]

E. Ostracized husband

I was a columnist for *Midweek Balita,* a Filipino newspaper published in Glendale, California, between 2006 to 2007. My column was about problems and issues immigrant parents and their Americanized children face. It was essentially an advice column a la "Dear Abby" style. One time, I received an email from an American husband whose wife was Filipino. His email thanked me for my column about shame because it was an eye-opener for him. He had his wife admitted to a psychiatric ward for depression. The next day he returned to visit her. To his dismay, she had been released. He ran to the nurses' station to inquire. He was told that his wife's parents came and were adamant that she be released. He phoned them, but they wouldn't take his calls. What's

---

[29](ibid.)
[30](ibid., 32).

worse, his wife's family ostracized him because to them, he had brought shame to the family honor. The family kept on meddling in their relationship until the couple divorced. No one bothered to explain to him what he did wrong. After he read my article on shame, only then did he understand.

My comment: In American culture and law, it is widely accepted that each spouse has certain legal rights to act on behalf of the other as he or she sees fit, and their relatives have no right or authority to intervene unless the spouse performing the action is somehow incapacitated. I told the husband that, in the first place, the hospital shouldn't have released his wife to her parents. They had no legal right to do so. On the other hand, I explained to the husband that he broke a Filipino cardinal rule when he decided to bring his wife to the psychiatric ward: do not put a Filipino family to shame. What family wants the public to know that their daughter or sister is crazy?! I advised him that he should have first considered what is deemed the propriety behavior since his wife is Filipino. Culture clash! The poor man didn't know any better. He was thinking in terms of his Western upbringing, with its norms of spousal agency and a Doing or "fix-it" orientation. It must have driven him crazy to realize the damage caused because he thought the right decision was being made. He loved his wife. True, he should have first consulted his wife's family before committing her. But how would such a thought possibly enter his mind, when he was raised to 1) be self-reliant, and 2) believe he had sole authority to act on behalf of his spouse. On the contrary, all Asian cultures hold family honor uppermost. It is imperative to keep projecting the status quo that "all is well" to the world.

As I noted in my first book, "For many Asian Americans, the concept of shame or 'face' is particularly important. *Haji* among the Japanese, *hiya* to Filipinos, *idz* to Chinese, and *chaemyun* to Koreans—these are terms that reveal concerns over the process of shame or the loss of face."[31]

"Many Asian Americans tend to avoid social services, the courts, medical care, welfare agencies, because it is a tacit admission that problems exist within the family and that seeking help may result in public knowledge and stigma. When confronted with emotional difficulties, Asian Americans are more likely to turn to their families and request outside help as a last resort."[32]

It was, therefore, no surprise to hear a Filipino American Deputy District Attorney of Riverside County, California mentioned the following in his speech during a Filipino American History Month event in October 2014 that there is zero crime in communities in his county with a high concentration of Filipinos. And yet, county law enforcers respond to numerous 911 calls from Filipino households and find domestic violence or suicide has occurred. Something doesn't add up. I will hazard a guess and say this holds true not only in Riverside County but nationwide. Crimes happen to Filipinos; they just do not report them. Because the stigma of shame is so great, Filipino families avoid seeking professional help until the problem is out of control.

A story I heard a long time ago illustrates a Filipino family's stubborn will to keep its problems among its members, believing that outside help was not an option. A daughter had recently reunited with her parents after being raised by her *yaya* (nanny) in the

---

[31]Lutie Orteza Lee, Culture Clash: The Americanized Teenagers, Implications for Parenting, Teaching, and Mentoring (NY, NY: Arbor Books, 2006),32
[32]ibid., 32-33

Philippines for 15 years. Soon she was having problems adjusting to her classmates and her younger, American-born sister. The parents tried to keep a lid on the problem, even as they struggled to solve it. One day, without her parents' knowledge, the daughter brought a knife to school to protect herself. She would later say for the next time she was teased and taunted as a "fresh off the boat" Asian.

The knife was discovered, school authorities called her parents, and law enforcement did an investigation. Afterward, the parents stood before a judge, who advised them that if they did not submit to family therapy as recommended by the court, their daughter would be placed in foster care.

In short, a problem that parents tried to keep under wraps grew a life of its own, eventually blowing up in their faces. What they didn't want the public to know became a soap opera of a scandal. The stigma of shame kept them from seeking outside help. Yet, had they sought help earlier, they might have been spared more painful consequences.

The Western impact of shame

The American teens and young adults whose worldviews have been formed in their U.S. environment cannot understand why we, their native-born Filipino parents, act as we do when they misbehave. What to them is no big deal is a big deal to us. We are in conflict with them because their perception of shame comes from a Western understanding, where shame has a moral dimension. And what they do is definitely not shameful in a moral sense. But for us, their parents, raised in the indigenous culture, shame has not only a moral but a social dimension as well. It considers what is propriety behavior in a particular situation, what behavior adheres to the status quo. That is where the "accommodative" in the "surface accommodative behavior" originates from, to accommodate or keep within the status quo.

Surface accommodative behavior is the scientific definition of the three Filipino core behaviors: *hiya, utang na loob*, and *pakikisama*. For example, one day my church pastor exclaimed in our Visayan dialect, "*Ay ka ulaw di ani* [how embarrassing], my members are already here!" He was late to a Sunday morning service, and some congregants got there first. So, in his mind, he broke protocol and what is considered to be propriety behavior for a pastor - you should be the first person in church on Sunday, always! So, there was a sense of *hiya,* but this kind of *hiya* has no moral dimension, unlike the Western notion. This distinction needs to be taught to our Americanized teens and young adults. We have to explain to them a fundamental cultural truth. Filipinos always want to come across as decent human beings and avoidance of *hiya* is very important, perhaps the most important thing in their lives.

Facebook

The social media site has become everybody's window display, the enabler of our universal obsession with being perceived as doing well. A happy family, sweet couple, achieving children, great career, hot body, cool tastes, regardless of what is actually happening in our real lives. Facebook is the number one manifestation of propriety behavior. However, there is more to those happy photos than meets the eye. To skeptics, Facebooking has become synonymous with showing off and living in denial.

I have a childhood friend whose marriage ended long ago. One day, I saw her Facebook post, which was a photo of the pair in a loving embrace as they danced. My heart skipped with elation. They have reconciled at last! So, I called to congratulate her. To my dismay, she said, seething with anger, that her grown children pushed them to get back together. They wanted to proclaim to friends that their parents were still very much married. And every chance they get, the kids snap photos of their parents and post them on Facebook! Those were just for show, she warned me. The fix is on folks. Be more discerning.

Recent reevaluation of shame

There appears to be a new understanding of shame that recently emerged from U.S. social research and is creating ripples in popular culture. In 2010, American scholar and best-selling author Brené Brown gave a TED Talk entitled "The Power of Vulnerability,"[33] which has gone viral. Her book, *Daring Greatly: How the Courage to Be Vulnerable Transforms the Way We Live, Love, Parent, and Lead* (2012) caught the attention of Oprah Winfrey, leading to an interview with the popular T.V. host. Brown's research into vulnerability, courage, shame, and empathy has become celebrated in academic, business, and media circles. Personally, I see such newfound interest as the dawn of a new day! Why? Traditionally, shame is a negative concept among Americans, a social disease to avoid. "Shame is an unspoken epidemic, the secret behind many forms of broken behavior," Brown said. Her TED Talk explored what can happen when people confront shame head-on. Because of it, shame is now getting positive press. Her original research into vulnerability led her to its birthplace, shame and fear, which in turn led her to study shame.

---

[33] "The Power of Vulnerability," talk given by Brené Brown, Ph.D. at TEDxHouston, June 2010.

Many of her talks and books are inspiring, but they are set in the Western context, not that of the indigenous Filipino culture. The American mindset of shame has always been singularly negative, whereas we Filipinos have viewed it as a duality, both negative and positive aspects. And yet, because of American culture's proximity to our own, not to mention the global media we inhabit, Brown's take on shame, American style, will fascinate the Filipino consciousness and, I fear, eclipse Enriquez' more organic concept. Alas, the latest Western shades will hijack our minds' eyes just when we were trying on our 20-20 vision of shame. Be on guard, my Filipino readers! Keep your colonial mentality in check. Just because America has a found new way of looking at shame doesn't mean we should buy their glasses. Keep in mind that it was only 70 years ago when Western-oriented researchers came to study Philippine culture and ended up defining our values for us! I am interested in the sample group that Brown studied, especially their ethnicity. I wonder if there were Filipinos or even Asians there, or were they mainly of American or European descent, born and raised in the United States and rooted in American culture?

Implications for Americanized teens and young adults

What implications does this chapter hold for our Americanized teens and young adults? When immigrant parents try to model the concept of *utang na loob* to our U.S.-born or raised children, we always end up disappointed, because it doesn't seem to work. Parents, we need to avoid calling them ungrateful because this is not their value. It is a foreign concept to them. We must let go of our expectations. We must learn to look at their behavior through their American perspective, not our Filipino lens. Their minds operate differently. What they respond to is something that's **earned**. Earn what, you ask. Well, parents. Now the tables are turned, now it's our turn to not understand! Here is an example:

A decade or so ago, there was an influx of special education teachers from the Philippines, in response to a chronic shortage in U.S. schools. I had the privilege of speaking to the first batch of these newly arrived teachers during a workshop organized for them. One of the teachers (let's call her Emma) ended up working in Maryland. A few years later, I got to meet Emma at a conference, and she shared her astounding experience teaching emotionally disturbed students. When she realized her students disturbing behavior was a symptom of a hunger for love, Emma went out of her way to love them UNCONDITIONALLY until she **earned** their love. She treated them as if they were her real children. The students felt her love. Emma wasn't just a teacher, she was mommy. Soon, they were attached to this tiny Asian woman who truly cared for them. The students told Emma they wanted her to be their mother. They started asking if she was going to stay. They didn't want her to go back to the Philippines. The transformation in their behavior was dramatic. The problem students were now calmer, happier, and everybody noticed. For these results, Emma was voted Teacher of the Year! She had **earned** everyone's admiration.

What happened here? Emma zeroed in on the Doing orientation so fundamental to American culture. Accomplishing something gets a high premium in a Doing society. To prove oneself, one must **earn** it. One must first earn love, then respect, and finally, trust, of someone to win him or her over. This is what Emma accomplished, and the rest is history. If immigrant parents expect U.S.-born or raised children to show respect, it has to first be earned. Unless we do, all our long-winded speeches about *utang na loob* will only fall on deaf ears. The more we take them to task for being disrespectful or ungrateful, the more we alienate them. On the other hand, if we work on earning their love, respect, and trust, our children will lavish us in kind. The challenge for Filipinos is to override our default orientation—Being—and go into Doing mode. The Being mode is essentially an attitude of just "being," not doing; the drive for accomplishment is not a big deal. Being-oriented people just accept what is without turning it into a project like Doing folks. Being-oriented parents feel they do not need to earn their children's respect because they feel they already have it by virtue of being parents. Respect, love, and trust do not need to be earned; they are automatic, built in based on one's age and position in the family, community, or society. This holds true if you live in the Philippines but not in the United States, where respect is earned.

Universal, cultural, and individual reactions to shame

If you are inclined to see everyday life as a series of isolated individual acts occurring without a context or background, you might see conflicts as just nothing beyond personal clashes. Yet, as our society becomes increasingly diverse, so does the likelihood of culture playing a part in these conflicts. My yardstick for determining whether an interaction is a culture clash or not is simple; is the interaction between two or more parties from different cultures?

Shame's stigma

Here is my own personal interpretation of the topic of shame. Let me preface it by echoing a universal concept. One doesn't go public with one's private life if it is avoidable. Put up a brave front, wear a smile, look gracious and in control, that's the universally held propriety behavior. Propriety means conforming to prearranged standards of behavior or morals. But how do you keep a secret when your spouse and another woman have gone public with their relationship? Or you have called the police for help when your teen daughter is missing from her bed in the wee hours of the morning? Well, that is exactly what I was hit with, a double whammy!

Everyone has a pain threshold. No matter the circumstance, pain is still pain, and it hurts. I know of a retired professor in a prestigious academic institution who kept her pain for 45 years. It was not until she wrote a book in her late 70s that she revealed she had been a "hidden child" during the Holocaust years[34]. The family who adopted her provided a new identity, which she lived under until the day she learned who she really was. In a presentation at her book launching, she admitted that she had only recently revealed her Jewish identity.

Why do we keep up a pattern of silence for many decades and then one day just decide to tell? Perhaps, it's more than just the pain of shame holding us back. I think over time, one builds up the strength to detach oneself from the pain and turmoil to reflect eloquently and rationally. I think I can speak for myself on that subject. For others, the strategy is to reinvent oneself, take on a new identity and forever leave the old one. I am not one of those people because I am breaking my silence now. It is my turn to share my shameful experience. I first told the story in my initial book:

> My story of ego-integrity and
> despair refers to my journey of learning
> to rise above the shame I went through

---

[34] Monique Saigal, *Hidden Child, Hidden Heroines,* Third Edition, translated from French by Anna Krasnovsky (USA: Self-published, 2015)

with my divorce and my daughter's rebellion. There was no way I could hide these events in the closet. It was public knowledge. My image as a wife and mother was tarnished. What choices were left for me? In the Filipino culture's ethos, no matter how many mistresses a husband takes, his wife stays in the marriage and becomes a martyr. When a couple separates, the wife is always at fault for being "unfit" as there is no such thing as an "unfit husband." When a child goes astray, the mother also takes the blame as there is no such thing as an unfit father, and no amount of blaming her child will make the problem go away. That being the case, I was both the unfit wife and unfit mother.

Like it or not, we live in a man's world. These were my despairing thoughts. I could feel the heat of people's judgment, the heavy energy, around me. One even said to my face—the meanest remark I would get in my life to date: *"Talagang totoo pala yung ating kasabihan na kung may taling ka sa mukha, kung nadadaanan nang luha, sawi ka sa pag-ibig."* This is translated as "So, it's true what they say, when you have a birthmark on your face where tears pass, you will be unlucky in love.

Despite this remark, I had no choice but to keep walking as if I were seven feet tall. I also received discrediting and fabricated stories about me. The worse were stories of me having an affair! I still wait for the day when stories that will be brought to my doorstep mirror who I am. As I struggled to face the world, I was not aware that my behavior was going through the process of transcending the collectivist self in me. I must rise above my culture's ethos to survive and in the process be reborn into a person with stronger character. I couldn't believe that I could go through the process of divorce. One must be able to have an individuated ego to do this, to be able to go against convention. I obeyed the push and pull of my true motivation.

I didn't know I was developing a strong individualist's character! When I look at myself today, I see both collectivist and individualist characteristics in myself, each of which emerges when the situation calls for it. This is what I meant by having a dual identity and being at home with being both a bicultural and bilingual person.

My divorce recuperation was short-lived because I was now pulled into a new problem. My teenage daughter was caught between her loyalties to me and her peers. I wasted no time in doing something before her life spun out of control and threatened her safety. From the West Coast, we moved to upstate New York. With God's grace, her life gradually seemed calmer after we withstood the storm between us. We survived. My daughter's life turning around and surviving my divorce were my ego-integrity and despair moments; I cannot tell only the triumph of the human spirit without telling my despair. These two will forever be life-defining moments, and I will keep turning to them for years to come. We cannot erase them from our memories. We simply learn to cope and accept. In time, the memory of pain no longer cripples or paralyzes. We begin to accomplish what we set out to do in our lives. Addressing and naming our pain, privately and collectively, empowers us in the end.

In conclusion, I believe my accomplishments defy the powerful cultural myth that no woman can ever be successful without a man behind her. As I've observed, Filipinos who know my story do not really know what to do with me! A friend said that because there was no man behind me, I had to rely on myself. I became a free thinker! The man behind her is supposed to define a woman's humanity. But I don't have a man in my corner, so who will endorse me? I am thankful to our Creator that there is one person who roots for me all the time, my precious child, my daughter.[35]

Shame and guilt

I want to stress that the feeling of triumph and empowerment one feels upon overcoming shame is a universal behavioral reaction that cuts across cultural boundaries. For me, that feeling of empowerment was accompanied by the restoration of my dignity, gratitude, and solidarity with the rest of humankind! However, at the same time, I want to emphasize that the American and Filipino responses to and motivation toward feelings of shame are not the same, even as both arrive at the same end—empowerment.

According to U.S. researcher and author Brené Brown, shame focuses on self, and guilt focuses on behavior. The guilt-based person will say, "I'm sorry, I made a mistake." The shame-based will say, "I'm sorry, I am a mistake." I understand this perspective because the focus of the American culture is always the individual experience; the autonomous self is of prime importance. It is therefore natural to relate shame to self. Everything is according to the point of view of the self.

---

[35]Lutie Orteza Lee, Culture Clash: The Americanized Teenagers, Implications for Parenting, Teaching, and Mentoring (NY, NY: Arbor Books, 2006), 39-41

In the Filipino indigenous culture, the point of view is always from the collective experience of the person, focused on others, away from the self. Thus, because the Filipinos are obsessed with the other—family, community, intimate circle, small group—shame responds to what is considered propriety behavior. Even if the behavior is wrong, there is no guilt because no one knows about it. Guilt feelings creep in once word gets out to the in-group—the people one cares about. Why? "*Nahiya na kasi, eh* (because one feels shame already)." One feels shame because one's behavior is exposed. There used to be a TV ad many years ago about alcoholics. The ad shows a person admitting he is an alcoholic because he is guilty of his addiction. I would hear Filipino friends make comments about this ad, saying how foolish of the Americans to tell the world they are alcoholics. He was doing alright when he kept his mouth shut but now everyone knows! Exposing oneself is not considered propriety behavior. So, a caveat to immigrant parents and their Americanized children is to be aware of what the stakes are in adopting the perspective of Brown's book. She comes from an individualist perspective, and her ideas are welcome within the confines of the American culture. But they become problematic once taken out of the American context, and inserted into the Philippine cultural, where the group good is the priority. As an ancient saying would remind us, "Know thy self."

PARENTAL TIPS & GUIDELINES

LISTENING

We grow up thinking our culture gives us a reliable yardstick for interpreting the world around us. Sometimes, this assumption is taken to the extreme, and we view opposing norms from another culture as threats meant to be shattered. Ideas and views collide—culture clash!

So, for Americanized children and their first-generation Filipino parents, the first tip is timeless advice in communication. **Listen** to each other. While the clash is occurring, the parent, the supposedly more mature party in the intercultural relationship, must lead by allowing the child to express what's on his or her mind. Avoid lecturing or preaching. Close your mouth, be quiet, and simply listen. If there is cultural clash, both sides may not hear each other rationally. Parents, I cannot stress this enough. A culture clash can be a teaching moment if you can just be quiet and listen, especially if you have the knowledge to explain what is going on. You will earn your Americanized child's respect because you've proven worthy of it by listening to him or her.

This reminds me of another event. If I was not wiser, I would have freaked out. My friends wanted to meet my new grandson. The opportunity came when my daughter and grandson came to town. She planned a picnic where she and my friends could come and see her son. My daughter wanted to set the main part of the picnic aside for her friends. After a discussion, I complied and invited my friends over for the dessert portion. We talked. Because I was gentle and calm in explaining, all went well and at the same time, feelings were freely expressed and addressed. No culture clash occurred. I had the time of my life with my grandson in Palm Springs while his parents went out on a date. Mother and daughter **listened**. Indeed, we have come a long way from 32 years ago!

Why do I stress **listening**, a time-honored virtue in communication? It is my experience that when culture clash is happening, both parties become irrational and neither side can hear what the other is expressing. They feel upset, hurt, and angry. Knowing what is going on and how best to address it is not a guarantee that one can solve the problem right there. In fact, trying to solve the problem while it is happening almost always fails. On the other hand, what works is pressing the "Pause button," focus on **listening**, and revisiting the clash another time when emotions have calmed down.

If you are in a multi-cultural family, culture clash can become even more severe at times. I suggest you seek opportunities for learning more about your situation. Go to workshops, seminars, or lectures. Participate in the open forum and air your concerns there. It is a safe space, a neutral ground where one can freely ask questions or express opinions. Having facilitated events like these, I can confidently say that the open forum portion is the appropriate context for the speaker or facilitator to answer questions without being perceived as defending one side or the other.

Some food for thought: When your ideas or assumptions are challenged, do you only seek to defend them? Or do you genuinely desire to be open to your assumptions being challenged, to understand opposing views as clearly as possible, and to accept them without judgment or disagreement? Think about it!

RESPECTED AUTHORITIES

Between a religious minister and secular professional, Filipino immigrant parents would find comfort being advised by the former, whom their community respects and reveres over the latter. More importantly, the community tends to have a stronger relationship with leaders of religious organizations. This is what moves Filipino immigrant parents. Religious ministers have the ears of communities big and small. In the United States, churches come in so many sizes, from cathedrals to garage chapels. I provide workshops to the clergy, who I count as my allies in the campaign to start the cultural conversation.

REFLECTION

> *Think about the soul we talk about when we say something like, "The music stirs my soul...Isn't that soul of ours just there? Isn't it our deepest subtle humanity? Isn't it a consciousness that can recognize; that can feel...gentle not aggressive? It does not scheme, is not political, is not ambitious, and is not evil. The soul is part of our everyday life!*
> —Deng Ming-Dao

CHAPTER 5

FLUCTUATING CULTURAL IDENTITIES

Ang taong hindi marunong lumingon sa kanyang pinanggalingan ay hindi makakarating sa kanyang paroroonan. (One who does not look back to whence one came from will never reach his destination.)
--Jose Rizal

These days, immigrants have been put on notice in our society. How will this dynamic affect the younger population, the impressionable minds who are witnesses to the current upheaval? This is crucial. When parents from Asia, Central and South America, Africa, and Europe immigrate to North America or Canada, the pressure put on their maturing teens in terms of who they are becoming is a constant stressor when they interact with the world outside the home. How will they characterize themselves in terms of their cultural and racial identity? Our foremost concern as immigrant parents is quickly finding jobs to feed, shelter, and provide warm clothing for the family. We have **no clue** about the world our children will face or their environment, especially the schools, classmates, and teachers. The need for teens **to fit in and belong** cannot be overstated. What they confront every day is quietly determining who they are and forming their ethnic identity in the minds of their peers and teacher. As time goes by, they juggle their identities, finally settling on what they feel comfortable with. Some children of immigrants emerge as typical Americans, but there are those who still remain insecure in their new identities. My first book addresses some of these issues:

> Wanting to find peace of mind, teenagers search for ways to find meaning in their self-identity. Some choose to live a *double life*. Inside the home, the obedient

167

immigrant child behaves in ways her parents want her to. Outside the home, she is an American down to cuss words. Others *reject* their Filipino heritage or the American side. Still, others practice total *denial* of their parents' culture. And still, others will *stay with their own kind*, without bothering to venture outside their Filipino peers. Everyone else is treated as *outgroups*.

However, most immigrant teens fluctuate between these behaviors. Those who do not venture outside may eventually come out of a moratorium and lead something of a double life. Oftentimes, leading a double life may result in a stage of rebellion or denial. These young people fluctuate—they do not behave consistently throughout the adolescent and young adult years. This fluctuation depends on the exposure to affirming or non-affirming experiences within the present groups, as well as exposure to new information and life-affirming feelings of self-worth."[36] Give them time and one day they will declare which cultural identity their "skin" is comfortable with. One day, while my daughter was in college, she said, "I'm really Asian American because my mom is Filipino, and my dad is Chinese." This is how she sees herself today.

In sociological terms, according to Nadal, these fluctuating identities would fall under "pan-ethnic Filipino identity seeing benefits by collaborating with other Asian ethnic groups: East Asians, South Asians,

---

[36] Lutie Orteza Lee, Culture Clash: The Americanized Teenagers, Implications for Parenting, Teaching, and Mentoring, (NY, NY: Arbor Books, 2006), 68

and Southeast Asians. Some Filipinos become "ethnocentric" choosing to associate only with people of their ethnic groups by placing importance onto calling themselves Filipino Americans.

"Filipino Americans identify with Latinos because of similarities of cultural values and colonial history. Some Filipino Americans identify with African Americans due to similarities in social class and connection with hip-hop culture. Other Filipino Americans identify as Americans with no feeling of connection to the country where their parents immigrated from but feeling the most pride in the country where they were born. Some individuals may learn to integrate all of these identities into one; they realize the importance of affirming Filipino American identity, while also maintaining coalitions with people of other racial and ethnic groups."[37]

"Fortunate are those students in high school who have the opportunity to exercise critical self-reflection about their identity. Many private progressive schools have programs on cultural diversity. One of my former graduate students at National University shared with the class her experience of attending a private school for girls that offered a course on cultural diversity. One exercise that left a lasting impression on her life was when her class played a game on how society programs used to relate to people according to their

---

[37] Kevin L. Nadal, Ph.D., "Who Am I? Ethnic Identity Development of Filipino Americans," Filipino American Psychology: A Collection of Personal Narratives, (Bloomington, IN: Author House, 2010), Introduction

stereotypes. The teacher pinned labels to the students' backs. They walked around talking to each person according to the appropriate stereotype (labels). The person then tried to guess her identity. Where it was 'mind-blowing' to my student was her realization that she knew all the right words to address the person who was trying to guess which stereotype he was given. My student had never used those words before, but she had them stored in her memory from having heard them. Since that experience, she has spent a lifetime undoing those stereotypes.

Do public schools provide room for self-reflection? Are teachers trained to provide this kind of activity? It is a shame when systems do not facilitate self-reflection and do not promote understanding of the dominant society from multicultural perspectives. Since parents are not usually equipped to do this and public-school education does not often provide these opportunities, many young people go into adulthood unarmed with the tools of self-reflection, walking in our midst with an **unnamed feeling.**

While it is frustrating to realize the lack of support in the public school system, parents can do a lot in this area. And even in schools offering diversity programs, teachers are not experts in all cultures. Therefore, may be unaware of important issues. Read the stories below to see the difference supportive parenting can make:

A. Maureen's Story, A Mestiza

Maureen's experience of growing up with mixed heritage having a Caucasian father and Filipino mother is exemplary. I had the honor of interviewing her and this is what she had to say about half of her culture being Filipino.

"Having an immigrant parent has been nothing but a blessing. I've always appreciated my mother's culture. My mother taught my brother and me humility and holds her faith close to her heart. Growing up, I was a little embarrassed when she would speak Tagalog too loud in front of my Caucasian friends, but as I got older, I learned to appreciate it.

I wish my mother was more adamant about teaching me Tagalog when I was young, but I have loved discovering my culture throughout my teen and college years. My mother only endeared her to me the first time I visited the Philippines. She took us to her hometown and showed us her humble beginnings. She's a special Mom."[38]

Maureen was the 2015 Miss Arizona and the first runner-up of 2017 Miss World contest. She is a contestant for the 2021 Miss Globe.

My comment: Maureen's story is a shining testament of success when a community nurtures one mestiza from cradle to adulthood. I marvel at the success of her "Miss Beautiful" story because her context in growing up was not in the Philippines! Those growing up *mestiza* and *mestizo* in the Philippines are put on a pedestal because of their good looks. They receive positive treatment by the society for being mixed race. They are quickly encouraged to go into the entertainment industry or to join beauty contests. The Philippines has become the beauty capital in the world. We can no longer count on our fingers how many beauty queens the country has produced in beauty contests around the world. They are often of mixed parentage. For proof, 2016's Miss Universe is from the Philippines, Pia Wurtzbach, has a Filipino mother and German father. A few years ago, Miss Hawaii was Filipino American, too. The diversity of genes among Filipinos strengthened Filipinos.

B. Susan's (not real name) Story, A Mestiza

Some *mestiza/mestizo,* however, have different perspectives living in two polar worlds. Here is the story of one woman, who I will call Susan, a professional in an academic community. She is still searching for how she can truly embrace her two worlds where they become one and to learn how to not behave as white when she's with white people and Filipino when she's with Filipinos. She neither

---

[38]Maureen Montagne, an interview, Chandler, AZ, 2016

feels wholly comfortable nor accepted among whites as they discover she's Filipino. Yet among Filipinos, she's perceived as white or *mestiza* and therefore she feels alienated from her cultural heritage. How do you reconcile your two-world orientations without denying either heritage while in your social group?

Susan was born in Philippines to a father from the East Coast of the United States and a mother from the Southern Philippines. She grew up basically in a Filipino household adopting the spoken Filipino language through her mother's family. But when she meets Filipinos outside her family circle and uses some of the words she came to know as common, the reactions of those who hear her was startling. This creates quite a bit of confusion because she grew up hearing these words and considers them normal. Is she going to change her language because it is considered uncouth in social circles? If she changes to adapt, she has no other words to replace them. What a dilemma!

I corrected her in those words such as *puday* (vagina) and *suso* (breast) which are not bad words per se but are reserved for intimate and informal discussions with close family and close friends. Only in those groups are the words deemed terms of endearment. Food was another area of concern. When it comes to food, she grew up eating *lumpia* (spring roll), *pancit* (noodles), *dinuguan* (pig's blood), *lechon* (roasted pig) etc., and she's a at natural cooking them. Now, how can she serve them if she has American guests coming? She can't serve dinuguan and assume they will love it. There is constantly split behavior in every aspect of her life. Her features are so pronounced on the White side that one can't guess she is half-Filipino. While we were conducting my interview, she said that she was able to be her authentic self while talking to me because she could express herself candidly. She feels acceptance in her White world if she acts "white enough" but that changes once it is known she is not White. She feels no acceptance in her Filipino world because she is not Filipino enough. What would she call herself being in-between these two worlds? Her response was, "I am lost. I am still searching."[39]

My Comment: When we first met, I experienced an embarrassing moment! A friend arranged for us to meet so that I could interview her for the book. My candid reaction upon first seeing her was to say, "You're White!" She replied, "Are you disappointed? This is me! I don't look Filipino enough?" Apparently, I have a preconceived notion of what *mestizas* ought to look like having a Filipino mother and American father. Embarrassed, I immediately apologized but she dismissed it because she said my initial reaction perfectly describes what she goes through each time a Filipino sees her for the first time. My reaction was totally honest because I just said it without giving it much thought. Yet, I did exactly what I don't want to do. I showed stereotyping but in the reverse. This is the epitome of what my book is also trying to convey, and I failed. Since that first meeting, we keep mentioning our initial exchange to one another with laughter. She proves her point! I can't help but wonder how Susan's life might have been different if she had grown up with the same openness and acceptance of being *mestiza*.

Our teenagers are here to stay. They are citizens or are going to become citizens of this country. Parents have the responsibility to help their teenagers cope with their identity issues, help them develop a strong ego identity [do not silence their voice], and help them appreciate their dual nature. They should let their children know where they come from and where they are going. The Filipino quote introducing this chapter reminds every Filipino not to forget her or his roots. Otherwise, one can't reach his or her destination. Do parents of Americanized teenagers really want their children to suffer such a fate, existing 'in limbo' in America? We find some of them in downtown Los Angeles jails for juveniles. Others are locked up in their bubble with the potential to blow up any time! A few years ago, I knew of a teenager while vacationing in the Philippines, without warning, who jumped from his

---

[39]An interview, name withheld, Claremont, CA 2017

hotel veranda. Our [teens] need our assistance in coping because society puts tremendous pressure on them when we make them feel we don't accept the who they have become living in this society. We have to help them attain a healthy concept of who they are, the product of our culture and America or sometimes simply America.[40]

STORIES HIGHLIGHTING FLUCTUATING IDENTITIES

A. ERACISM

The son's first trip home after being away for a full semester in college (shared by his parents) had them reeling in shock upon seeing him in the airport wearing a t-shirt that said "ERACISM!" His parents' church community prepared a welcoming party with a banner and all the works. They were not ready to meet a college student with long hair and a beard, wearing baggy pants and a t-shirt with that 'word' written it on it!" *"Ano bang nangyari sa iyo, anak?"* he exclaimed. (What happened to you, my child?)

My comment: Perhaps, this son left for college as a "prim and proper" student, and he changed overnight? As this story was shared by the father, my response was that he has no idea what has truly been going on in his son's mind during middle school and high school. The college experience liberated him to announce to the world his new identity. He may have been a compliant child at home but, once outside he attended meetings on student activism. It is a typical occurrence. This happens to many young people when they leave an authoritarian home and go to college, whether Filipino, American, or other ethnicities. The authoritarian parenting style has not taught them to make choices as young adults.

---

[40] Lutie Orteza Lee, Culture Clash: The Americanized Teenagers, Implications for Parenting, Teaching, and Mentoring, (NY, NY: Arbor Books, 2006), 68-70

I attended a meeting of this nature in downtown L.A. where I met around 20 college-age students who were up to date on social concerns and justice issues around the world, especially in the Philippines. Almost 99% of them told me their parents had no idea about their involvement in social justice issues. One student told me her mother had shared that as a college student in the Philippines, she was also involved in campus activism. Since then, the two have become close because her mother is quietly supporting her cause. At the same time, her mom does not want to have issues with her job which would occur if she were to openly join her daughter.

B. I DON'T WANT TO BE A FILIPINO, ANYMORE

"My son came home from school and announced, "I don't want to be a Filipino anymore," said a mother. The mother got mad at his remark and answered him, "*Ano, tayo parang mga damit na isusuot at itapon pay ayaw mona? Baliw, kaba?'* (What, are we like clothes that you will discard if you don't want anymore? Are you crazy?)

My comment: Wrong response! Be thankful that your son was open with you, acknowledging what was going on in his mind. Be appreciative of his openness and encourage him to say more so that you can find the root of this statement. His classmates may have ridiculed his culture, his features, or there may have been class discussion, and the teacher failed to include him. However, with that kind of a response from the mom, her son may have sought to find answers elsewhere.

C. RACIST CURRICULUM

A Filipino couple who are tenured professors have a college-age daughter who was attending the university where they taught. Their daughter, who aspired to be a journalist, would write essays attacking some courses offered and describing them as a racist curriculum. She also condemned other campus issues that called for social justice. Her essays were published in the campus weekly newspaper. The poor couple did not know how to behave in the faculty lounge! The problem was solved when their daughter voluntarily transferred to another school. There, she could write freely without worrying about the impact on her parents.

My comment: Definitely, this daughter was born and raised in the United States. She's all-American. It's her right to speak her mind and have freedom of speech. She has no *pakiramdam* (shared inner perception) of "propriety behavior". Upon graduation, reality sank in! She could not continue to write about topics that offend mainstream society if she wanted to be hired. Eventually, she found employment abroad and had the time of her life teaching English as a Second Language.

D. I AM A FILIPINO BUT...

I visited a college-roommate who is a resident on the Big Island of Hawaii. She's a high school English teacher. She invited me to be a guest speaker in her classes. During the informal conversations among her students, I noticed a pattern among those with Filipino features saying, "I am a Filipino, but I am also part Portuguese, part Japanese, part White, etc." I waited for someone to just say, "I am a Filipino." It seemed to be a status symbol of Filipinos to have foreign blood running in their veins.

My comment: Apparently, these students already figured out how they want to be culturally or racially identified. What was disheartening was the fact that they were more Filipino-looking than mixed heritage. Some of them, I am sure were mixed. I hope that someday when they reach adulthood, they will come to terms with their "Filipinoness" and be proud of it. For now, the slave-mentality is alive and kicking!

E. ENGLISH ONLY

Upon the arrival of a Filipino couple with their toddler, they made it clear to the relatives that from now on, they were only going to speak English to her. They wanted their child to grow up devoid of the Filipino accent! They strictly enforced their rule. The poor elderly relatives felt awkward speaking in their *baluktot* (crooked) English to the toddler!

My comment: This is a very unfair rule! Your child is growing up in an English-speaking environment. She will eventually speak English without a Filipino accent, even without this rule. Other parents struggle to enforce speaking the Filipino language at home, and this couple wants to eradicate it! Strive for bilingualism and biculturalism, and your child will thank you. One of my interviewees is very proud that his parents took pains to ensure observing the Filipino culture and language at home. Jeff told me that as soon as they enter the house, their dad would say, "Leave your English outside and speak Tagalog!"

YOUNG IMMIGRANT'S FUTURE

There is a nationwide coalition of churches concerned with addressing Filipino human rights abuses in the mother country along with other related political issues. I collectively interviewed some members of this coalition made up of college students and young professionals.[41] The afternoon session I had with them became a therapy session because they were able to air grievances about their parents. One young woman broke down in tears because she was finally able to vent to a sympathetic audience. "My parents declared that I am a lost soul," she said. I learned that immigrant parents need to be enlightened because being involved with social concerns does not necessarily spell "communism." They think their children are now lost causes. They don't understand and think their children are wasting time on these gatherings instead of focusing on earning more money. "Why can't you write a check to a group in the Philippines instead of going to rallies here and there?" said the parent of one student. Because parent and child do not see eye-to-eye, the unmarried young adult feels like a boarder in his parents' house; he comes and goes. Immigrant parents do not realize that these

---

[41] Group Interview NAFCON (National Alliance of Filipino Concerns), Pasadena, CA, February 2015

young adults are more comfortable with their newfound identities. Let them be, accept them, love them even if their worldview is unlike yours. One of them is only a fourth Filipino, but she found her new community, so she hangs out with them. The irony is her immediate family is the white folks she goes "home" to. Thus, she does not share her social concerns with them. Parents give them time, as they are finding their bearings. The day will come when they settle on who they are and who they have become. In their fluctuating journey, your unconditional love will be met with challenges by the very children that you are nurturing to adulthood.

OUR RESILIENT YOUTH

A word that has come into popular usage is "outlier." I want to consider a less popular meaning that relates to our youth, as one who stands outside the immigrant parents' values, norms, and traditions. They are outliers. How do they negotiate their emerging values contrary to their parents as they develop their identity? As I have listened to several groups, I can confidently say that without the interference of parents and society, their world is just as secure as anybody else. They have no problem with identity but may only appear to have such problems because of pressure from their parents to conform to code and from the dominant society to adopt its values as encouraged by mass media.

"Growing up as an Asian American teenage girl requires an evaluation and analysis of often conflicting ideologies. You pick and choose what works for you. The result is not assimilation, but the creation of a culture that is not entirely American and not entirely Asian."[42] Such a strikingly pragmatic statement reflects the notion that, indeed, American children of immigrants live in two worlds, yet they can juggle the two worlds in such a way that both realities are compatible, fusing them to become one world according to the

---

[42] Lutie Orteza Lee, Culture Clash: The Americanized Teenagers, Implications for Parenting, Teaching, and Mentoring, (NY, NY: Arbor Books, 2006), 68

child's perspective - neither his parents nor society's idea of what this child should be. Such amazing **resilience** must earn them our trust. Eventually, Filipino American teenagers create this third culture that they can call their own.

Unfortunately, researchers often portray immigrant children as having lost their identities because they live in two conflicting cultures. They focus on the negatives much more than the positives. It is precisely because of that assumption that they become attractive subjects for grant studies. The resulting research then predicts what these teenagers would become, and the perception will determine the treatment. Here is a quote from research done in 1992 by D.L. Sam:

> Growing up in a society where their parents' values apply to a minority group, these children can experience an acute sense of shame in practicing their parents' culture in a society where mainstream people have different values and norms. Nevertheless, rejecting their parents and their norms can be painful and result in extreme emotional problems. The child may experience guilt feelings, anxiety, and loneliness. On the other hand, rejecting society and taking sides with the parents may also create another form of loneliness—alienation. Inability to integrate different cultural norms and values, with the child, impelled to choose (or reject) sides, makes the maintenance of the ego identity difficult and the child susceptible to identity disorders."[43]

---

[43] D.L. Sam, Ph.D. A quote from the 1993 article of Sam in the Internet: Adaptation of Immigrant Children to the U.S.: A Review of Literature, https://www. Researchgate.net/publication/24117033_Adaptation_ of_Immigrant_Children_to_the_United_States_A_Revi ew_of_the_Lit

The idea stemming from this research invades the public consciousness that sets the stage in assuming these children are candidates for identity disorder even if some of them are healthy-thinking individuals. Tragically, such ideas become a self-fulling prophecy for teenagers who have not been raised with the dominant culture's highly valued traits, of independence, self-reliance, self-sufficiency, and self-esteem to be a great person. If their behaviors do not demonstrate these valued traits, they are primed in applying the psychoanalytic personality theory when it comes to identity disorders. Who is responsible for this assumption and coining the phrase, "identity disorder" or "identity crisis?"

ERIK ERIKSON

In my master's degree in Bicultural Development, one of the theorists we studied was the child psychologist extraordinaire, Erik Erikson. He coined the concept of "identity disorder" and "identity crisis." He was considered a "giant" during the 50s and continues to influence 21st-century thinking in human development theories, especially his eight stages of human development and youth identity crisis.

I find that Erik Erikson's work on youth identity disorders would be misleading if it were to be applied to Americanized teenagers' behavior. Their behavior might just imply that they are going through the struggles or adjustments of living in two worlds, their immigrant parents and society. When counselors use the language of identity disorders in describing the youth's behavior, they are labeled for life in that the connotation usually implies some degree of abnormality. I agree that these youth are experiencing an identity crisis which is temporary but to label them as possibly having identity disorder is not appropriate. It is not fair. Why? Erikson projected his personal identity issue in his life.

In my initial book, I wrote extensively about his personal life. I learned about the man behind the theories, only after my graduation. My class was focused on his work, and our professor did not include teaching us why Erikson was passionate about the subject of identity crisis. Here is an excerpt:

Apparently, Erikson went through serious identity struggles in his own personal life, having an adoptive (Jewish) father and growing up Jewish. His adoptive father and mother were Danish-Jews. [He] was a tall, blond blue-eyed boy. His mother was previously married to his biological father before she married his adoptive father. At temple schools, he was teased for having Nordic features. At his grammar school, classmates teased him for being Jewish. In his adult life, he eventually embraced Christianity. Originally, he was named Erik Homberger. He changed his last name to Erikson when he was granted American citizenship. He never granted personal interviews of his life except relating to his work. It became his life-long quest to search for the identity of his real father. It is no surprise that his identity problem became a passionate object of study. So much so, that in turn he developed the eight stages of human development and coined the term identity disorder which today has become one of our psychoanalytic terms. I would suggest using the term, identity disorder, only if we are looking at juvenile behavior on a clinical ground, already showing pathological behavior. Let us, therefore, use it sparingly if we are only referring to our ordinary, regular Americanized teenagers going through regular struggles."[44]

---

[44] Lutie Orteza Lee, Culture Clash: The Americanized Teenagers, Implications for Parenting, Teaching, and Mentoring, (NY, NY: Arbor Books, 2006), 62

STAGES OF ADJUSTMENTS

The Stages of Adjustments from my first edition introduces various stages of adjustments as we shift to a new culture. This shift is especially important for our youth to absorb. I find the work of Derald Wing Sue and David Sue appropriate for my concern when it comes to our Americanized youth and young adult struggles of living in two conflicting worlds." I prefer the term adjustment which implies a temporary behavior whereas disorders suggest permanence.

One textbook that grabbed my attention in my master's study was Sue and Sue's *Counseling the Culturally Different* (1981). The resource book is now in its 5th edition with a new title, *Counseling the Culturally Diverse* (2008). I prefer the later edition. The excerpts from that edition use inclusive language.

CONFORMITY

According to Sue and Sue, **conformity** is the first stage that occurs in the racial/cultural identity development among minorities. This is the period when immigrant teenagers adopt everything American, everything Filipino is rejected. White Americans in the United States represent their reference group, and the identification set is quite strong. Lifestyles, value systems, and cultural/physical characteristics that most resemble White society are highly valued, while those most like their minority group may be viewed with disdain or may hold low salience for the person.[45]

My word for this stage is also to **reject** one's culture because the need for acceptance and belonging in the new culture is so greatly valued. Becoming pro-American is the

---

[45] Derald Wing Sue and David Sue, *Counseling the Culturally Diverse,* (Hoboken, NJ: Wiley & Sons Inc., 2008), 96

new attitude. Even though **conformity** is desired, there is also the need to stick with **one's own kind**, their ethnic group, for security while the individual is in the process of conforming to the values of the dominant culture. What's the first-order task to tackle? The accent! Overcoming a Filipino accent when speaking English becomes of paramount importance. Who wants to be a laughingstock among their peers? If our children continue to speak with an accent, their American peers will taunt them. In fact, a, the newly arrived five-year-old child who only speaks her birth language will suddenly stop speaking to others. This happened to my five-year-old, upon our arrival from Taiwan, she only spoke Chinese to her Chinese-speaking grandma! Among the grown-ups though, it could be a source of culture clash, because if you arrived in the United States as an adult, overcoming one's accent could be difficult. One *Lola* (grandma) reported that in their church choir, the group of *lolas* are often reprimanded by their Americanized choir conductor because of their accent and pronunciation.

DISSONANCE

Next comes the **dissonance** stage. "No matter how much one attempts to **deny** his own racial/cultural heritage, an individual will encounter information or experiences that are inconsistent with culturally held beliefs, attitudes, and values. An Asian American who believes that Asians are inhibited, passive, inarticulate, and poor in people relationships may encounter an Asian leader who seems to break all these stereotypes. People generally move into this stage slowly, but a traumatic event may propel some individuals to move into **dissonance** at a more rapid pace."[46]

I vividly remember a traumatic encounter when it was assumed I was a classroom aide while I was waiting to sign the contract papers as a newly hired classroom teacher. I was made to wait forever and when I asserted myself because I needed to get back to my assigned school, only then did I find out that the clerks at the personnel office perceived me to be

---

[46] Ibid., 101-102

a classroom aide. Therefore, they did not attend to me right away despite the fact I arrived before the others. I exclaimed, "Whaaat, me an aide?!" The clerks were surprised as to why I would be upset! I could not understand until my co-teacher explained that my features resembled that of aides. It was normal to be stereotyped that way unless my identity was known. My new teacher friend just said, "Welcome to America, you'll survive!"

RESISTANCE AND IMMERSION

The **resistance and immersion** stage follows. "The person seems dedicated to reacting against White society and **rejects** White social, cultural, and institutional standards as having no personal validity. The desire to eliminate the oppression of the individual's minority group becomes an important motivation of the individual's behavior. The three most active types of affective feelings are guilt, shame, and anger. There are considerable feelings of guilt and shame that in the past the minority individual has sold out his or her own racial and cultural group. The feelings of shame and guilt extend to the perception that during the past sellout the minority person has been a contributor and participant in the oppression of his or her own group and other minority groups. This is coupled with a strong sense of anger at the oppression and feelings of having been brainwashed by forces in White society. Anger is directed outwardly in a very strong way toward oppression and racism."[47]

INTROSPECTION

Then comes the **introspection** stage characterized as: "First, the individual begins to discover that this level of intensity of feelings (anger directed toward White society) is psychologically draining and does not permit one to really devote more crucial energies to understanding themselves or to their own racial-cultural group. Second, the minority

---

[47] Derald Wing Sue and David Sue, *Counseling the Culturally Diverse* (Hoboken, NJ: Wiley & Sons Inc., 2008), 103

individual experiences feelings of discontent and discomfort with his group's views that may be quite rigid in the **resistance and immersion** stage. Often, to please the group, an individual is asked to submerge individual autonomy and individual thought in favor of the group. Many group views may now be seen as conflicting with individual ones."[48]

In my perspective, the individual is now developing **a dual/double** identity. Standing upon one's cultural belief may defeat the unity the group aspires to. So, to have peace within, the new immigrant youth/young adult finds solace in a dual/double behavior. In my interview with an Americanized college student, he said he chose to be the compliant, obedient son in the family, but outside he is the fast-talking expletive-filled conversant with peers, Filipinos or non-Filipinos. The individual is almost in the **integrated awareness** stage. In dual/double identity, the individual keeps see-sawing to please both groups.

INTEGRATIVE AWARENESS

Finally, the minority individual reaches the **integrative awareness** stage. "Minority persons in this stage have developed an inner sense of security and can now own and appreciate unique aspects of their culture as well as the US culture. Minority culture is not necessarily in conflict with White dominant cultural ways. Conflicts and discomforts experienced in the previous stage become resolved, allowing greater individual control and flexibility. There is now the belief that there are acceptable and unacceptable aspects in all cultures, and that it is very important for the person to be able to examine and accept or reject those aspects of a culture that are not seen as desirable. At the integrative awareness, the minority person has a strong commitment and desire to eliminate all forms of oppression."[49]

I want to emphasize that these stages do not imply that one proceeds rigidly. The person may go back and forth between stages, until the **integrative awareness** becomes

---

[48] ibid.,104-105
[49] Ibid.,106

clear because of life-affirming events. These stages are guideposts of the adjustment process. The example below demonstrates how this person reached **integrative awareness**, but not without a price. According to Sue and Sue, people generally move slowly from the **dissonance** stage to **resistance + immersion**, unless a traumatic event occurs, then they move on to **introspection** and **integrative awareness.** This stage indicates the person finally feels **at home** expressing to the world who they have become, the **integrated** individual.

Sue and Sue's stages of racial/cultural development remind me of the four Hs of cultural adjustment that immigrants face and that I learned from attending a conference sponsored by the University of Hawaii, Manoa campus in Hilo, HI many years ago. The speaker explained quite simply, all immigrants go through these stages of adjustment depending on the strength of their personality but may spend a shorter or longer time in each stage. The four stages are:

Honeymoon stage: The immigrants are in the euphoric stage of finally landing in the United States and are having a good time going to Disneyland, Sea World, Universal Studios, etc.

Hostility stage: Something happens that propels the immigrants to realize that some values and established beliefs and customs in America are not similar to theirs, at home in the Philippines. They notice the difference. For instance, in a typical middle or high school classroom, it is not customary for students to stand up when called to give an answer. Imagine the humiliation when the newly arrived Filipino immigrant stood up to answer the teacher. Laughter was heard in the background!

Humor stage: As time goes by, the immigrants start to see some humor in the things they do and why they do them. They begin to see the importance of learning to adjust and may even tease themselves when they make a mistake. Friends in a similar situation may even share stories of life in the States. Here is one: In a McDonald's restaurant, the newly arrived immigrant noticed that, when in line, if you said, "to go," the food appeared. When it was his turn and the cashier asked what he wanted, he said, "To go!" He was embarrassed when he realized his mistake.

Home stage: The immigrants finally feel at home in two worlds. They can switch themselves, off and on, American or Filipino depending on the situation. I interviewed a bicultural Filipino, as he claims to be, who explained that when he is with Filipinos, he observes the protocols, the propriety of doing, such as applying "opo" to respect older adults. But with Americans, he becomes casual or informal in how he relates, such as calling people by their first names, even those much older than him.

The four Hs of adjustment are easy to remember and self-explanatory: honeymoon, hostility, humor, and home. Sue and Sue's stages of adjustment require deeper thought about the meaning: conformity, dissonance, resistance + immersion, introspection, and integrated awareness. The four Hs are easy to discuss in a light conversation and leads to a more candid sharing of one's adjustment experience. The four Hs are light table talk whereas Sue and Sue's would call for more serious thought, perhaps, at an academic discussion.

When discussing levels of adjustment, it must be considered as in the case of the four H's and Sue and Sue's if they apply to all socioeconomic classes of immigrants. "People from the middle class find it easy to locate the appropriate agency for help and redress when dealing with frustrations stemming from public bureaucracy. There is always an economic issue that shapes the culture of immigrants. Even those Asians who are "loaded," still deal with problems."[50] With this narrative in place, let us go to the acculturation of our teens and young adults.

ACCULTURATION

Acculturation is the ongoing development of adapting to the dominant society's values and culture but also keeping

---

[50] Lutie Orteza Lee, Culture Clash: The Americanized Teenagers, Implications for Parenting, Teaching, and Mentoring, (NY, NY: Arbor Books, 2006), 77-78

the culture of origin. There are two levels, high acculturation and low acculturation. High acculturation implies that the individual exhibits more of the values and culture of the new society and less of the original culture. Whereas low acculturation implies less of the American ways and values and the individual retains more of the culture of origin. (If the reader of this book is American and has been residing in the Philippines for many years and may have adapted Filipino ways, their context would be different: the individual's high acculturation would be adapting more of the ways and values of the Filipino culture and less of the original culture. Or, the low acculturation would mean, the individual continues to retain the ways and values of her/his original culture and less of the dominant society's, the Filipino.) An interview I conducted with Jerry, who is in his late 20s and has been in the United States less than five years, revealed that his adjustment is typical of someone exhibiting less acculturation. Every time he greets the elders after the church service, he takes the time to do *amen* to us. This is a Filipino practice of showing respect to elders by taking their hand and lifting it to touch one's forehead. He also includes *po* while speaking to show a gesture of respect to someone much older. Problems arise in the parent-child communication because chances are, the parents are still very Filipino while their children have already adapted to the host society. "Children of Asian descent who are exposed to different cultural standards often attribute psychological distress to their parents' backgrounds and different values. The issue of not quite fitting in with their peers and being considered 'too Americanized' by their parents is common."[51] This leads us to assimilation.

ASSIMILATION

For greater clarity, the metaphor of acculturation and assimilation is like a salad bowl where the various ingredients

---

[51] Derald Wing Sue and David Sue, Counseling the Culturally Diverse, (Hoboken, NJ: Wiley & Sons, Inc., 2008), 368

have not totally lost their individual flavor, the taste of tomatoes, lettuce, scallions, shredded meat, raisins, and carrots remain creating a palatable flavor. This is acculturation. One's identity is not totally lost. Assimilation is like simmering stew. All ingredients are thrown in the pot to create one dynamic flavor, with all ingredients melting into one mouth-watering taste.

"The newly-arrived Filipino immigrant child not only has to contend with the rigors of learning to speak American English but also the pressure to adjust to his new culture. His need to belong and be accepted by his new culture drives the new immigrant child to conform—the first stage in identity development. The school curriculum adds to his burden to assimilate, this being the hidden agenda.[52]

"The new curriculum drives this idea clearly, drilling students solely on academics, disregarding the cultural and psychological adjustment they face in schooling. Sadly, as one teenager complained in an interview, immigrant parents have no idea of the multiple adjustments, a new language, curriculum, ways of the peers, that they face in school, especially if they are not Caucasian."[53]

McLaren wrote, "Student struggle is one that involves their history, language, and cultural discourse as they fight against being conditioned to accept the familiar as the inevitable. Worse, they are too often denied a voice with which to be counted in the world. They are made invisible to history and rendered powerless to shape it."[54]

The American classroom is often an unsafe place for immigrant students to develop their bicultural voice. The school environment may discourages expressing their bicultural voice. Teachers, especially in high school, are

---

[52] Lutie Orteza Lee, Culture Clash: The Americanized Teenagers, Implications for Parenting, Teaching, and Mentoring,(NY, NY: Arbor Books, 2006), 85
[53] ibid., 86

[54] ibid., 86

responsible for providing an atmosphere where healthy cultural dialogues among students take place. Is this happening? In my interview, one teenager said that sometimes her teacher, who is Caucasian, asks a question about cultural diversity but is unable to control the discussion when it goes on a tangent.

For instance, one day she asked us what being American is all about. There was silence. She asked, "Who in the class is American?" Still, there was silence. Finally, she remarked that this was the first time no one raised a hand. We started to respond almost in unison, saying we call ourselves Americans only if we are in a foreign country or at war! Then we began speaking from our different points of view, but she didn't know how to sort out the varying perspectives. We were frustrated. Some blurted "Duhhh!" If our teacher had asked me, I would say I was born in the Philippines. So, am I a Filipino? I will say I am Filipino American because there is a difference. I don't speak Filipino; my mannerisms are different than Filipinos in the Philippines. So, am I American? I think the reason why no one raised his hand was that when you say you're American that means you are like everyone else. But we know we are not. We have all kinds of backgrounds. So, I think many of our teachers are not trained to teach about culture and identity issues. How can we even discuss holidays of importance to us? Like Cinco de Mayo, which is special to my Hispanic classmates, but our teachers don't really know how to seriously discuss the history of this holiday. What is Cinco de Mayo anyway?

Mexican food and dancing to Mexican music? Is that all?[55]

When children of immigrants arrive home, parents tear them apart, condemning their Americanized behavior. But the Americanized youth can't help it, they are going through the process of assimilation. As a public-school teacher, I taught my class how to express their opinions with gusto. It was part of my scripted lesson. Therefore, immigrant parents, when your children express themselves as if they are your equals, trust me, they mean no disrespect. They are just expressing their opinion in a calm rational manner. They have become American, in other words, assimilated into the dominant culture. Assimilation takes place when an individual or group completely takes on the traits of another culture, leaving behind the original cultural identity.

The pressing problem schools face when it comes to celebrating diversity is how to raise awareness instead of reinforcing stereotypes of races and culture. Given the large number of immigrant cultures, it becomes impossible for any one teacher to be knowledgeable about all cultures. Which results in surface support, at best. The common themes of cultural diversity, what have been known as the big F's, Famous people, Fashions, Festivals, Flags, and Food, simply function as entertainment.

Despite the school system's agenda of assimilation, immigrant children still face many reminders that they are not Americans, thus contributing to their confusion. If only they were left alone to discover who they are without pressure from society and friends, I firmly believe these children might develop into regular human beings with a healthy self-concept of themselves.

Asked to bring a sample of their family's favorite food to class. John recalled the teacher's shock that he brought hamburgers. "This is not your food," his teacher told him. When John wrote American under ethnicity on the school emergency notification card, a counselor corrected him

---

[55] ibid., 86

saying, "No, you're Filipino." The incident forced John to realize that society's view of him did not necessarily mirror his own. "You strive so hard to be an American, but all the time there are reminders that you are not," he said. "People kept telling me that I was a Filipino, but I really didn't know what one was, so I had to search for it."

The adolescent years are often a time of painful adjustment. But for many Asian American youngsters like John, it becomes especially difficult. They have two cultures to reconcile and a dearth of Asian American role models to identify with. Many know little about their heritage or find themselves at odds with parents who push them to adapt.

As for John, the boy took his search seriously. He became chairman of Youth and Student Taking Action in Neighborhood and got involved in community issues such as the plight of Filipino World War II veterans. Today, he is proud of his trip to the Philippines.

"I used to believe that if people perceived me as Filipino, they would think they could take advantage of me," said John, who dropped out of high school to help support his family. "But it's different now. It's more like, 'You won't take advantage of me because I know who I am.'"[56]

The need for critical self-reflection cannot be overstated. Without giving ourselves time for serious reflection, we go from one meaningless event to another, living shallow lives. Identifying your experience and connecting it with a higher purpose empowers and liberates us. My commitment to cultural diversity and making a difference in the lives of American teenagers does not wait for big monetary gains. I am committed because it feels right to me. I come alive when I engage in cultural diversity topics.

Assimilated children of immigrant parents who have become naturalized United States citizens may not be interested in reminders of their ethnicity, but they can thrive

---

[56] Lutie Orteza Lee, Culture Clash: The Americanized Teenagers, Implications for Parenting, Teaching, and Mentoring (NY, NY: Arbor Books, 2006), 87- 89

with counseling. But the acculturated children may be suspicious of Western-based therapy as they relate to their identity issues according to Sue and Sue. One of my parent interviewees remarked that she never imposed or taught Filipino values and culture to her children. She emphasized only Christian values because to her that was more important than the Filipino values and culture. I would then surmise that her children who were raised here are assimilated into the dominant culture and are Americans in thought, word, and deed. The Filipino culture becomes foreign, and this book may not even be of interest to them.

With that narrative, it would seem that the assimilated immigrant population would not trouble themselves with identity issues as opposed to those with acculturation identity. So, individuals undergoing acculturation conflicts may respond in the following manner:

1. **Assimilation.** Seeks to become part of the dominant society to the exclusion of his or her cultural group.
2. **Separation.** Identifies exclusively with the Asian culture.
3. **Integration/biculturalism.** Retains many Asian values but adapts to the dominant culture by learning necessary skills and values.
4. **Marginalization.** Perceives one's own culture as negative, but is unable to adapt to the majority culture.[57]

ACCULTURATION VS ASSIMILATION

Before I go to the current consciousness of acculturation and assimilation, I want to remind us that since time immemorial, in the Bible, assimilation and acculturation have been ongoing. It's not a new thought. We have simply

---

[57] Derald Wing Sue and David Sue, *Counseling the Culturally Diverse* (Hoboken, NJ: John Wiley & Sons, Inc., 2008), 369

evolved to where we stand today in this phenomenon. When armies conquered their enemies, the enemies become captives and slaves, living under the new rule they abandoned their culture to make room for their master's way of life. The Jews were exiled for 500 years in Babylon. After their release and return to Jerusalem, although this was gradual and did not occur as one single event, some were already assimilated to the Babylonian way of life, and some had managed to retain their Jewish heritage along with adopting Babylonian values. Without going too deeply into Biblical history, the returning deportees found that there were still inhabitants in Judah, not everyone left 500 years ago! Therefore, there was now a mixture of assimilated Jews of Babylonian culture and acculturated ones, along with the traditionalists who kept pure Jewish culture. This is the background of Jews who rebuilt Jerusalem and set forth the birth of Judaism. It's the same wavelength when we discuss current thoughts of acculturation and assimilation in the United States. Some are assimilated, others have high or low acculturation, and still, others are totally one with the dominant culture having been born and raised in the United States and have a total disconnect with the home country of their parents.

After reading, *Becoming Bicultural: Risk, Resilience, Latino Youth,* by Smokowski and Bacallao (2011) I felt concerned about the impact on the targeted population, Latino youth. Becoming bicultural is desired because of the benefits, but what if the reader does not feel this way? Are they not okay from the author's perspective? Is there more work that they must do? It becomes acculturation versus assimilation. Can we just let them BE if they have reached an appropriate age and settled for acculturation and assimilation as they become a contributing person to society? Once again, we see an either/or way of thinking. Which one is better? Biculturalism would be acclimated to acculturation. There are situations where it is better off for one to be acculturated and other situations where it is better to be assimilated. Let them do the switching, instead of making a pronouncement according to the research. "Bicultural individuals especially those with high levels of bicultural identity integration, may benefit from having developed wide behavioral repertoires of social skills and mastery of cognitive frame switching that allows them to handle diverse cultural situations."[58] At the same time, many assimilated adults are thriving in their chosen profession. They are happy with who they have become, so be it. For an in-depth look, I recommend Sue and Sue's book, *Counseling the Culturally Diverse.*

The story below could be a teaching tool for educators on culture clash and how one learns to live "cross-culturally.[59]

THE PARABLE OF THE PRINCE and THE MAGICIAN

Once upon a time, there was a young prince who believed in all things but three. He did not believe in princesses, he did not believe in islands, and he did not believe in God

His father, the King, told him that such things did not exist. As there were no princesses or islands in the father's domain and no sign of God, the prince believed his father.

But then, one day, the prince ran away from his palace and came to the next land. There, to his amazement, from every coast, he saw islands, and on these islands, strange creatures, he dare not name. As he was searching for a boat, a man in full evening dress approached him along the shore.

"Are those real islands?" asked the young prince.

"Of course, they are," said the man in evening dress.

"And those strange creatures?" added the young prince.

"They are all genuine and authentic princesses," the man replied.

"Then, God must also exist!" cried the prince.

---

[58] Paul R. Smowkowski and Martica Bacallao, *Becoming Bicultural,* (New York & London: New York University Press, 2011), 185

[59] John Fowles, "The Parable of the Prince and the Magician," *The Magus*, (NYC: Dell Publishing Co., Inc., 1965), 499-500

"I am God," replied the man in evening dress, with a bow.

The young prince returned home as quickly as he could.

"So, you are back," said his father, the King.

"I have seen islands, I have seen princesses, I have seen God," said the young prince reproachfully.

The King was unmoved. "Neither real islands, nor real princesses, nor real God exists," he said.

"I saw them!" cried the prince.

"Tell me how God was dressed."

"God was in full evening dress."

"Were the sleeves of his coat rolled back?"

The prince remembered that they had been.

The King smiled. "That is the uniform of a magician. You have been deceived."

At this, the prince returned to the next land and went to the same shore, where once again he came upon the man in full evening dress.

"My father, the King, has told me who you are," said the prince indignantly. "You deceived me last time, but not again. Now I know that those are not real islands and real princesses because you are a magician."

The man on the shore smiled. "It is you who is deceived, my boy. In your father's kingdom, there are many islands and many princesses. But you are under your father's spell, so you cannot see them."

The prince pensively returned home. When he saw his father, he looked him in the eye.

"Father, is it true that you are not a real King, but only a magician?"

The King smiled and rolled back his sleeves.

"Yes, son, I am only a magician."

"Then the man on the other shore was God."

"The man on the other shore was another magician."

"I must know the truth, the truth beyond magic."

"There is no truth beyond magic," said the King.

The prince was full of sadness.

He said, "I will kill myself."

The King, by magic, caused Death to appear. Death (an image of a skull and crossbones) stood in the door and beckoned to the prince. The prince shuddered. He remembered the beautiful but unreal islands and the unreal but beautiful princesses.

"Very well," he said, "I can bear it."

"You see, my son," said the King. "you too, now begin to be a magician."

THE PARABLE SYMBOLISM

This story was written by British fiction writer John Fowles, from his collection of stories in *The Magus* (1965), little did he know that the story would turn out to be rich in symbolism on multiculturalism or culture clash.

We all begin looking at the world through the lens of the culture we are born into. Our birth culture provides the guiding force in our lives. It is our comfortable reality, a reliable yardstick to measure the world. It gives us security. Our culture creates our notion of reality giving shared meaning to our interaction with each other within our culture. It supplies the familiar, allowing us to understand our environment. We have the shared values and assumptions of our culture. The prince's first culture is his father, the King. All of us are the prince.

But we move to a new country, the USA, and something happens. We become aware that what we believe is the "way" is not the "way" in America. We gain a new awareness of our differences and other perspectives. The spell of our culture is broken. In the story, the prince encountered the man in evening dress who represented the breaking of the spell. Culture clash!

Now the prince is dealing with the conflict of culture, his first and the new one. The prince is dealing with this inner conflict. He is having difficulty accepting the validity of other cultural perspectives. A lot of ambiguity is going on and he struggles with these differences. His security is threatened. We all go through these experiences when we first arrive in the United States. We want to reject new and unfamiliar rules. The prince is so troubled by the new norms that he threatens to kill himself. Can you relate to the feelings of the prince, not necessarily that you want to commit suicide, but feeling deeply troubled?

Finally, the prince learns to cope. He thought of the beautiful but unreal islands and the unreal but beautiful princesses. He learned to accept the similarities and differences. After all, both were magicians, the King and man with the long evening gown, but with different beliefs.

The prince said, "Very well, I can bear it." He had learned to deal with culture clash and became willing to live multiculturally. He became a magician too! He learned to accept new knowledge, new skills, and to have an expansive vision of the world. All of us who have been here for many years have become magicians. We have a broader outlook and can see the world from many angles. We are on our way to becoming multicultural or bicultural in our worldview!

BECOMING BICULTURAL

When someone becomes bicultural or multicultural in their worldview, one may assume that they have gone through the process of "jumping many hoops" in their journey and can now claim their bicultural worldview. I interviewed two gentlemen who were bicultural and bilingual.

"My mom was always there, rain or shine to meet my needs. I had done my share of giving her problems in my younger years. What I remember now is how she handled my brother and me. She did it with so much love. I married early and when the marriage broke up, she was there to support me and to take care of my daughter. My daughter lived with her *Lola* for many years because I have a trucking business that I manage. So, I work long hours. Yet, this is not a problem for Mama. Many nights I end up sleeping at Mom's. I live in two worlds, the Filipino world and my trucking world. My brother lives in two worlds, too. He owns a successful seafood restaurant in Texas. Our father died when we were very young. Our mother single-handedly raised us. She's the reason we are able to live happily in two worlds, the White and Filipino."[60]

Another bicultural Americanized Filipino was born in Toronto, Canada, and moved to the U.S. when he was 18 years old. He is now 43 and a successful occupational therapist. I was impressed by his fluency in speaking Tagalog. He said he is very appreciative that in his formative years, his parents were strict in insisting everyone speak Tagalog at home. The rule was to leave English outside the door. He is at home in the two worlds he lives in, the White and Filipino. His parents were involved in all traditional Filipino get-togethers: Sto. Nino, Independence Day, Simbang Gabi (nightly worship) leading to Christmas Day, birthdays, anniversary parties, mahjong, etc. The family was very active in the Filipino community. He loves the Philippines and always enjoys his time when he visits the country because he feels right at home with Filipinos. Speaking the language is a plus!

He intends to keep the Filipino language and learn Spanish as well. He speaks Spanish at work because he has many Spanish-speaking clients. He is thinking of establishing residence in the Philippines when he retires. He said that most of his Filipino friends are in the Philippines. Here, his friends are very diverse. He does not mingle with Americanized Filipinos because he finds them *ma-arte* (show-off). He interprets the behavior as overcompensation for what they have been lacking in their previous Filipino life. He cannot stand the need for material acquisition and showing off the brands of this and that! I asked if this is what he meant, *"Pare, pasensya kana, huli ako, na flat tire kasi ang BMW ko."* (Bear with me Buddy, I am late, my BMW had a flat tire.) He laughed out loud because I nailed what he meant. He prefers a diverse group of friends who were born and raised here because of their casual demeanor. He has less patience with formalities, protocol, or observing propriety behavior unless he is with old folks and then his *"opo"* comes out.

He was once married but it ended in divorce because of culture clash. He wanted to be Filipino as a couple but his

---

[60] Interview, Chandler, AZ, 2015

wife, who was born and raised in the Philippines, wanted to be American. This coming summer, I am bringing our son to enjoy the Philippines.[61]

You have just read the stories of seasoned bicultural and bilingual Filipino Americans.

Parents, especially mothers may not realize that we hold the key to shaping the fundamental worldview (not necessarily cultural) of our children, whether a winning or losing formula, nevertheless, we are responsible. My daughter sent me her last Christmas card six months before she married the love of her life. Her last Christmas card that she signed was music to my ears because it summarized a worldview that she learned from me. The card said:

Christmas
Isn't about things
It's about moments,
Beauty,
And love.
You taught me that, Mom,
Thanks.

PARENTAL TIPS and GUIDANCE

CREATE A COMMUNITY

I am a firm believer that it takes a village to raise a child, to borrow an African proverb. If the family abandons their young because they no longer adhere to our culture of origin and society rejects them for not mirroring, tall, fair skin, straight hair and an aquiline nose, there might be regrettable and irreparable consequences. Our young people begin to feel rejected by both sides—by both their parents and society. As an advocate of avoiding culture clash, no matter how different they have become from their parents and society, we must never stop our support or they will run to their friends. Our failure may have permanent adverse consequences down the road. The teens will exist feeling deeply wounded inside, thus, becoming psychologically vulnerable to outside forces, such

---

[61] Interview, Fort Lauderdale, FL, 2016

as gang violence or ISIS recruitment. Be intentional when you nurture your child in a community and not only just with your nuclear family. Have a community of kindred spirits that your child may rely on.

HAVE A CHECK-IN OR KEY TIME WITH YOUR TEENAGERS

Be intentional when you check in with your teenagers and select a specific time of the day, preferably before going to bed. Every member shares a high and low point of the day. Keep communication open and pleasant. The rationale of this daily ritual is to develop the habit that you are open and interested in their experiences outside the home, both big and small. Show that you can **listen** without judgment. Chances are your children will come to you when challenging or disturbing events happen. Nevertheless, don't be deterred. Stick to it, you are the mom; you are the dad. Assert your authority and insist everyone observe the check-in time.

One Korean mother shared her experience with her Americanized son and daughter. She's a pharmacist and works hard. Her husband, an architect, also works hard and comes home late in the evening. One afternoon, she hurried home to cook the meal for her family. After she set the table and put the meal out, she called to her two teenagers. They came, put food on their plate, and left her. They went back to their respective rooms to continue watching their TV programs. She was furious. She went to each of their rooms, pulled the plugs of their TVs, and demanded that they eat together as a family. She called her husband to come home early because they needed to have a serious discussion to determine if they could truly be a family that sits together, eats together, and prays together. From these talks, the family had a turnaround.

The husband sold his architectural firm and his wife sold half of the pharmacy business. He entered seminary to earn a doctoral degree in ministry. While on one of his hikes to the foot of Mt. Baldy, he saw a property for sale. After three years of searching, longing, and struggling for the next direction in his life, a light bulb came on. He had the wild idea of building a residence with a retreat facility, an eco-sustainable, spiritually nourishing retreat center. The husband designed and built their "sustainable" house. His children resented the loss of their entertainment, the TV. There was only one communal TV in the family room of their new home. Before going to bed, they would come together as a family for their "check-in" time. During the construction of their residence-retreat house, their son and daughter helped in making a sustainable garden. Eventually, the children also had a turnaround. The daughter entered seminary and is now an associate pastor and the son became a lawyer. In retrospect, said Sung, the father, the lasting legacy of what he and Myra did was being intentional in observing "check-in" and "key" times with their children before retiring to bed. When they really **listened** to their children as they shared the day's events, the children began to invite their peers to meet their parents. Come visit Myra House, spend your weekend with them. The arrangements can be made through Airbnb.[62] If you are in Claremont, California, go see the place on Mills Avenue, going north to Mt. Baldy.

WHAT'S INSIDE THE TRASH?

You might find scraps of paper thrown in the bedroom trash that your teens scribbled on. Pick them up and in your free time read them but return the notes to their trash basket. This is one way to find out what is concerning your teenagers. In a non-direct way, initiate conversations about what you have read. Never let it be known that you picked up trash from their bedroom. Do it when they are away. Respect their privacy in that way. A story was shared during a Q&A session wherein the mother's move backfired! The mother panicked upon reading the scribbled notes she found in her daughter's room because it implied, she was contemplating suicide. So, she addressed it only to find out that they were the

---

[62] Myra House is an eco-sustainable-spiritual-nourishing retreat center built and designed by Rev. Dr. Sung Sohn located on 3643 N. Mills Ave, Claremont, CA 91711

lyrics of a song. Despite the upheaval that ensued, it served as the springboard for the daughter to express her bothersome thoughts of growing up.

EMBRACE THEM OPENLY

No matter how they are developing, wholeheartedly, embrace your teens and young adults. Some of them are figuring out their conflicting feelings in terms of how they want to be identified in the long run. You should be more mature, so lead by loving them first not the other way round. Meaning that you don't wait until they initiate loving you. Be firm in your authority but never act out harshly when expressing your feelings. I guarantee they will follow your lead. Whether they agree or disagree with your statements, you hold the power to silence or empower them.

REFLECTION

Is the life you are living, the life that wants to live in you?
-from the book, *Let Your Life Speak*

CHAPTER 6

NOW WHAT?

The fact is that the greatest people who had the greatest impact on humankind, who have helped the greatest number of people, are those who have consulted their own inner feelings, rather than follow what everyone else is doing to feel what they are feeling. Instead, the likes of Jesus, Gandhi, King Jr., Twain, Thoreau, Siddhartha, [Mother Teresa] went against the climate of their times and made a difference.

—Wayne Dwyer

Now that I've spelled out the five culture clash points, it is time to share my story, my personal truths that I want to leave with you, my readers. I want to impart lessons and insights I discovered during my journey as a mother and teacher. What ultimate equation of parental guidance can I spell out to help with your journey that will make sense of it all? Ah, if only.

PART I
My Mother and Daughter

A. IT TAKES A VILLAGE TO RAISE A CHILD

With the current upheaval in immigrant communities, our anchor in our anguish and sorrow is our respective communities of family, relatives, and friends. I recall my own anguish in keeping my daughter from falling into bad company thirty-two years ago. I needed to act fast before she suspected that I was removing her from the situation. It was time to relocate far, far from Pasadena, California. But how could I accomplish it so that she would cooperate? It took a village of friends, school officials, and relatives synchronizing in perfect harmony to make the move. Without their support, I don't know what the outcome would have been. I only have a mother's wild imagination running amok to answer the question, "What if we had stayed."

Two people advised me, one a professional "friend" and the other a co-teacher. The professional friend, my therapist, reminded me the power of peer pressure cannot be underestimated. I must act immediately while my daughter would still listen to me because that has become a "thin-thread." The wise counsel from my co-teacher was, *"Ang trabaho'y pwedeng maiwanan at pwede ring mabalikan, pero ang buhay na bata ay minsan lamang."* (Work can be dropped and resumed, but a child's life happens only once.)

With these thoughts, I decided the next step was to move, but where? My therapist suggested the place must be as far away as possible from where we were living. In other words, out of state! Unbeknownst to me, a distant cousin of mine whom I will call Eric and his wife, Meg, had already consulted his big sister about my predicament. They agreed that we must move to the East Coast. Sonia, the big sister, called another sister, Rachel, who was married to an American ordained minister, Shawn, on the East Coast and shared my story. They agreed they would welcome us to move in with them temporarily until we settled in our own place. The next action was setting the stage so my daughter would agree to come. If I were a Catholic, I would say, "You have no idea how many Hail Mary's I said!"

The Catholic Church in my area was preparing a big celebration honoring the church's anniversary, and the Filipino community was going to have a food booth. The Filipino youth were making plans to participate in the affair. I thought this would be the perfect day to leave without the group noticing. I no longer trusted her friends. I went to my principal and told him what was going on and let him know that I needed to resign. I also informed her father of my decision. I went to my district's personnel office and signed resignation papers. The head of personnel said that if I wanted to return, I was always welcome. I did in 1994. After resigning, I went to see the principal at my daughter's school. I told him what was going on and that I was transferring my daughter to a school on the East Coast. The principal was very supportive and instructed his staff to prepare her school transcripts right away. With her transcripts in my hand and the flight arranged, the only thing left was to convince my daughter. Another prayer was needed.

My dramatic performance late that Friday night deserved an Oscar! I told my daughter I had been so stressed with what had been going on that I applied for a 10-day vacation to New York. She perked up with this news. I told her that because my budget was limited, I could only afford to buy standby tickets, and so we had to pack immediately so we could leave at the crack of dawn. Eric came and drove us to the airport. Our ticket was not standby. It was the first early morning flight. I gave her no time to tell her friends and, thank God there were no iPhones at that time. Before lunch that Saturday morning, we arrived in Upstate New York. Rachel was at the airport to welcome us. We lived there for four years. Upon my daughter's high school graduation, she stayed for college while I returned to Southern California to begin seminary.

It is only fitting to now tie my story with my daughter's. She wrote the following essay during her junior year of high school. She gave it to me as a Christmas present. It was an entry she submitted to a contest in 1993, according to her.

The Sacrifice of Caring

"I have a very special friend who cared so much, she made a great personal sacrifice. This special person who cared was my mother.

I lived a little outside Los Angeles. I was a young impressionable kid. I went to a private Christian school, and when I was inside the school, I was very quiet and disciplined. Because my school had strict rules, all students had to abide by them.

Once I was outside of the school, I was a much different person. My rambunctiousness was free to come out. I had friends a lot older than me, my "homies."

All these friends were getting into the gang scene, and I was also on the way. I'd ditch school to chill with my homies. We'd go cruising down the streets in L.A. looking for walls to 'tag' (write our names on). While we cruised, we kept our eyes 'scoped' for any potential trouble to start. We were out to do anything that was even remotely rebellious.

My mother slowly grew aware of this. We went through time and time again of arguing because I wanted to be with my homies, and all I wanted to do was go out. She didn't want me to fall in the line of gang life at the tender age of 12 ½. My mother tried everything to get me to stop spending time with my homies, but I wouldn't listen.

"Why do you want to go out with these people? Don't you see they'll bring you down? All they do is get into mischief. Do you want to end up with a police record?" my mom would yell at me each time we got into argument.

"I don't care. They're my friends. What we do isn't really that bad. All we do is go cruising," I would retort. I knew I was lying because we were deeper into the gang scene.

My mom tried taking me to a child therapist to get me to talk, but stubborn me wouldn't speak a word.

My mom had a very secure job as an elementary school teacher. She had gained a tenured position and was loved and respected by all in school. Then, one day it happened. My mom said goodbye to her career, and we moved to upstate New York. It came as a surprise to me. I didn't even know we were moving until we were already there. In the town where we moved, lived a distant relative married to a minister and so my mom felt comfortable relocating there. I hated the place because it was such a small quiet suburban town. That year of transition was a big change for me. It was nothing like what I was used to.

I realized now my mom went through this only because she cared about my welfare. She gave up a secure job in Pasadena so that I could live elsewhere and grow up in better surroundings. My mom thought she could get a teaching job in New York which she did, but because she wasn't tenured, she was the first to go when the district had cutbacks.

Teaching was my mom's life. She taught kids way back in the Philippines before I was born. If it wasn't a classroom setting, she was teaching English, ESL (English as a Second Language) students at a private school.

My mother sacrificed a lot for me. I'm 16 and now I really thanked her for her sacrifice. I've spent about three years in this good ol' town, and it's not so bad. I've picked up values like respect for authority, love for education, and most of all, love for my mother. If my mom had not cared enough to get me out of the life I was living, I'd probably be just another statistic for teen pregnancy or gang-related activities.

I love my mom for caring enough to get me out. I wish my friends had the same chance. I admit I still miss my friends, but I wouldn't want to live where they're living right now. The future to come is still a question mark, but because my mom cared so much, at least I still have a future.

To add a beautiful ending to my daughter's story, on her high school graduation, her Dad came from Southern California to attend. He surprised her with a cashier's check to buy a brand-new car for college. The next day, they went out to pick a Honda Coupe.

It is now 2021, in retrospect, indeed, the African proverb of "It takes a village to raise a child," rings true in my journey with my own daughter. I don't want to take all the credit. I have put in three groups of friends and relatives who were there for me (their names appear on the Acknowledgment page with a subsequent statement to cite their help)—the primary, secondary, and tertiary roles of support I received during those turbulent years.

B. A MOTHER'S AGONY in HER GETHSEMANE GARDEN

For the completion of our mother-daughter story, I must recall my agony waiting for my daughter's safe return in the wee hours of the morning, not knowing if my teenager would come home by 5 a.m. or 6 a.m. or not at all. It became my own Gethsemane. The police officer assured me that if she did not intend to run away, she would be back. Praying earnestly, I felt soaking wet with perspiration. While I was engulfed in the sea of human emotion, I experienced the human side of God. As I suffered and perspired, I related my perspiration to Jesus' own when he, too, bargained with God "to remove the cup from him but nevertheless not my will, but Thine be done." I shuddered when I silently whispered the same words that Jesus did. Total surrender to God's will at that moment, being ready for what was to come! God's indwelling presence was there, as I suffered. I felt cradled in a warm embrace by His "presence." And in turn, I cradled my daughter with so much love upon seeing her returned safe and whole. At that very moment, God became the deep empathy; the great compassion for us. I was joyous, just embracing her with so much love. No wonder the father of the prodigal son upon seeing his son return celebrated and ordered his servants to kill the best calves for a feast. Choosing the indwelling lure of God, love abounded instead of violence (her friends' parents did not have similar reactions) upon seeing her alive that early Easter Sunday morning. A childhood hymn I loved to sing became my anchor:

> Jesus, Savior pilot me
> Over life's tempestuous sea
> Unknown waves before me roll
> Hiding rocks and treacherous shoal
> Chart and compass came to me
> Fear not, I will pilot thee.

Parenting is messy, there is no clear-cut guaranteed solution. But would that knowledge relieve one of the desire and the belief in a "happy ever after" ending to you and your children's relationships? Life is like a game of catch, and once in a while, God throws you a wild pitch. All of a sudden, you're scrambling after it. Heretofore blissfully and rudely disrupted. Yet even when you fall on your face, you must keep the faith. Believe in a boundless God, a God that never ceases to surprise you, and will surprise you again. "Lo, I am with you always to the very end of the age" (Matthew 28:19). Where there is God (life), there is hope.

PART II
My Personal Truths

1) Listening to One's Inner Voice
Over the years, I've talked to many of people. One out of five people want to write a book. If you have that

inner longing, go for it. Read Dr. Steve Price's book *Dream Making in a Dream Taking World.*[63] Look for signs directing you that now is the time to do it. Listen to that inner voice. J.K. Rowling did! She persevered even after 20 rejections from publishers before her final breakthrough with *Harry Potter and the Sorcerer's Stone.* Success is built on failure, frustration, and sometimes catastrophe, according to the media mogul, Sumner Redstone, owner of CBS, BET, and Paramount Studios.

My decision to write a second book on culture clashes did not come without a price. I lost friends and affiliations with organizations I was once actively involved in. But once you decide to start living the life that wants to live in you, without compromising your integrity, you become your own standard, not someone else's. Right now, I am willing to be unpopular. To quote the well-known Christian hymn, "All Is Well with My Soul."

2) The Integrity of the Other

There was a serendipitous encounter with Jewish-French philosopher Emmanuel Levinas while working as a program staff of the headquarters of my church denomination from 2007 to 2010. In March of 2008, the team where I belonged went to our book depository. We were to do an inventory of books and other church resource materials and to decide which ones were to be discarded. In one pile, books were being sold for $1.00. It was a bargain. My colleagues and I were now on a shopping spree! I bought *Pastoral Theology in an Intercultural World* by Emmanuel Y. Lartey (2006). His Chapter 5, "Pastoral Theology at Work in the

---

[63] Steve Price, *Dream Making in a Dream Taking World* (Tampa, FL: INTI Publishing, 2001)

World," introduced me to the writings of Jewish-French Philosopher Emmanuel Levinas. I was taken aback that he was discrediting the work of philosopher-theologian Martin Heidegger. Whaat? Heidegger was among the "classic theologians" we were required to read in seminary. To read a philosopher discrediting another philosopher's thoughts was tantamount to blasphemy. Nevertheless, I was drawn to reading Levinas' work. I was intensely enamored with this man's thoughts and his ideas. His philosophy gave me the language of the Other.

"The most significant aspect of Levinas' work emerges out of his dissatisfaction with the phenomenology of Husserl and Heidegger. His philosophy came to revolve around the one decisive and far-reaching theme, a concern that Western philosophy has consistently practiced suppression of the Other."[64] Why? Because in Western thought the Other is regarded or viewed by the Self as someone that ultimately through education and development will be eventually reduced to become one with the Self. If the Other is irreducible, then, the Other suffers the aggression of the Self! Annihilation or destruction!

Levinas is protective of the Other. He postulates, "The Other lies absolutely beyond my comprehension and should be preserved in all its irreducible strangeness."[65] His career came to be dominated by one question, What does it mean to think of the Other as truly Other? A poignant example to prove his argument is the true drama in the movie, "The Zoo Keeper's Wife." Polish zoo owners, Jan and Antonina Zabinski resolved to save as many Jews as possible. The Jews could move

---

[64] Emmanuel Y. Lartey, Pastoral Theology in an Intercultural World, (Cleveland, Ohio: The Pilgrim Press, 2006), 130

[65] ibid., 131

from the Warsaw ghetto and hide beneath the tunnels of their property until they could be relocated to a safer place. They saved over 300 Jews. During the Nazi occupation in Poland during WWII, the Others were Jews, along with gypsies and gays. The Zabinski's were Polish, but they desired to keep the "integrity of the Others." The husband-and-wife team were compelled to help against all odds.

I am committed in my own small ways to also respect and keep the integrity of the Others even before my knowledge of Levinas' work. My circle of intimate friends is not confined to my own kind, in fact, it is diverse. I have read further writings of Levinas, and I learned that Heidegger and Hitler were good friends, and his worldview may have influenced Hitler. I will never know, however, the depth and extent of Heidegger's influence.

Nevertheless, let's hope that some of us strive to keep the integrity of Others. God is full of surprises.

PART III
PARENTAL GUIDELINES

1) Fearless Living of a Transparent Life

No matter how hard some of us may try to keep them private, the narratives of our lives are like planes or ships traveling in the night, giving out flashes or beeps for others to see or hear. Wholly or partly, we betray our personal truths in our comings and goings. Some of us live our lives fearlessly, with unapologetic passion. Some of us live in trepidation. The former, I've found, tend to be emotionally and culturally grounded individuals. Those in the latter are the risk-averse folks. A transparent family life is one that is devoid of concern

214

about the appearance of righteous living and perfect parenting. A life that lives for the fullest expression of one's authentic identity produces children who are grounded and reasonably fearless. Consistent transparency within the family functions like a feedback loop, constantly alerting its children on how to behave with their parents, and without realizing it, changes their worldview even as it is forming in their minds. It's a wonderful reality-checking mechanism that transparent families have given to their children.

A. Sandra K. Hester

I was in for a big surprise when I commented to a well-known, local public personality, a gutsy public policy advocate, that she must have had a great role model growing up. Her reply jolted me! "I thought for a long time that my mom had the biggest impact on my life," Hester said. "But one day, I had an aha moment. It had been my dad all along. He was my role model!" She went on to explain that her mother was indeed a great role model and that they were a lot alike in temperament, beliefs, and actions. In fact, her career followed in her mother's footsteps of serving in non-profit organizations, working to improve the quality of life of a wide range of people.

However, she said, her dad was an Archie Bunker type (the famously racist dad in the 1970s sitcom, *All in the Family*) who grew up in a small Wisconsin town that was divided along ethnic and religious lines. "He was raised in a wealthy household with servants and grew up believing that others who were not like them were lesser individuals," she said. "It was this privileged lifestyle that shaped my father's character. He thought that his consistent racist remarks were normal, and others were less than him. His behavior made me see how unjust and unfair his comments were, he never even knew the people or group he was pontificating about with his racial remarks!

"It was in [as a reaction to] this environment that I began standing up for others no matter what their circumstance, their race, or religion was, and speaking back to him," Hester continued. "I knew his remarks were wrong and I was constantly refuting him. I was mad at him for speaking the way he did about [people who were different from him]. We love each other, but his [attitude and speech] made it difficult for me to look up to him. Much later in my adult life, I realized how his bad behavior had subconsciously created the opposite trait in me. For example, one day I was with a group of friends, all of us white, and one of them made a racial comment, so I called him out in front of everybody. He tried to defend it by saying that it was what his parents had taught him, and implied that I was insulting them because he was merely quoting them! I just quietly said that maybe they didn't know any better, and as soon as I did that the whole group seemed to gasp, afraid of what he might do. But he did nothing. We all sat there in silence for a few moments, then I declared, looks like it's time for dinner, and we all got up and went to the table and broke bread together. That was the end of it. No one in that group ever made racial slurs in my presence again. I secretly thanked my dad for inadvertently shaping my sense of fairness deep in my heart. I realized how life-altering his influence was on me only after he had passed away."

Sandy spends her valuable time living her truth by being active in social justice issues no matter what race, gender, disability, or creed is involved. At 73, she continues to advocate on behalf of minorities in the arena of public policy in several capacities: vice president of the Democratic Club of Claremont, chair of the Los Angeles/Orange County region of California Senior

Leaders Alliance, Volunteer District Liaison for AARP in California, vice president of the American Institute for Progressive Democracy (a West Coast think tank involved in public education forums), and member of the NAACP-Pomona. She opens her home for coffee with local political candidates and various groups meetings. In fact, she has created an annual tradition: Open House for friends and strangers who want to have a Christmas meal and dessert at her house on Christmas Day! With her sweetheart, John Ammon (a member of Tsnungwe Tribe of South Fork, Hupa, California), Sandy is developing a program to help youth 18 to 24 years old transition out of the foster care system and into adulthood. The Turtle Medicine Lodge Training Academy helps these young people develop personally and professionally through programs with a Native American perspective.

Sandy entered my life at a much-needed time when I was all but ready to throw in the towel in my efforts to understand white folks. She disproved my notions (i.e., they are not all intolerant and xenophobic), and thus became my saving grace. I thought, wow, there must be others like her too! (This book is dedicated in part to Sandy and like-minded souls.) She is a vision of a human being who continues to cross barriers of discrimination. No stone is left unturned.

In a functional family, rules are clear, and transparency is a must: children and parents both see each other's character for what it is: the good, the bad, and the ugly. Parents have no qualms about displaying their flaws; they definitely don't go around pretending to be a perfect mom or dad. In my book, Sandy's dad lived fearlessly with a capital "F" no matter how wrong his views were.

I don't expect you, the reader, to agree with this personal truth. I contend that Sandy's dad was not in the business of modeling how a father ought to be to his children. But some people are excellent role examples of what shouldn't be done, and his transparency allowed his daughter to see that. As a result of his example, Sandy made fighting racism her life's work, with true serendipity, a happy unexpected consequence of her dad's absolute honest expression of who he was in front of his children. He lived transparently with the world and his children. Sandy grew up constantly watching her father's worldview but with the benefit of socialization and education she rejected it. Eventually, she had children of her own to display her worldview to. The radical honesty of Sandy's dad helped her carve out her own blueprint for her children, one that is strongly grounded in reality.

Some readers will dismiss my argument by asking this: Well, if you're rich, you can afford to be fearless and honest. I'm reminded of a Chinese saying, "money is the guts of the hero." Indeed, Sandy's dad came from a very rich family. Perhaps he could more easily afford to live fearlessly and honestly. Yes, if I agree to this logic, I discount one of my foundational truths. The key to having grounded children is being a transparent and honest parent.

Still, on the rich argument, there is a temptation to conclude that Sandy came upon her more inclusive worldview because of a good education that her rich but racist father paid for. That, somehow, wealth can buy wisdom. To which my reply is, not necessarily so. Witness the countless rich children who fall into lives of dissolution and make more bad choices than their poorer counterparts. The truth that I am indicating has nothing to do with riches. It is all about transparency: How honestly and openly does a parent exhibit his philosophy, his beliefs, and views to his children? My theory states that when children can form their own worldviews that support or oppose those of their parents, they create a realistic blueprint to stand on without myths.

To expound on my theory on another level, what can you say about a dirt-poor family in the Philippines that produced four incredible daughters who went on to become successful, thriving career women in the United States? They lived in a tiny house with a dirt floor. Yet, they were raised with a clear vision and philosophy. We rise together or fall alone. Education is the ticket to success. They studied hard and excelled in class. Their teachers would ask them to check test papers, and in return, the girls received free lunches. They also applied their talents in business to augment their parents' meager incomes. During grade school, they would sell homemade candies (locally known as *tira-tira*) to their classmates. One girl learned to sew and alter clothes, and another one was good with flower arrangements. They plied their trade around the neighborhood and started getting jobs. The third daughter had a knack for dancing and began teaching dance classes in the neighborhood park. The fourth set her sights on the city, and with her looks and height got modeling gigs. All four girls learned how to give manicures and pedicures, building a loyal clientele. Amazingly, even as they hustled to earn money, they were going to school and earning excellent grades. Eventually, their parents followed their own advice and went to college, even sitting in the same classes with their daughters! Through their determination, education, and skills, they were able to immigrate to the United States, where they are now partners in a successful real estate business. Billed as humble millionaires, they credit their success to their parents and God. Perhaps, readers, you will say this story, while inspiring, is the exception to the rule: It is mostly those who are born rich who go on to become rich. The key point I want to drive home is the importance of role modeling by parents, whether they are rich or poor, to promote the success and happiness of their children.

When parents model fearlessly with passion, openly bearing their flaws and strengths, their children form a realistic view of what they want out of life and who they want to become, because they are constantly presented with an unvarnished knowledge of who their parents really are. If they like what they see, they will adopt it. When they see a flawed characteristic, they have an opportunity to correct it in their own lives. They don't want to pass on unflattering traits to their own children. They have no illusion about their parents' true character. When parents are not concerned with the image of being the perfect parents or the good guys, but are natural and authentic, children see them for who they really are, and that is healthy. The latter will then base their worldview not on abstract ideas but on the reality they see in their parents. I imagine Sandy going through something similar to the above.

B. Ambrocia T. Ociones

In the Philippines, it is quite common to have a *yaya* (nanny) who will raise you while your parents are out working. I am a product of this practice. From the bottom of my heart, I am forever grateful to my mother that she wisely chose Ambrocia T. Ociones to be my surrogate parent while she went back to school. I call her *Manang*, an honorific title for an older female family friend or neighbor. *Manang* was my second mother. She practically raised me during the first five years of my life. We became so close, that I am fairly sure I acquired some of her personality traits. Like *Manang*, I have a temper (I try to keep it in check!). I can be feisty with a stubborn streak, outspoken to a fault, and committed to social justice and fairness. I want to highlight the last

220

attribute, which I believed was shaped by her early life growing up during the Japanese occupation in World War II. As a 10-year-old-girl, *Manang* became a courier for the Filipino guerillas fighting the Japanese soldiers, delivering messages from one camp to another. She would recall walking by the Japanese barracks to go to the other side of town, carrying secret documents that she would deliver to the guerillas, and then walking back the same way, this time with a new set of papers. I was scared for her and amazed at her bravery—to me, *Manang* was an unsung hero. Later, she put her culinary skills to good use by running a restaurant. Her husband raised hogs, and with their meager earnings, the couple sent their three daughters to the country's premier educational institution, the University of the Philippines at Los Banos, Laguna. All three are now accomplished professionals.

Manang will turn 86 in December 2021, I intend to be there in our hometown to join her in celebrating this big day. Her memory sadly has dimmed with age, and she has to be reminded it would be devastating otherwise. Nevertheless, I count myself blessed to have such a role model in my life, someone who lived fearlessly and with a passion.

Living fearlessly with a passion is no easy feat. One must be ready to live with a lot of negative consequences: hurt feelings, bruised egos, broken relationships, even physical danger. It's the cost of discipleship to follow Jesus, "take up your cross and follow me," he said. But the dividends are golden. To go back to my thesis: All things considered, transparent and fearless living and parenting will likely produce emotionally grounded, courageous, and socially responsible children. God may still surprise you.

2) **Empowered Voices**

In the Philippines, our child-rearing practices are authoritarian. Parents have absolute authority over their children as long as the children are dependent upon them. Parents are in charge of a child's life. Children belong to parents. No ifs and buts. They make all significant decisions in a child's life, even up to a college major and yes, a life partner.

But I challenge the parents, especially those raising children born in the United States. To consider the bigger picture, how many of us really believe that we own our children? Isn't it true that we only have them for a fraction of their total life here on earth, while they spend the bulk of it out in the world without us? If that is the case, shouldn't we raise them in such a way that we don't silence their voice but empower them to use it? How do we do it? Simple: Encourage debate and let them speak their minds without being patronizing or condescending. If you do this, you will earn your children's respect.

It's important that the protagonists in this family dynamic, Philippine-born parents and the U.S-born children they impose their worldview on, come to an understanding. An empowered voice is essential for both parties. Equally important is that both sides have the freedom to express what they want without repercussions. Ultimately, the family setting becomes the training ground for children to practice expressing opinions without regrets or apologies. Without such freedom, conversations degenerate into shouting matches, and the message is never heard by either side. This is a telltale sign of a dysfunctional family.

A pattern that emerged during many workshops I have conducted is the youth chose to be silent in the presence of their parents, and no amount of coaxing them to speak works. So, I said to parents, "In a few years, your children will graduate and enter the working world. Will they leave your home empowered to express their opinion and make their mark? Or should you be concerned that because they were silenced at home, they will remain silent when they leave home?" Empowering our children begins with us, the parents.

A couple expressed bewilderment when their adult children settled for what they considered to be mediocre careers. They thought their kids lacked ambition as both parents held doctorates. "*Ang dudunong naming! Bakit ganito lang mga anak naming, matatalino naman.*" (How smart we were! But so were our children! So why did they come to only this? They lack ambition.) If only these parents attended my workshop, perhaps they would stop wondering!

The ongoing revolution in personal technology, the internet, and social media has put older parents at a disadvantage. Our grown children are now beyond our comprehension, sometimes even our command! They grew up in the American culture, which taught them to be self-reliant. While that's a good thing, it also made teenagers lose patience more easily with their parents who need help using an iPad or navigating the Web. Perhaps they've become too absorbed with the technology-driven life they are living, where results are instant and the answer is here right now. They simply cannot afford to spend time teaching their technologically inept parents. But there is an exception to this rule. If we had been authoritative and not authoritarian in raising our children, our relationship with our children might result in the children being patient enough to help us.

Authoritarian parents expect blind obedience from their children, authoritative ones afford their kids room to express their opinions, giving gentle guidance.

Authoritarian parents conduct one-sided conversations with their children, whose voices are silenced and remain that way even after they leave home.

So, parents, what parenting style will it be: authoritarian or authoritative? I suggest the latter. While it doesn't guarantee a happily-ever-after ending for your family, it is still more likely to result in family members being loving and respectful to each other.

3) **Total Surrender**

What do I mean by total surrender? It is to relinquish our human will wholeheartedly to God's divine will for our lives. If you believe God is the one who knows you better than anyone because he created you, the One who knows what's best for you, and the One who's in total control of your life at every moment, then what are you fighting for? Why not make it easy on yourself and just fully surrender to God's divine intervention and depend on God's divine providence. We let go and let God! The exasperated parents cry surrender to their children this way: "I don't know what to do with you anymore! I've done everything I know!" I know. You're only being human. But you have to realize that you are the grown-up in the house, and your child is a baby by comparison. Such outbursts don't help; they only make your child's situation darker. Imagine the pressure you are putting on your child.

Surrender to the Creator, not to your child. Let God do God's work! Psalm 62 is my life. Verses 1-2: "For God alone, my soul waits in silence; from him comes my salvation. He alone is my rock and my salvation, my fortress; I shall never be shaken." Verses 5-8: "For God alone, my soul waits in silence, for my hope is from him. He alone is my rock and my salvation, my fortress; I shall not be shaken. On God, rests my deliverance and my honor; my mighty rock, my refuge is in God. Trust in him at all times, O people; pour out your heart before him; God is a refuge for us."

For that one moment in my life that I felt emotionally bankrupt and didn't know who to turn to for help, I held on to those precious verses. And they got me through, in the most amazing way. Divine intervention appeared in the vision of a giant round onion. Yes, an onion! One by one, the layers of the onion peeled off and fell to the ground. And on every layer were scrawled the words, "go with the flow." This philosophical attitude that I adopted from the Chinese culture did not sustain me. As I got to the core of the onion, only the seed was left. On the seed was written, "FAITH." I held the seed, and from somewhere I heard a whisper: "Have faith, you will be okay." This vision comes to mind every time I read Psalm 62. I hope its words offer comfort to you. Still, I must say that in parenting, there is no guarantee of a happy ending. As was my experience, I hope that God will surprise you as well.

4) Relationship vs. Honesty

At what cost do we keep our relationships with our friends, relatives, children, professional colleagues, or business clients? We must be aware of what is at stake. What makes a relationship worth keeping? Are you going to put on a false front, hide or bury your fear and anger just to keep a relationship? Are you ready to compromise your honesty, your truth? Often, in American culture, the premium is on honesty. Get straight to the point. Have authentic and genuine communication. If that ruins the relationship, you have to take that risk. The thought is it is better, to be honest and lose a friend; he or she is probably not worth it if you can't be truthful.

In the Filipino context, relationships are valued over honesty. In fact, relationships are so highly valued that in order to preserve them, lying or deceit is overlooked. I know of U.S.-based Filipinos who have entrusted their Philippine properties to their relatives who use the same in shady dealings for their benefit and keep the owner in the dark. But these situations have a way of coming to light, and when they do, the owner has two choices: Get angry and sever the relationship with the relative or forgive and try to understand (perhaps the guy needs the money to feed his family or pay off a debt) and keep the relationship. Most of the time, keeping the relationship wins.

Our Americanized children find this attitude mind-boggling! "Why do you still send money to them when they cheat you?" they lecture their parents. "Just say NO!" Sometimes, it seems that Filipinos are running in a popularity contest, they are obsessed with being liked. They want and need the approval of others. Which begs the question: Can you really be free if you are always seeking approval from others? In a collective society such as the Philippines, relationships take a premium over honesty. Some might disagree, but they are a tiny minority.

While we disdain politics for putting relationships over integrity, we go easy on families that behave the same way. Yet if we believe that honesty begins at home, how do we expect public officials to serve honestly if they were raised in a family that values smooth relationships over truthfulness? Reform family values first, and eventually there will be more honest governments. In turn, more honest officials go home to their families and reinforce the same family values. The two systems are interconnected and reinforce each other, like a self-perpetuating loop. If there is cheating in the family, then there will be cheating in the government. The same goes for justice. Families and governments have to make a conscious decision: relationships or fairness?

Yet again, a more enlightened parenting, one that favors honesty and fairness over a relationship, is no guarantee of a happier family life. Again, I say, Just believe. God may surprise you yet.

5) Form and Substance

What are my personal statements about form and substance in the context of relationships? Forms are the rituals, the outward expressions that we undertake to keep relationships going, without necessarily cultivating the substance or meaning behind them. Gifts, greeting cards, phone calls, text messages, social media chats, these are the expressions or rituals we observe to keep the relationship from falling apart, without having to do the hard work of nourishing the substance at the core of the relationship. For instance, it has become a common practice for grown children to visit their parents. And yet, because they have not resolved or at least found clarity in the issues that have divided them over the years, the visits have become rituals. They're just going through the motions. It's tragic in a way. The substance, what gives meaning to the ritual, what nourishes the relationship and makes it alive and empowering, is slowly dying. What keeps it alive is substantive sharing of inner thoughts, feelings, dialogue about things that really matter. Without the hard and sometimes messy work of meaningful and honest communication, relationships wither into an empty husk of rituals and expressions. Just gestures, no meaning.

I believe the success of any parent-child relationship lies in honest communication. Parents have the responsibility to maintain an equal emphasis on form and substance. Alas, I found in my interviews and conversations, many of the young adults raised in the

United States are emotionally impoverished. They are deprived of meaningful conversations with their immigrant parents. Their daily interactions have been reduced to rituals. Some live with their parents but behave more like renters, coming and going as they please. What's ideal is to have both form and substance in the relationship. In between the rituals and gestures, parents must engage their children in the discussion of difficult and sensitive topics. Now that my daughter is an adult, our relationship has become much better, because we engage in those hard conversations and share our perspectives with more understanding hearts. When you become more understanding, you become less judgmental. Form and substance complement each other resulting in a more meaningful whole.

As parents, we are called to provide form (organize birthdays, write letters, make phone calls) and substance (initiate dialogues, encourage the honest sharing of feelings) in our relationships with our children. But as I've said before, Keep trying and believe. Who knows? God may surprise you yet.

6) Cultural Awareness

Sometimes, we may wake up thinking, today I am going to study culture. As if there's me and there's my culture, like a book I'm taking off the shelf to read. Yet the reality is that our relationship to our culture is more profound than that. Indeed, our culture is part of the air we breathe. It is our way of being. But our culture and worldview are circumscribed by our reality, our current circumstances. The challenge, therefore, becomes how to expand our reality by venturing out into the realities of others who are not like us, who live in a geography, economy, and society different from ours. Conversely, we will be enriching the other side with our own realities. The effect of this venturing out is cultural awareness. It is how we make ourselves and our fellow human beings live more fully. It works and it is quite easy to do.

As the story goes, one day Robinson Crusoe encountered another human being living on his island. Culture clash occurred because each believed his way of being was the right one. In reality, both were right of course! However, each only knew his way. Living in a multi-cultural society like America, we encounter a diverse variety of people and cultures. I stress the importance of going out and relating to those outside of your own culture. Try it and you will see your own culture more clearly.

Here is an example that supports my point. I learned from the Chinese culture that when it comes to giving, you give the best, the best quality, the biggest expense. If you don't have an awareness of this, you can't relate to the Chinese custom. An American husband goes to a Chinese-speaking Christian church because his Chinese wife is a member of the church. He is appalled upon hearing an announcement of a bidding contest to raise funds for the church. If one family gave $5,000 another family would go higher by giving $10,000! It is a Chinese tradition that when you are invited, you come bringing an expensive gift. That's one trait of the Chinese that makes them who they are culturally. My ex-husband is Chinese. When we were still married, at one point I stopped reminding him that it's the thought that counts because every time I did, he would say that it was absurd. In the Chinese culture, gift-giving defines relationships. If you really care for your friend or relative, you will spend a handsome sum on a gift. Visit empty-handed and you will be crossed off the next party's guest list. In any important life event, weddings, birthdays, baby's birth, funerals, the customary gift is money. The bigger the amount, the higher esteem you will be held in. Word gets around and soon you will be on everyone's guest list.

And yet, I must counsel that part of cultural awareness is always seeing the big picture. This saves us a lot of trouble and helps us figure out how to solve the everyday problems. Like many of you, I love playing video games on my cell phone. As you know, most of these games progress to levels of higher difficulty. When you complete one level, the next one is tougher. I started playing this game I really liked. As soon as I understood the objective of a level I could breeze through to the next level. Playing became so much fun. I connected this awareness to the rest of my life—it is the same scenario.

So, in video games as in culture clashes, learn right away what the big picture is all about, then proceed to master it. In culture clash do not explain to the injured person that a clash is going on because chances are that person is irrational at the moment and will not hear you. In fact, you will be perceived as defending one side. Rather, consider the big picture: Just listen and let the person air his or her gripes. When all is calm and quiet, then you can initiate a discussion to trace where the culture clash began. Cultural awareness is about stepping out of the clash and looking at it from above to get the bigger picture so you can resolve it.

Yet, even upping one's cultural awareness is no guarantee for immigrant parents and their U.S.-born or raised children of nirvana. But keep aiming for it. Believe it can be achieved. After all, God never runs out of surprises.

7) There is More Than Meets the Eye

As I progressed in my research, I noticed parents tended to claim they spoke from the perspective of their Americanized children, that they spoke for them. But when I had the opportunity to hear from these same children, I found their perspectives were totally different than their parents reported. "There is more than what meets the eye," I quietly told myself. In fact, out of respect for intimate friends, I stayed away from interviewing their children. In the same vein, when I began to experience the rebellion of my 12-and-a-half-year-old teenager, I immediately recognized the after-effect of my divorce. It was not just our culture clash. But this book is about the culture clash that occurred before and after my divorce. To have included the divorce story would have changed the narrative. This book is about the parent-child journey. The contents in this book speak about our relationship.

My daughter was searching for a replacement for her family that was there no more after the divorce. She found them in the circle of her homies, as she called them. Unfortunately, at her age she did not realize that she had a false sense of security with friends who were falling into bad behavior. I had to act fast before it was too late.

Fortunately, because I was in therapy when her rebellion surfaced, I had first-class professional advice from Huntley, my therapist. She told me adamantly that I must relocate as soon as possible to get my daughter away from her friends while I still had a hold on her. Thankfully, a distant relative wholeheartedly welcomed us to join their family on the East coast.

Divorce is often the blame when teenage children rebel, but teenagers do not need a divorce to rebel. There are many factors are the cause teenage rebellion and one is the culture clash dynamic of the immigrant family. My daughter's friends came from intact families whose parents were married. yet they still have an irreversible scar as a reminder of their teenage rebellion years. Be kind to struggling children from divorced parents, something beautiful could come out of them.

No family escapes dysfunctional behavior, there's more than what meets the eye, and this observation is always left unspoken. Our ever full-of-surprises God, however, may lead us to authentic behavior. Just believe. I do.

8) Love

After my grandson was born, I stayed with my daughter and son-in-law for a month to help. Memories of my daughter's birth came back to life. My life came full circle: first, there was me and my daughter, now she too is a mother. Now we start a new circle, this time with my grandson and me as his *Lola*. Just before I left the new family, I wrote a note giving her a few nuggets of wisdom. One was about parental love and how it differs from friendship and marriage. I told her that as her son grows, there will be instances when parental love is challenged. Friendship and marriage thrive on reciprocal love, but parental love is unconditional. The love you have for your child is pure love. Giving and giving, expecting nothing in return. The reward is love itself.

Had I not succeeded in loving my daughter unconditionally, there would not be this book. Let me repeat a quote, "I don't have a fat bank account. I don't own a house. I have no car to get me around. But I know the world is a little different because I was important in the life of a child." I can rest on that thought until I cross over to the other side, satisfied that all is well with my soul.

Most parents want to give the very best to their children. We want to hope we are giving them a passport to a life of happiness. Yet, there are no guarantees. As parents, we have to be prepared that Life may throw us off and turn us upside down! But have hope. Have faith, God may surprise you yet.

PART IV

FEEDBACK

We were unaware before coming to the United States with our children of the coming head-on collision of our child-rearing practices and the egalitarian orientation of the American culture. One parent said, "In less than six months, my children grew horns!" But we cannot make blanket statements because some kids will choose to be obedient sons and daughters. Two different teenage sons, both decided that to have peace they must abide by what their mothers and fathers expected of them.

Three young adults shared that, now, since they have their own children, some mellowing is taking place. Becky said, "I am beginning to realize how right my mom was with her parenting style. Now we have more harmony than conflict." Alice's perspective is different. She learned to be bicultural with her parents. She knows how to make them feel they are needed to help parent their *apo* (grandchild). Her parents love this and there is more harmony in the house. When she wants to be independent, she doesn't push too far because she knows her parents need to feel needed. Shelly's situation has something to do with her career. She wants to explore by applying for different positions until she finds her niche. But her mom is worried she might not land another job if she keeps changing careers. Shelly wants to explore, she's young, single, and wants to land her dream job, but her mother wants her to settle for a job right away for guaranteed income.

NUGGETS OF WISDOM

1. LISTENING
Strive to listen with the heart in culture clash scenarios. It's humbling. Ego listening brings out arrogance and self-righteousness, "I'm never wrong!"

2. CULTURAL AWARENESS
If you know only one culture, you know no culture.

3. AWARENESS
In real estate: location, location, location
In culture clash: awareness, awareness, awareness

4. DIAMOND RULE
When it comes to culture clash, the Diamond Rule applies: **Do unto others as they would have you do unto them.**

5. COLLECTIVIST and INDIVIDUALIST
Collectivist: I am because we are and because we are, therefore, I am. Individualist: I think, therefore, I am.

6. SELF-ESTEEM
For the collectivist: "I belong."
For the individualist: "I found myself."

7. SHAME
Collectivist orientation: "I broke what's considered a propriety behavior."
Individualist orientation: "I made a mistake."

8. MENTORING

You can't be both parent and mentor to your children. Be intentional in helping them find mentors among your esteemed friends, relatives, and colleagues. Mentors play significant roles in our children's lives.

9. WORKSHOPS

The ideal place to address your burning questions is in workshops, a neutral place. No one is on the "hot seat."

10. CULTURE CLASH

Distinguish culture clash from universal and personal behaviors. Learn and understand that culture clash is real, and it exists.

11. AUTHORITARIAN VS AUTHORITATIVE

Authoritarian Rule: There are no "ifs" and no "buts." It is "I say what goes!"
Authoritative Rule: Allows room for reason. Be firm and avoid harshness.

12. *PAHIWATIG* (THE ART OF INDIRECTION)

Filipinos thrive on ambiguous clues. It's the art of indirect communication. *Pakikiramdam muna.* (Practice "shared perception" first.)

13. THE TRIAD

The Filipino core values:
hiya (propriety/dignity);
pakikisama (companionship/esteem);
utang na loob (gratitude/solidarity).

These core values operate as a triad, like a stool, remove one leg in the triad and the Filipino personality is whole no more.

14. OPINION and FEELING
Opinion statements come from the mind, a belief or idea. Feeling statements come from the heart. Americanized teens and young adults express opinions, while immigrant parents express FEELINGS.

15. RESPECT: BUILT-IN? TO BE EARNED?
Be aware that in hierarchical societies, respect comes with one's birth order, title, and position in society. Among egalitarian societies, respect is to be earned!

16. BEING and DOING
Being mode - it's enough just to be. Doing mode - if there's a problem, fix it!

17. ASSIMILATION and ACCULTURATION
Assimilation is the "simmering stew," whereas acculturation is the "salad bowl."

18. CULTURAL ADJUSTMENTS
Our cultural adjustments go by stages:
A. Conform, Deny, Rebel, Dual/Double life
B. Conform, Dissonance, Resistance +
Immersion, Introspection, Integrative awareness
C. Honeymoon, Hostility, Humor, Home

19. LOVE and COOPERATION
Children receive unconditional parental love while the successful parent-child relationship

requires parents have the cooperation of their children.

20. SELF-RELIANCE

The unifying cultural value among Chinese when disaster strike is: Give a man a fish and you give him food for the day. Teach him how to fish and you give him food for a lifetime. I propose let's adopt this value as Filipinos to become our "battle cry" too when misfortune hits us.

21. WITNESSES

The direct witnesses of our public and private "personas" are our children. They see and hear us when we drop our guard. They know us. Some chose to be silent, but others are vocal witnesses. Be careful with your public statements.

22. BOTH/AND; EITHER/OR

Complicated problems are solved by both/and logic; simple ones are solved by either/or.

23. WHOSE PERSPECTIVE?

Do not speak for your children, chances are, when you ask them, the answer will not be your perspective.

24. SURRENDER TO A HIGHER POWER

Surrender to God, not to your child.

25. CULTURE CLASH CAUSES
    a. Conflict orientation of the self
    b. Highly verbal and nonverbal cultures
    c. Authoritarian and egalitarian orientations
    d. Considering what's the propriety behavior
    e. Fluctuating cultural identities

26. FAMILY REFORMS

Reform family values and the government operations will reform, too. Corrupt family dynamics will extend to corrupt government. They are inseparable.

27. LOOB (INTERIOR)

When our good deeds come from our loob, our acts are priceless. There is no utang (debt), that we will expect from others, galing sa loob eh (it's coming from our interior self). That's agape, unconditional care, and love for others. PURE FILIPINO CORE VALUE.

28. IT TAKES A VILLAGE TO RAISE A CHILD

It's an illusion to conclude that you and you alone raised your child

29. LAUGTER, THE BEST MEDICINE

Where there is acceptance of one another, eliciting humor comes easy.

REFLECTION

The moment of impact. The moment of impact proves the potential for change. Has ripples effects far beyond what we can predict. Sending some particles crashing together. Making them closer than before. While sending others spinning off into great ventures. Landing them where you've never thought that you've found them. That's the thing about moments like these. You can't, no matter how hard you try, control how it's gonna affect you. You just gotta let the colliding parts go where they may. And wait. For their next collision.

—From the movie *The Vow*

EPILOGUE

*We all make choices in life. The hard thing is
to live with them. And ain't nobody who can
help you with that.*

From the movie: *The Words*

I went to extreme measures to remove my
daughter from a situation that I feared would lead to
grave consequences, literally taking her out of the
California suburbs and moving to rural New York, as far
away from anything as you can imagine. In those
moments, I felt just like a mother hawk swooping in to
protect her young. I did what I had to do no matter how
difficult it was for me, no matter how extreme my actions
were to my friends. My efforts to reach out to her and
understand her behavior took me on a journey that would
eventually lead to me writing *Culture Clash* in 2006.
You could say the book grew organically out of our
crisis, because the conflict between us, as it turned out,
was mainly cultural. So, culture clash has become my
passion!

Today, I am comforted in my soul knowing that
my daughter and I went through a terrible crisis and came
out okay, and now enjoy a meaningful mother-daughter
relationship. Our process was the key. **Together, we
explored where and how our culture clash intersected
and we took the time needed to create a new basis for
understanding and communication.** My daughter is
now a successful marketing professional, happily
married, and so madly in love as she raises her five-year-
old and one year old sons, my grandsons, my *apos*. For
now, we are content with our lives. That's as much as I
can ask for.

REFLECTION

Here's my pain, my joy that gave birth to
this book. These are my words.
--Lutie Orteza Lee

INDEX

REFERENCES

Alexander, Eben, Ph.D. *Proof of Heaven: A Neurosurgeon's Journey into the Afterlife.* New York, NY: Simon & Schuster, 2012.

"Attributions and Attitudes of Mothers and Fathers in the Philippines." http://www.ncb.nim.nih.gov/pmc/articles/PMC3150789/.8/21/2015

Augsburger, David W. *Conflict Mediation Across Cultures.* Louisville, Kentucky: Westminster/John Know Press, 1992.

Baumrind, Diane. "The Authoritative Parenting Style: Warmth, Rationality, and High Standards" 11/27/2015 http://www.parentingscience.com/authoritative-parenting-style.html.

Bellah, Robert N. et.al. *Habits of the Heart: Individualism and Commitment in American Life.*Berkeley, Los Angeles, London: University of California Press, 2008.

Blanco, Marivi Soliven. *Suddenly Stateside.* Quezon City: Milflores Publishing, Inc., 2002

Brown, Brené. *Rising Strong.* New York: Spiegel & Grau, 2015. "The Power of Vulnerability." TED at TEDxHouston. http://www.ted.com/Talks/brené _brown_on_vulnerability, June 2010.

Brown, Brené and Randow-Tesch, Margarethe. *Women & Shame.* Austin, TX: 3C Press.2004.

Burpo, Todd. *Heaven is Real: A Little Boy's Astounding Story of His Trip to Heaven.* Nashville, Tennessee: Thomas Nelson, Inc., 2011.

Cameron, Charles. *The Comparison Board*. Game and Original Board, hipbone@earthlink.net.1995,'96, 97.

Chua, Amy. *Battle Hymn of the Tiger Mother*. New York, NY: Penguin Books 2011.

Conde-Frazier, Elizabeth. *A Many Colored Kingdom*. Grand Rapids, USA: Baker Academic 2004.

Church, Timothy A. and Katigbak, Maria. *Filipino Personality and Indigenous and Cross-Cultural Studies*. Manila, Philippines: De La Salle University Press, Inc., 2000.

Darder, Antonia. *Culture and Power in the Classroom*. Westport, CN: Bergen & Garvey 1991.

Dolezal, Rachel. *In Full Color: Finding My Place in a Black and White World*. Dallas, TX: Ben Bella, Inc., 2017.

Dossey, Larry. *Prayer is Good Medicine*. New York: Harper Collins Publishers 1996.

Elizondo, Virgilio. *The Future is Mestizo*. Colorado: University Press of Colorado 2000.

Elms, Alan. *Erikson's History*. New York: Scribner 1999.

Enriquez, Virgilio G. *From Colonial to Liberation Psychology: The Philippine Experience*. Manila, Philippines: De La Salle University Press, 2004.

Fallows, James. "A Damaged Culture: A New Philippines". New York: Atlantic Monthly. November 1987issue. http://www.theatlantic.com/magazine/archive/1987/11/a-damaged-Culture/505178/

Farley, Christopher John. *Introducing Halle Berry*. New York: Pocket Books, 2002.

"Fil-Am girl kills self, apparently after online shaming by her father." World wide web: http://globalnation.inquirer.net/124209/fil-am-girl-kills-self-apparently-after-online-shaming-father.9/6/2015.

Freire, Paulo. *The Pedagogy of the Oppressed*. New York: Continuum Publishing Corporation 1982.

Galef, Julia. "Why You Think You're Right—Even If You're Wrong." Talk at TEDxPSU February 2016.
http://www.ted.com/talks/julia_galef_why_you_think_you_re_right_even_if_you_re_wrong.

Gladwell, Malcolm. *Outliers: The Story of Success*. New York, Boston, London: Back Bay Books, Little Brown Company 2008.

Gibran, Khalil. *The Prophet*. New York: Alfred A. Knopf 1923.

Guthrie, George and Jacobs, Pepita Jimenez. *Child Rearing and Personality Development in the Philippines*. Manila, Philippines: The Bookmark, Inc. 1967.

Hall, Edward T. *The Dance of Life*. New York: Anchor Press Double Day 1983. *The Silent Language* 1973; *Beyond Culture* 1967; *Hidden Dimension* 1966.

Hess, Carol. *Caretakers of Our Common House*. Nashville: Abingdon Press 1997.

Igloria, Luisa A. *Not Home But Here: Writing from the Filipino Diaspora*. Pasig City, Philippines: Anvil Publications 2003.

Jobs, Steve. YouTube: "Stanford Commencement Speech 2005"

Kim, Eun Y. *The Yin and Yang of American Culture: A Paradox*. Yarmouth, Maine: Intercultural Press, 2001.

Kluckhohn, Florence and Strodtbeck, Fred. *Variations in Value Orientations*. New York: Row, Peterson and Company 1961.

Kujawa-Holbrook, Sheryl. *God Beyond Borders: Interreligious Learning Among Faith Communities*. Eugene, Oregon: Pickwick Publications 2014.

Lartey, Emmanuel. *Pastoral Theology in an Intercultural World*. Cleveland, OH: The Pilgrim Press 2006.

Lee, Lutie O. *Culture Clash: The Americanized Teenagers, Implications for Parenting, Teaching, and Mentoring*. New York: Arbor Books, 2001.

Lee Lutie O. Teaching Cultural Diversity Through Children's Literature: Applying the Kluckhohn Model. Quezon City, Philippines: New Day Publishers, 2006

Lochte, Ryan. "Dancing Saved Me". New York, NY: US Weekly Issue 1133. October 31, 2016.

Maggay, Melba P. *A Clash of Culture: Early American Protestant Missions & Filipino Religious Consciousness*. Manila, Philippines: Anvil Publications, 2011

Maggay, Melba P. *Pahiwatig:Kagawiang Pangkomunikasyon na Filipino*. Manila, Philippines: Ateneo de Manila University Press, 2002.

Maggay, Melba P. *Understanding Ambiguity in Filipino Communication Patterns*. Quezon City, Philippines: Institute for Studies in Asian Church and Culture, 1999.

McDaniel, Jay. "Suns, Moons, Bodies Creative" *Creative Transformation* Vol. II No.2 2000.

McIntosh, Peggy. "White Privilege: Unpacking the Invisible Knapsack". *White Privilege & Male Privilege: A Personal Account of Coming to See Corresponds Through Work in Women Studies*. Wellesly, MA: Wellesly College Center for Research in Women 1988.

McLaren, Peter. *Life in Schools: An Introduction to Critical Pedagogy in the Foundation of Education*. Boston: Pearson Education, Inc. 2003.

Mlodinow, Leonard. Ph.D. "How Your Unconscious Mind Rules Your Behavior," at TEDxReset talk 2013.

Moorjani, Anita. *Dying To Be Me: My Journey from Cancer, To Near Death, To True Healing*. Carlsbad, California: Hay House, Inc., 2012.

Mukshani, Raj. "Chapter IX *Pakikiramdam*: A Critical Analysis" February 2, 2009:

Nadal, Kevin L. Ph.D. "Who Am I? Ethnic Identity Development of Filipino Americans". Section I *Filipino American Psychology: A Collection of Personal Narratives*. Bloomington, IN: Author House, 2010.

Ocampo, Christian Anthony. Ph.D. *The Latinos of Asia: How Filipino Americans Break the Rules of Race*. Stanford, California: Stanford University Press, 2016.

O'hearn, C.C. ed. *Half Half*. New York: Pantheon Books 1998.
Park, Jung Young. *The Trinity in Asian Perspective*. Nashville: Abingdon Press 1996.

Pascale, Richard Tanner and Athos, Anthony G. *The Art of Japanese Management*. New York: Warner Books 1981.

Pigafetta, Antonio. *First Voyage Around the World.* Translation from Portuguese originally written in 1536. Pigafetta was Ferdinand Magellan's chronicler who was one of the survivors of
Magellan's crew after he was killed by Mactan chief's Lapulapu men. Manila: Filipiniana Book Guild, 1969.

Price, Steve. *Dream Making in a Dream Taking World.* Tampa, FL: INTI Publishing 2001.

Proctor, Frank. ed. *What Matters for Children and Families: Engaging Six Vital Themes of Our Faith.* Cleveland, OH: United Church Press 2009. This resource is a project developed under the Leadership of Lutie Orteza Lee, Minister for Children and Families in the Congregational Vitality and Discipleship Ministry Team, Local Church Ministry, United Church of Christ.

Rizal, Jose. *The Indolence of the Filipinos.* The Project Gutenberg EBook The essay itself originally appeared in the Filipino forthrightly review, *La Solidaridad,* of Madrid, running from July 15 to September 15, 1890. It was a continuation of Rizal's campaign of education in which he sought by blunt truths to awaken his countrymen to their own faults at the same time that he was arousing the Spaniards to the defects in Spain's colonial system that caused and continued such shortcomings.

Roces, Alfred and Grace. *Culture Shock.* Portland, OR: Graphic Arts Center Publishing Co. 2003.

Saigal, Monique. *Hidden Child, Hidden Heroines.* 3rd ed. Translated from French by Anna Krasnovsky. Self-published, 2015.

SIPA (Search to Involve Pilipino Americans) "Encouraging Togetherness and Better Communication in The Filipino Family." Talk given Los Angeles, CA in Historic Filipinotown, July 25, 2015.

Smokowski, Paul and Bacallao, Martica. *Becoming Bicultural: Risk, Resilience, and Latino Youth*. New York, London: New York University Press, 2011.

Stewart, Edward C. and Bennet, Milton, J. *American Cultural Patterns*. Yarmouth, Maine: The Intercultural Press 1991.

Sue, Derald and Sue, David. *Counseling the Culturally Diverse*. 5th ed. Hoboken, NJ: John Wiley & Sons 2008.

Sue, Stanley. Online Readings in *Psychology and Culture* Unit 3 Chapter 4 "Asian American Mental Health: What We Know and What We Don't Know." Retrieved July 4, 2004.

Tamaki, Julie. "Cultural Balancing Act Adds to Teen Angst: Asian American Youth Face Perils of Adolescence While Coming to Grips with Issues of Identity." July 28, 2003. The *Los Angeles Times* on the web (online newspaper)

Tomas, Andres, *Positive Filipino Values*. Quezon City, Philippines: New Day Publishers 1989. *Management By Filipino Values* 1985; *Understanding Filipino Values* 1981; *Understanding Values* 1980.

Triandes, Harry. *Individualism and Collectivism*. San Francisco, Oxford: Westview Press, 1995.

Trifonovich, Gregory. "Culture Learning/Culture Teaching," *Educational Perspective* Vol. 16 No. 4, 1980.

Wang, Jianglong. "Knowing the True Face of a Mountain: Understanding Communication and Cultural Competence." Readings in *Psychology and Culture* Chapter 4. Online available) http://www.Ac.wwu.edu/-culture/Wang.htm 4 July2004.

Watts, Alan. *Tao: The Watercourse Way*. New York: Pantheon Books, 1975.

Wink, Joan. *Critical Pedagogy: Notes from the Real World.* New York: Addison Wesley Longman, 2000.

Wright, Gerry. "Why Y'all Trippin? It's Just Ebonics!" a written paper submitted as required assignment of the course TED 667 Diversity & Reform: A Critical Pedagogy. National University, San Bernardino Satellite, May 2004.

Zaide, Sonia M. *The Philippines: A Unique Nation.* Cubao, Quezon City, Philippines: All Nations Publishing Co. Inc., 1999.

APPENDIX A

The iceberg concept of culture

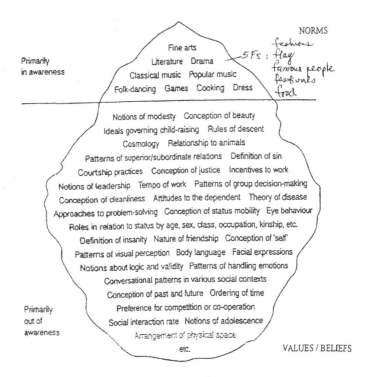

Culture the 'medium' of our social interaction, a convention developed by any group of humans
who are in regular contact, incorporating language, social style, agenda of concerns, etc.

APPENDIX B

The Comparison Model

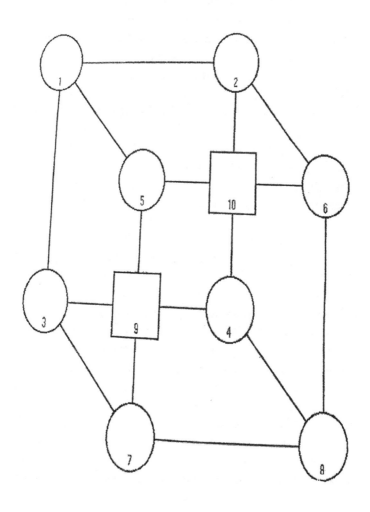

Positions 1, 2, 3, and 4 circles, comprising square 9 are for moves that have to do with the first of the paired concept, idea, value, etc. Positions 5, 6, 7, and 8, comprising square 10 are for corresponding moves exploring the second. Now, positions 1, 5, 2, and 6 are linked. And positions 3, 7, 4, and 8 are linked. Positions 9 and 10 are for more "general overview" links between the two: concepts, values, or ideas, etc.

For example, to apply this game, the instructions are:

Today's comparison is about the American values of the youth or young adults and immigrant parents. The youth/young adult will write cultural values on positions 1, 2, 3, and 4. The immigrant parents will write on positions 5, 6, 7, and 8. (Before this game is done, list down on the board American values and immigrant parents' values.) When all the positions are written on all the circles on one paper, there will be "new" positions when, 1, 5, 2, and 6 are linked. And when 3, 4, 7, and 8 are linked a "new" position is created. Position 1, 2, 5, and 6 will have square 10 while positions 3, 4, 7, and 8 will have square 9. Holding positions 1, 5, 2, and 6, you now come up with an activity to write on square 10 that will help both youth and parents understand or prevent culture clash to escalate (general overview). Perform the same thing to those holding positions 3, 4, 7, and 8 on square 9 (general overview).

Added instruction:

There will only be one paper to answer for youth/young adults and parents. Parents wait for the youth to write positions 1, 2, 3, and 4. After time is up, the papers are given to the parents to write positions on 5, 6, 7, and 8. Collect the papers, then, ask the youth and parents to form a pair. This will work best when there is the same number of youth and parents.

APPENDIX C

*THE KLUCKHOHN MODEL

Value Orientation-Ranges of Variation in Value Orientation

Human Nature	Mixture (Good & Evil, mutable and immutable	Good	Evil
Human Being-to-Nature	Mastery-over-nature	Subjugation-to-nature	Harmony-with-nature
Time	Present	Future	Past
Activity	Doing	Being	Being-in Becoming
Relational	Linearity Authoritarian	Collaterality Collective decisions Collectivism	Individualism Individual choices Equal rights

*Do not interpret the table by looking for some linear evolution of development. This table has been modified according to a non-linear **worldview of development. The value orientation of different cultures are simply stated, implying no order of development. This is simply the varied cultural orientations of human societies. This table does not appear in** the same way Kluckhohn and Strodtbeck arranged it in their book, *Variations in Value Orientations.*

APPENDIX D

ABOUT THE AUTHOR

Lutie Orteza Lee is a lifelong educator/teacher, born and raised in the Philippines with a passion for understanding the push and pull of her Filipino culture while also seeking to understand others. She wrote a Culture Clash column for *Balita,* a weekly newspaper in Southern California and has written two books, *Teaching Cultural Diversity Through Children's Literature: Applying the Kluckhohn Model* and *Culture Clash: The Americanized Teenagers,* the current book is a 2nd edition with a new twist. She was a recipient of an educational travel grant through a writing contest, "Making Teachers Smile" given by Pasadena Educational Foundation which enabled her to visit London, England to observe International Baccalaureate elementary schools. She holds a Bachelor of Science in Elementary Education and Master of Arts in Bicultural Development and Religious Education. She taught for 30 years in the Philippines (2), Taiwan (5), and the USA (23 – HI, CA, NY). Before retirement in 2010, she was the Minister for Children and Families Programs of the United Church of Christ (UCC) national office in Cleveland, OH. Visit her website to know more about her culture clash passion and about its WHY story: CultureClashCoach.com. Lutie lives in Southern California. She has one daughter who is happily married with two sons.

Check out Lutie Lee on social media and the web:

Website: cultureclashcoach.com
Twitter: lutie_lee
Instagram: leelutie; cultureclashcoach
LinkedIn: Lutie Orteza Lee

ACKNOWLEDGMENTS

Books are completed by including the acknowledgment of a village of supporters. For this second book on culture clash, 2021, the groups and names that appear below have been involved in one way and another in their support.

I want to start by first thanking those individuals who volunteered to contact and organize various groups where I can give seminars to Filipino American churches. Those who recommended I attend group meetings of activists and Filipino student associations to speak at a Filipino-American association anniversary celebration, in whom both parents and children were in attendance, and opening their homes to hold the workshop. They are first on the list because without their support, how could this book project endeavor take flight?

Dr. Sheilachu P. Gomez for contacting the UF Asian Pacific Islander Multicultural and Diversity Affairs, Filipino Student Association and the Philippine-American Association of Gainesville and Surrounding Areas (PAG-ASA) in Gainesville, FL.

Amy Calumpag for inviting me to attend NEFFCON (National Ecumenical Forum for Filipino Concerns) enabling me to interview some young adult professional activists in Los Angeles, CA. Amy was also instrumental in connecting me to the Perris Filipino-American Association in Perris, CA.

Rev. Josiah Ang of the Alliance International Church in Pasadena, CA. I met members of his church on several occasions to discuss culture clash.

Christian Joseph Esteban for sending me to a meeting of the Anak Bayan group, allowing me to meet the college activists and have conversations with them after their meeting in Los Angeles, CA.

Dr. Oscar Monera and Dr. Eulalio Orteza, Jr., for organizing and contacting a United Methodist church in Houston, TX to hold a workshop.

Oscar and Ruth Avila for organizing (twice) my interview with parents and their young adult children at Cosmopolitan United Church of Christ in Carrolton, TX.

Rev. Teogenes Tawagon for holding many workshops at his church, Moreno Valley Faith Community, UCC in Moreno Valley, CA.

Maria Christina Sanchez for holding a workshop in her home, Jacksonville, FL.

Dr. Sheryl Kujawa-Holbrook and Lea Appleton for arranging a workshop at the Claremont School of Theology, Claremont, CA.

Zette Woodward for connecting me to NANAY Center, enabling me to meet the founders and to interview their young adults in Miami, FL.

Emma Buot for holding a workshop in her home which was attended by Filipino mothers in Chandler, AZ and enabling me to interview several young adults including the Director of the State's cultural affairs.

Grace F. Orteza for an in-depth interview, Alexandria, VA.

Blanca Gomez from Arcadia, CA for an informal interview of her diverse friends from other countries and agreeing to read one chapter.

`   Rachel G. Silliman for her invaluable suggestions.

Words of appreciation to Claremont School of Theology through the office of Academic Dean Dr. Sheryl Kujawa-Holbrook for conferring on me, the title of Visiting Scholar for two years, 2014 to 2016 so that I could use the CST library and could also access other Claremont colleges' libraries.

Deep gratitude to Dr. Melba P. Maggay for her book review.

In alphabetical order, these individuals have been involved in my book-writing project as attendees of the workshops, willing readers and critics of chapter manuscripts, one-on-one interviews and mainly supportive of my project always rooting for the success of this endeavor: Jeff Abenina, Joy Abiera, Chita Acio, Ali Aguarino, Yvonne Aguarino, Emma Alaestante, Dimy Alexander, Ernie Almiro, Fe Almiro, Violy Amano, John Ammon, Cristina Ang, Josiah Ang, Vangie Ang, Dolores Angeles, Ronnel Angeles, Wendy Anson, Favie Antiporda, Samuel Arda, Nathan Arias, Oscar Avila, Ruth Avila, Jonathan Ayson, Bernard A. Bassig, Wayne rose Bandoy, Ana Maria Balayon, Leopoldo Balayon, Gani Barias, Jr., Norbie Berdin, Jeremy Bituin, Maribel Blasco, Petronio Blasco, Sharon Brammeo, Eleanor Brown, Raymond Brown, Joyce Bruce, Carmen Buot, Emma Buot, Joan Bynum, Domie Cabanilla, Fely Cabanilla, Freddie Cabico, Lydia Cabico, Antonio Calantas, Corey Calaycay, Dollores Callejo, Samuel Callejo, Loreta Caluyan, Mely Caluyan, Cesar Catan,Elizabeth Catan, James Catan, Lidia Catan, Marina J. Catipon, Krislam Chin, Cade Codina, Dexter Colorado, Hexel Colorado, Lura Colorado, Maxwell Colorado, Ray Colorado, Antonette Conception, Bea Cruz, Redd Cruz, Darryl Damaso, Debbie Damaso, John Damaso, Reggie Dancel, Joey Davide, Julie Davide, Carmen D'Cunha, Vida de Guzman, Michelle Delmastro, Jef Demetrio, Linda Demetrio, Delia V. Digan, Joycee Domingo, Karen Droegemueller, Vanessa Durand, Cyril Empig, Gali Encabo, Andrew Esposo, Abe Estaban, CJ Esteban, Gabe Estaban, Susan Esteban, Marc Eli Faldes, Matt Andrew Faldes, Josie Faustino, Ronald Faustino, Broderick Floresca, Ethan Floresca, Jun Floresca, Mavel Floresca, Wolfgang Floresca, Celestin Friend, Coucessa Friend, Kristina Frost, John Frost, David Gagne, Rica Gagne, Dina Garcenile,

Ramon, Garcenile, Charles Gaviola, Elsa Gomez, Toddy Gomez, Sandra Hester, Janice Hizon, Divina Himaya, Elizabeth Hoffman, Catherine Iguipas, Christine Iti, Larcy C. Jarmin, Cecile Jimeno, Madison Kelly, Rey Lao, Anastacia Layas, Dominador Layas, Miriam Lim, Lope Lindio, Annalon Lingat, Keith Macalino, Cristina Magahis, Dion Magahis, Rhodora Maligalig, Jurgette H. Malonzo, Aubrey Manahan, Marion Maningo, Antonio Marero, Rowena Martir, Delia Marzan, Andy Mercado, Maria Miranda, Linda Monera, Oscar Monera, Annabel Montagne, Maureen Montagne, Betsy Moscal, Lee Munroe, Ernalyn Navarro, Mario Nazareno, John Nguyen, Nicole Obar, Cherry Orteza, Evelina M. Orteza, Jun Orteza, David Otal, Marissa Otal, Em Ozoa, June Ozoa, Arelyne Pacho-Ramos, Pilar Packer, Tess Padlan, Jerico Pagdilao, Joffer Pagdilao, Marivic Pagdilao, Robert Pagdilao, Perla Paniamogan, Samuel Paniamogan, David Pantesmuchl, Eduardo Pascual, Jun Pascual, Pilar Pascual, Sonia Pascual, Cisa Payuyo, Maria Pitt, Ephraim Pongan, Mirga Pongan, Pearl Ramiro, Bab Ramirez, Ed Ramirez, Charmaine Ramos, Agripina Rasco, Melita Reddish, Bernadette Reed, Deverette Reed, Marivic Reyes, Letty Riley, Persi Rivera-Mendez, Emerlinda R. Roman, Amy Romero, Eduyll S., Mariepet Sabal, Virginia Salao, Rachel Salgado, Dennis Sanchez, Iona Sanchez, Maria Sanchez, Hoher Sepijio, Ronelle Sepijio, Lily Sevilla, Carlos Sevilla, Michael Sun, Flora Talam, Rene Talam, Cara Tawagon, Joy Tawagon, Teogenes Tawagon, Wil Tawagon, Cyril Valencia, Puring Valencia, Badeene O. Verora, L. Villanueva, Alexis Villas, Sharon Walborn, Rufina N. Ward, Sally Willis-Watkins, Michelle Wells, Joy Woods, Zette Woodward, Ruth Yandell, Rowena Yumol, Ronald Yuson, CherryLyn Zafaralla, Marianna Zapanta, and Haidee Lisa Zmenzlikar

I want to make special mention of the following friends:

Gani Barias, Arelyne Pacho-Ramos, and **Amy Romero**, we racked our brains to come up with the final book title.

Ching P. Gomez, who at the very start believed in this book-writing project. She was always ready to assist in anyway despite her heavy schedule. She was my initial reader and edited the first three chapters of raw product of my brain. **Grace F. Orteza**, who edited a chapter. **Amy Calumpag,** who assisted in many ways including gathering activists for interviews, reading and critiquing one chapter, and recommended me as speaker. **Sandy K. Hester**, who edited all chapters, except Chapter 5. She constantly marketed my book-to-be even as it was still in the raw writing stage and she shared her life story with transparency about Dad in Chapter 6.

I want to make special mention to the "real players" who reached out to my daughter and me in our "culture clash" exemplifying the meaning of our Filipino core value: *utang na loob* (gratitude and solidarity) showing what it means to "value which moves to recognize, respect, promote, and at times defend the basic dignity of each person." You did all this by being you, and I thank you from the bottom of my heart. Tessie Camiling, Alma de Guzman, Huntley, Ephraim and Mirga Pongan, Nancy and Wi-chan Ritnimit, Delza and Rick Weir, and Kristi White.

To my Foreword writer, Dr. Michael Tan, thank you for graciously agreeing to share your valuable perspective on culture clash.

To Claremont Mayor, Corey Calaycay, his down-right sincerity in recommending Kathryn Dunn, Claremont Courier's editor after my first editor suffered a heart attack.

To my valued professional editors, James Saspa, the former editor of *Balita* who captured the essence of the Filipino indigenous cultural roots after commenting that Chapter 4 was the hardest to edit and Kathryn Dunn, the heaven-sent editor of Claremont Courier for accepting the baton to edit the last of the chapter and for stringing together all chapters to become one file from the Introduction to the Appendices. She read the entire manuscript doing edits as needed, I extend a heartfelt thanks to her. Her initial comment of my work was, "You bring out my humanity."

To my feisty no-nonsense book agent, Linda Peavy who upon reading the first edition called and told me the potential and promise of the book for a second edition. She never wavered in her support. Her mantra was: Write in your own time and space—never write when you are pressured, stressed, and tired. No deadlines for me. Take your time, whatever it takes to finish your work. I officially started in November 2013 and completed editing of the manuscript in March, 2019. It's been six years!

To my one and only daughter, Bing Sahulee, without her wholehearted support, this book would not be, *Culture Clash: A Guide for Filipino Immigrants Raising American Children.*

To my editor, I want to express my appreciation beyond measure to Anchor Book Press, Ltd for working painstakingly in editing my book to reach the Gold Standard of a published book. Their mission statement of being an author-centered publishing press cannot be overstated. What could have been contentious passages were turned into a gold mine of discussion. Thank you, Carol Pirog, you delivered, sprinkled with honesty concern for the book's impact on the readers, and accompanied with an attitude of love and care.

Finally, I thank God, the original owner of this work. I am the vessel. A friend said to me that God has ways for us to listen and to do things in God's own good time, not ours. I needed to finish my book writing project that was already approaching its sixth year. There were setbacks that I encountered discouraging me to keep on. Book-writing required patience, determination, and perseverance. Richard Paul Evans, who wrote *The Christmas Box,* described his encounter with God in his Introduction. In despair, he questioned God: why all he kept getting were rejections from publishers. And God sent a thunderous reply! "Who wrote this book? This is my book. If this book won't be published, I will be devastated first!" Evans was shaken to hear this voice from nowhere. He knelt and cried, whispering, "not my will but thine be done." Listening to the still-speaking God, it meant I stay put and quietly and diligently finish my manuscript. I worked closely with my editor with hardly any interruptions and distractions. To God, be the glory!

To all whose names and groups that appeared here, my grateful heart is etched in yours. If I failed to mention some names, please forgive me, it is not my intention. Blame, senior moment!

Praise for Culture Clash

"Mobility and migration pose great challenges to individuals, mainly in terms of adjusting to a new environment and culture...
Parenting guides rarely consider these challenges that come about from mobility and migration. Lutie Orteza Lee's book is timely."

Michael L. Tan, Ph.D.
U.P. Chancellor
University of the Philippines,
Diliman, Quezon City

"While immigrant Filipino parents may be the primary audience for this book, multicultural families from many backgrounds will appreciate Lutie Orteza Lee's insights into Filipino culture, as well as her "Nuggets of Wisdom" that can guide any parent. She provides convincing support for authoritative rather than authoritarian parenting, giving children clear and high expectations, as well as strong emotional support. Sprinkled liberally with love, humor, and honesty, Ms. Lee's book is almost like sitting in the corner of one of her workshops."

Jill S. Grigsby, Ph.D.
Richard Steele
Professor of Social Sciences and
Professor of Sociology, Pomona College

"Lutie Orteza Lee draws out the culture themes that usually figure in the tensions between parent and child in Filipino-American households...The book opens up a discourse on parenting third-culture and bicultural kids..."

Dr. Melba P. Maggay, President
Institute for Studies in Asian Church and Culture

"As Filipino culture thrives in different parts of the world, culture clash occurs inevitably within the family. A must-read for every Filipino family as it gives a deeper meaning to that hard earned Balikbayan Box – that repatriate box containing canned goods, assorted clothes, shoes, etc. But to every Pinoy, that box contains love, care, and tight hugs."

Lenette Doria
Immigrant Filipino mother raising her teenagers

"This is a comprehensive well-thought of facts and testimonies about culture clashes among native Filipinos and Fil-Am Heritage. The testimonies were well-said and true to life. I can relate myself being one of them. This book is great and should be read by all."

Erlinda B. Juliana, M.Ed.
Professor and Filipino Language Specialist
University of Pennsylvania

"Lutie Orteza Lee speaks with profound passion and wisdom about the struggles faced by Filipino immigrants, raising children in America. Her insights offer the reader a needed view into the reality of every immigrant group that comes to this country and must raise children in a strange and sometimes hostile environment."

Rev. Paul Hobson Sadler
Sr. Senior Pastor, Mt. Zion, UCC
Cleveland, OH
Founder and Director
Sadler for Justice, Equity, Diversity, and Inclusion
Cleveland, OH

Made in the USA
Monee, IL
23 August 2021

75800459R00157